A
GREAT
PLACE
TO
WORK

A GREAT PLACE TO WORK

WHAT MAKES SOME
EMPLOYERS SO GOOD
(AND MOST SO BAD)

ROBERT LEVERING

Random House
New York

Grateful acknowledgment is made to the following for
permission to reprint previously published material:

Franklin Insight, Inc.: A chart that was originally
published in Franklin's insight. Copyright © 1985
Franklin Insight, Inc. (page 261).

G. P. Putnam Group: Excerpts from Pink Collar Workers:
Inside the World of Women's Work by Louise Kapp
Howe. Copyright © 1977 by Louise Kapp Howe.

Harper & Row, Publishers, Inc.: Excerpts from In Search
of Excellence: Lessons from America's Best-Run
Companies by Thomas Peters and Robert Waterman, Jr.
Copyright © 1982 by Thomas Peters and Robert
Waterman, Jr. Reprinted by permission of Harper and
Row, Publishers, Inc.

Random House, Inc.: Excerpts from A Passion for
Excellence: The Leadership Difference by Thomas J.
Peters and Nancy K. Austin. Copyright © 1985 by
Thomas J. Peters and Nancy K. Austin.

Transaction Books: Excerpts from The Humanist
Temper: The Life and Work of Elton Mayo by Richard
Trahair. Copyright © 1984 by Transaction, Inc.
Reprinted by permission of Transaction Books.

Library of Congress Cataloging-in-Publication Data

Levering, Robert, 1944–
A great place to work.

Bibliography: p.
Includes index.
1. Personnel management—United States.
2. Job satisfaction—United States.   3. Quality of
work life—United States.   4. Work environment—
United States.   I. Title.
HF5549.2.U5L385   1988   331.2'0973   87-43226
ISBN 0-394-55725-5

Manufactured in the United States of America
24689753
First Edition

To my grandmother,

Elsie Marion Schlaegel

(1888–1987)

for her gift of curiosity

and

To my mentors,

Stewart Meacham, Larry Scott, and George Willoughby,

for the example of their lifelong commitments to

peace and justice

PREFACE

Good workplaces are worth examining, if for no other reason than that they enrich the lives of the people working there. Everyone, after all, would prefer working in a pleasant working environment to an unpleasant one. Since most of us spend the greater part of our waking hours at work, this is no small matter.

At the same time, the quality of our workplaces has major social implications. We're all familiar with the symptoms of bad workplaces—the personal stress, the erosion of physical and mental health, the lower productivity. A society of good workplaces, where people feel turned on rather than turned off to work, would be a superior place for everyone.

It's curious, therefore, that no one has analyzed the dynamics of a good workplace or tried to ascertain its essential characteristics. Business journalists tend to ignore the workplace. They are writing for investors or managers, not for employees. Even in-depth articles about individual companies rarely describe what it's like to work there. The audience of investors isn't interested. Investors' overriding question is whether to buy or sell stock in specific companies. Workplace conditions don't fit into that scheme of things.

Modern economists, too, have steered clear of the workplace. They prefer looking at subjects that can be reduced to numbers and mathematical formulas, like the nation's money supply,

GNP, savings rates, and so on. What a far cry from Adam Smith, whose masterpiece *The Wealth of Nations* opens with a detailed description of the manufacture of pins in eighteenth-century England. Or Karl Marx, whose *Capital* includes numerous memorable passages about the working conditions in nineteenth-century textile mills.

Two groups do focus on the workplace—managers and trade unionists. Neither has looked at the phenomenon of great workplaces, but for entirely different reasons.

Management consultants and business-school professors have written countless books and articles about workplace issues, ranging from personnel administration to theories of motivation. They write for managers who want tips they can apply to their own jobs. Rarely is there any attempt, however, to see how the various techniques or policies fit together as a whole. Nor is there much interest in the underlying *attitudes* that frequently determine whether a technique succeeds or fails.

The burgeoning genre of management literature has an unstated us-versus-them stance: How do we (the managers) get them (the employees) to do something that we want them to do? Thus, improving the working conditions can be justified only if it appears to be a means to another end—improving worker productivity. The implicit manipulative ethic involved distorts workplace relationships, as shall be discussed at length in this book.

Also missing in this equation is the obvious point that managers are employees, too. Their lives are affected by the workplace just as are the lives of those they supervise. A working environment that's full of tension and hostility takes its toll on all concerned. It may be worse for those on the bottom than those on top, but it still takes its toll. Not only are nonmanagerial employees subordinated to the quest for an ever-fatter bottom line, so are the managers.

Trade unionists, unlike managers, view the workplace from the employee perspective. Unions have been thorns in the sides of insensitive employers, and they have rectified countless injustices. Still, we can understand why trade unionists have little to offer to a discussion about good workplaces. Unions aren't products of happy work environments. Trade unionists spend most of their energy trying to eke out small gains through confrontation. Conflict certainly exists in the best of workplaces. But adversarial battle is not the only reality of the workplace.

Yet if any group could benefit from a clearer concept of what makes for a good employer, it is the union movement. Its rapidly decreasing membership reflects its lack of vision. Nearly 40 percent of the American work force was unionized in the mid-1950s; less than 20 percent is under union contract today. It may well be that the union movement needs to articulate more clearly what it is fighting for, not just against. Most of the younger people in the work force are sophisticated enough to realize that merely having a union doesn't make for a good workplace. Unions may need to develop an analysis that demonstrates how they relate to that objective before they can attract many of the people who are turned off by a rhetoric that sounds a half century out of date.

The huge body of Marxist and socialist literature is also ostensibly written from an employee viewpoint. There's a long tradition of such work in this country, dating from Upton Sinclair's horrifying tales in The Jungle, about meat packinghouse workers in turn-of-the-century Chicago. Those who have sought fundamental changes in the economic and political system have often pointed to the sorry state of working life as their primary recruiting tool. Some insist that capitalism inherently produces bad workplaces and argue that the emancipation of workers requires the overthrow of the capitalist system. Two points. First, capitalism has no monopoly on bad workplaces, as the shipyard workers in Gdansk, Poland, have dramatically demonstrated. Second, this book offers evidence that good workplaces are possible within the capitalist system, though creating a good working environment often requires major structural changes within organizations relating to the sharing of power, profits, and ownership.

If there is an ideological bias here, it is a Gandhian one—that the means determine the end. In a great workplace, the means are the end. How people are treated is important. Creating a good working environment is considered a valid objective of the company. This contrasts with the conventional business assumption that the only legitimate objective of a company is to increase profits. In a great workplace, both goals are seen as compatible. Indeed, good employers would argue that creating the best possible workplace may enhance a firm's ability to perform well financially. But they insist that having a good workplace cannot be merely another strategy to make money. Quite the reverse. Rather than stifling employees' lives to make money, a good workplace also sees profits as a means of enhancing employees' lives.

Finally, this book is an exercise in vision. It puts forth a model of a good workplace. Consider this analogy. A psychologist can approach the personality by working from either a model of an unhealthy mind or from a model of a healthy mind. Major schools of psychology base their practice on each of those models. The same can be true of the workplace. Until now, those who have bothered to look at the workplace have concentrated on what's wrong and how to fix it. It's time for the opposite approach—looking at what is right and how to learn from it.

ACKNOWLEDGMENTS

Employees of good workplaces made this book possible. Literally hundreds of them took the time to explain what makes their workplaces tick when my coauthors and I were researching *The 100 Best Companies to Work for in America*. In addition, I am especially grateful to the many people I interviewed at the twenty companies that I revisited specifically for this book. Among those who helped me were: Jerry Sanders, Elliott Sopkin (Advanced Micro Devices); James Ewing (Delta Air Lines); Delayne Giardini, Douglas Strain, William Walker (Electro Scientific); Charles Hartness, Tom Martin, Nancy Neil, Jim Perkins, Ted Sartoian, Fred Smith, Roy Yamahiro (Federal Express); Robert Burke, Richard Menschel, Ed Novotny, Frank Smeal, Roy Smith, John Weinberg (Goldman Sachs); Bill Gore (W. L. Gore & Associates); J. D. Goodwin, Donald Hall, Charlie Hucker, David Hughes, Bill Johnson, Ellen Sloan, Linda Smith, Robert Stark (Hallmark Cards); Mary Anne Easley, David Packard (Hewlett-Packard); Ed Connolly, Gerald Holder, Ewing Kauffman, Fred Lyons, Michie Slaughter (Marion Labs); Lewis Lehr (3M); Henry L. Bertram, Helen Braun, David Cromwell, Leonard Langer, Frank Rosenbach, Michelle O. Woody (J. P. Morgan & Co.); Joan Lloyd, Robert Ninneman, Kris Roepsch, Robert Roska, Susan Zintek (Northwestern Mutual Life); Jan Erteszek (Olga); George B. Harvey, Thomas R. Loemker, Thomas McGarry, William Redgate, Carole St. Mark, Janine L. Salvey, Al Salvino, Lee Shlaefer, Robert Vanourek (Pitney Bowes); Norman Bennett, Howard Bradshaw, Mike Callahan, Marcia Carroll, Joyce Cohee, Bill Hastings, Bruce Kennedy, Logan Kerr, Jerry Meredith, William Potter, Rosemary Pinder, Sandy Redd, Larry Regosch, Richie Storck, Billy Terrell (Preston Trucking); Mark C. Hollis, George W. Jenkins, James Rhodes, Edward H. Ruth (Publix Super Markets); John Fowler, Helen Pauly, Larry Quadracci, George Ryan, Joanne Scherer (Quad/Graphics); Walter Lowenstern (ROLM); Patricia Becker, James Treybig (Tandem Computers); Joe Floren, Dave Friedley, Al Foltz, Susan Stone, Earl Wantland (Tektronix).

Two others made this book possible—Milton Moskowitz and Michael Katz, my coauthors for The 100 Best Companies to Work for in America. This book is a natural outgrowth of that book. Milton Moskowitz generously shared his thoughts about the phenomenon of good workplaces during the years we were crisscrossing the country researching the first book, and he made many helpful comments on the manuscript as this book progressed. Michael, who is now a literary agent, patiently critiqued every draft of every chapter. Even more important, he offered moral support at every turn for which I will always be deeply grateful.

Not many authors are so fortunate as to have their manuscript undergo critical readings by a corporate executive, an entrepreneur, a psychologist, and a poet. So I consider myself particularly lucky because my four brothers (Gordon, Gary, Jim, and Donald) were willing to read the manuscript from those four very different perspectives. Each of them made extremely useful and detailed comments, as did our parents, Lois and George.

Others who read various drafts of the manuscript were Bob Eaton, Jay Elliot, Juliana Fuerbringer, Terrell Jones, Cathy Miranker, Raymond Pfeiffer, Bonnie and David Snedeker, and Harry Strharsky. Not only did they spot major and minor problems, but they also took the time to discuss their own ideas about what makes for good and bad workplaces based on their own experiences. Many of their ideas have been incorporated into the book in one way or another.

At various stages of the research, I got help in transcribing and cataloging the more than sixty hours of interviews, or in tracking down and indexing the more than five hundred books and one thousand newspaper and magazine clippings and studies on workplace-related issues. My thanks to Layla Bockhorst, Lucy Collier, Takla Gardey, Clara Lusardi, Marian Staats, and Cheryl Vradenburg. I also appreciate Lucy's and Marian's perceptive comments on the manuscript.

From my editor, Carolyn Reidy, I received a terrific lesson in the kind of trust discussed in this book. From the beginning, she expressed enthusiasm for the project and confidence that I could do the job the topic deserves. She gave me the space and time I needed to sort out my own thinking, and when I needed help she was there. Most important, her sharp editorial comments have let me know that her trust was of the genuine variety: It was coupled with high expectations. Based on my experience, Random House is an awfully good publisher to write for.

Finally, I wish to express appreciation to Susan Barnes for all the extra child care she endured because of the book and to our son, Reuben, who continues to be a constant joy.

CONTENTS

VI WORKPLACE AND SOCIETY

INTRODUCTION

Nearly six years ago, I started interviewing employees in their offices, factories, and cafeterias for the book *The 100 Best Companies to Work for in America*. As the book's title suggests, my coauthors, Milton Moskowitz and Michael Katz, and I sought to identify the best employers of the land. In all, we visited about 125 companies in 30 states and talked with hundreds and hundreds of employees about their workplaces.

When we first started, we weren't sure what we would find. My impression, based on more than a decade as a business and labor journalist, was that most companies are pretty lousy to work for. I assumed that working for a company, especially a large one, implies a Faustian bargain—security and/or money for a piece of your soul. That conviction came early in life, when overhearing my father talk about work life at a major airline, where he worked for forty years. My own work experiences had further soured me on the possibilities of an uplifting working environment. My longest employment (six years) had been with a weekly newspaper in San Francisco. Employee turnover there was almost 100 percent a year. At one point, the entire nonmanagerial staff went out on strike over the working conditions and lack of job security. In the end, I was fired for objecting to another employee's being terminated for refusing to do more work for less pay.

Several of my friends or acquaintances have reported similar—or worse—encounters with their employers. Those stories have been the exception. More typical have been the offhand comments with which people indicate a feeling of alienation at work. Most people I've known have eventually found themselves making unpleasant compromises, ones that affect their feelings of self-worth. It's seen as part of the job.

Many social observers have reinforced these subjective impressions. In his best seller Working, Studs Terkel relates interviews with more than a hundred people talking about their working careers. They paint a picture of a workplace full of "daily humiliations." What's especially depressing is that most of Terkel's people say they want to do a good job; they want to feel pride in their work. But such yearnings rarely can be fulfilled in the contemporary American workplace.

Another keen social commentator, pollster Daniel Yankelovich, has gathered some impressive statistical evidence showing that if anything, the workplace is getting worse. In a survey conducted in the late 1960s, Yankelovich found that more than half the respondents felt they got personal fulfillment from their job; by 1980, when the same question was asked in another survey, only 27 percent were able to say that their job turned them on. Despite these figures, Yankelovich, like Studs Terkel, discovered that most Americans still want to do a good job. Over half of all working Americans still endorse the work ethic, agreeing with the statement "I have an inner need to do the very best job possible, regardless of pay." There's a mismatch, then, between what most of us want to do during our working hours and what we are allowed to do in our workplace. This discrepancy translates, on a personal level, to a profound feeling of alienation. Socially, it represents a tragic waste of human energy.

I was surprised, therefore, when our research for The 100 Best Companies to Work for in America led us to some really terrific places to work—where the experience of work was fulfilling rather than alienating. Especially convincing were the positive comments made by people whom you would not expect to be singing praises of their employer—secretaries at Goldman Sachs in New York City, steelworkers in a Nucor mill in Utah, electronics assembly-line workers at Tektronix in Oregon, insurance clerks at Northwestern Mutual Life in

Wisconsin. Employees talk about a "people orientation" and sense of community (sometimes called "family") at especially good workplaces.

To examine the phenomenon of good workplaces for this book, I have relied first and foremost on interviews with employees. Their observations form the backbone of the book. It is their experience at work that this book aims to explain.

After completing *The 100 Best Companies to Work for in America*, I revisited twenty especially good workplaces (the best of the best, if you will). In addition to further interviews with lower-level employees, I made a point to talk with the top officers and, where possible, the founders. I wanted to find out why and how they thought their companies had become great places to work. Among the people whose insights I obtained were top executives and/or founders of the following companies: Advanced Micro Devices; Delta Air Lines; Electro Scientific; Federal Express; Goldman Sachs; W. L. Gore; Hallmark Cards; Hewlett-Packard; Marion Labs; 3M; J. P. Morgan; Northwestern Mutual Life; Olga; Pitney Bowes; Preston Trucking; Publix Super Markets; Quad/Graphics; ROLM; Tandem Computers; and Tektronix. The fifty transcribed interviews that resulted and the follow-up visits to those companies provide much of the material presented in this book. Nearly half of this book, in fact, is devoted to detailed descriptions and analyses of the workplace practices at seven of those firms.

To place the phenomenon of good workplaces into a broader context, I have read widely about workplace and work-related issues. This has included more than three hundred volumes on management theory, industrial psychology and sociology, economic history, and social and moral philosophy, as well as more than a thousand articles from newspapers, magazines, and professional journals about contemporary workplace issues.

Much of this reading has concentrated on one simple question: Why are most workplaces so bad? Part of the answer can be found by examining the roots of American management styles, especially the ideas of influential management thinkers. It's not enough to criticize others, however. So this book also puts forward an alternative analysis of the workplace that may have some relevance to those interested in a nonmanipulative approach to managing.

It is my hope that the information and analyses in this book can assist those with practical concerns. With an awareness of what makes for a good employer, job seekers can have a better idea of what to look for in a workplace. They would know which questions to ask and which types of employers to avoid. Those with jobs could get some notions about how to improve their own working situations. And most important, having a clearer idea of the characteristics of a good workplace can help shed light on the daily experience of working for an organization. It can help people get a fix on what is possible to expect from their workplace.

This exercise may also be of great help to well-meaning employers. If they can be shown what makes an organization a great place to work, they might be able to recreate the conditions. Or at least make a stab at it. They would have some tools for analyzing what is wrong with their own workplace.

No discussion of this phenomenon would be complete without an attempt to spell out some of the social implications inherent in the notion of a great workplace. This is, after all, a nation of employees. Just as most Americans consider themselves middle class, most also think of themselves as employees. Indeed, less than 10 percent of the U.S. work force is self-employed. The rest work for companies, government agencies, or nonprofit concerns. So the quality of life within organizations not only has a major impact on each of us personally but on the society as a whole. How we treat each other during our working hours defines what kind of society we have.

Good workplaces provide beacons in a fog of mediocrity and insensitivity. They offer a different vision from the dog-eat-dog, each-man-for-himself, free-the-entrepreneur philosophy that enjoys widespread currency today. A great workplace is one where everyone, employees and management, is pulling together. It makes the workers feel better. It makes the managers feel better about the roles they play. And it helps society in general. In short, the attitudes implicit in this volume can do much to revitalize, and possibly even transform, American society.

PIECES
OF
THE
PUZZLE

In order to get a handle on the phenomenon of great workplaces, we first must
consider how people talk about the experience of working for a good employer.
We can then begin to spell out the defining characteristics of a great workplace.

1
INSIDE
GREAT
WORKPLACES
What Employees Say

When you ask employees of good workplaces what makes their companies so good, they typically talk first about attractive benefits—like the free lunch at the J. P. Morgan Bank in New York City or the generous profit-sharing plan at Hallmark Cards in Kansas City or Hewlett-Packard's ten different company-owned recreation areas for employees, from mountain resorts in California and Pennsylvania to a lake resort in Scotland and a ski chalet in the German Alps to a beach villa in Malaysia. Or they may go on at great length describing some of the unusual practices at the company—like the free Saturday night first-run movies at Merle Norman Cosmetics in Los Angeles or the "pig picking" (pig-on-a-stick) company picnics at Lowe's in North Carolina. In other words, employees first tell you what is different or unique about their company, just as a tour guide would take any tourist to the distinctive sights of a new city.

The information about benefits and unusual customs provides some idea about what the company is like. But it doesn't really give much of a picture of the experience of working there. So I found myself prodding employees more deeply on this question. After interviewing literally hundreds of employees at dozens of such companies while researching *The 100 Best Companies to Work for in America*, I noticed something unusual. I discovered that I was repeatedly hearing

nearly identical characterizations of working environments—
even among companies that superficially had nothing in
common. Employees at a printing plant in Wisconsin (Quad/
Graphics), a space shuttle components manufacturer in California (Odetics), a midwestern stock brokerage (A. G. Edwards), and a Texas real estate developer (Trammell Crow) all
talked about their companies as "fun" places to work. Employees at similarly divergent companies used the same terms:
*trust, pride, freedom, family, being treated fairly, being al-
lowed to make mistakes,* and so on. In other words, employees
began talking about the atmosphere of the workplace—the distinctive ways in which people work and relate to each other.
That people used precisely the same words and phrases indicated that their experience of work was similar. It was my
first clue that there is a distinctive quality that good workplaces
share. It was an indication that there is such a thing as the
phenomenon of a great place to work.

If I had heard these phrases only once or twice in my travels
across the country, I probably would not have thought much
about them. But because they cropped up so frequently at such
different kinds of workplaces, it was perhaps inevitable that I
would do a lot of thinking, trying to see what was behind the
words. Since these phrases were the starting point of my own
inquiry into the meaning of a great workplace, it seems that
sharing some of these phrases and some of the thoughts they
have provoked is a natural place to begin our discussion of
this phenomenon.

Examining the five phrases that follow will give more of a
feel for what it's like to work for a good employer. At the same
time, our discussion of the five phrases that follow will reveal
themes we will be touching on throughout the rest of the book,
providing us with some of the essential pieces of the great
workplace puzzle.

A Friendly Place

At Tektronix, a maker of oscilloscopes and other electronic
instruments based in Oregon, Valerie Cullen, a junior electronics technician, said this: "The part about Tek I like the
most is that I can walk up to anybody and say hi to them and

expect a friendly response. When I'm in the chow line in the cafeteria, I can turn around to just about anybody and enjoy talking with them."

It may sound trite, but friendliness appears to be one of the distinguishing characteristics of good workplaces. People seem to enjoy each other's company. This is not an insignificant issue. Work for an organization is, after all, work in a group setting. It's very different, for instance, from the mostly solitary work of a novelist or a painter. When you work for an organization, other people don't disappear. You are forced to interact with others, with your co-workers and your boss or your subordinates. What you think about your workplace has to do largely with the quality of those interactions.

Robert Schrank, a Ford Foundation sociologist, wrote an autobiographical book about his extraordinarily varied work experiences, ranging from farmhand and auto assembly-line worker to union organizer and government official. One of his jobs was working as a machinist in an electric powerhouse substation. Though not a particularly good employer, the workplace had its pluses:

> I found that one of the best things about being a machinist or a toolmaker was the freedom to move around, to schmooze. Often when a machine tool has been set up for an operation, there can be considerable time to schmooze with the guys around you—go get coffee, a Coke, or a smoke.

Schmoozing—informally chatting with others—is an accepted part of everyday life at good places to work. The important part of that sentence is the word *accepted*. You don't need permission to do it. There is no sense of having to look over your shoulder to make sure the boss doesn't catch you talking to someone on company time.

The relaxed attitude toward ordinary socializing springs in part from the relative lack of social hierarchy in good workplaces. Few of the *100 Best* companies, for instance, have executive dining rooms, executive parking lots, or other executive perks prevalent throughout corporate America. It is common to see people of all ranks mixing naturally with each other in spots like employee cafeterias. Company presidents at many of these firms, including some quite large ones, like

Armstrong World Industries, carry their own trays and eat in the employee cafeterias with everybody else. Schmoozing isn't restricted to one's peers.

The apparent social egalitarianism is only part of what is going on here. Good workplaces are not country clubs. Employees invariably insist that they work hard at these companies. Those who have worked elsewhere often say they work as hard or harder than at their previous place of employment. What's different, they say, is that people do not feel compelled to prove their industriousness to each other by "acting busy." The underlying mutual respect people have for each other—the assumption that everyone is a responsible adult—makes such pretenses pointless.

There Isn't Much Politics Around Here

An atmosphere of mutual respect also affects how people handle power struggles endemic to every human organization. In the workplace, people compete over promotions, choice assignments, and recognition, among other things. Competition can be healthy for both the individuals and the organization—but only if, to use a sports metaphor, the playing field is level. The field tilts when employers tolerate favoritism or practice outright discrimination against people because of sex, age, sexual preference, nationality, religion, etc. But even when the field is level, subverting others is the way to get ahead in some organizations, making employees feel there are no rules or referees.

At good workplaces, employees don't seem concerned about backstabbing. It's in this context that one expression heard repeatedly at good workplaces takes on meaning: "There isn't much politics around here." By that, people mean employees aren't constantly jockeying for position, trying to curry favor with the high-ups, worrying about the impact of their actions on their chances for moving up in the company, or looking over their shoulder to make sure someone else isn't setting them up to destroy their career.

After working for several other *Fortune* 500 companies, Carole St. Mark joined Pitney Bowes in 1980 and was named a top vice-president five years later (one of the few women in such a high position in corporate America). St. Mark found the lack of politics at Pitney Bowes the most refreshing aspect of the place:

> People who play political games are real obvious here. People say what they believe, and they are not punished for that. What's unique in my experience is the openness. People say what is on their minds, and the management will listen.

St. Mark contrasts the openness with the "cutthroat politicking" at her previous employers. She said the politicking got worse as one moved higher in the company hierarchy.

Indeed, those in charge of the organization are often responsible for encouraging a politicized working environment. Some openly promote rivalries among managers vying for higher positions. More common, however, are top officers who simply turn a blind eye to actions that contribute to politicizing the company. Politicking, for instance, is fostered whenever someone is fired (or demoted) for what appears to others in the company to be a personality conflict rather than deficiencies in work performance. Such episodes teach a powerful lesson to others—that loyalty (personal loyalty, not corporate loyalty) is the supreme virtue. Those who are loyal get rewarded; those who are not loyal get exiled, or worse. Instead of the "openness" St. Mark appreciates at Pitney Bowes, employees become careful not to offend. After all, their work may be judged not on its effectiveness to the organization but on how it affects their standing with the powers that be (or the powers that want to be).

Left unchecked, politicking affects everybody's behavior. Rosabeth Moss Kanter, an industrial sociologist and Harvard management professor, wrote insightfully of this problem in her book *Men and Women of the Corporation*:

> An interest in corporate politics was a key to survival for the people who worked at [the company]. . . . First, individual careers rose and fell, and people found the "top" more or less open to them, through dealings in power. Sometimes, crossing the wrong person could be dangerous. . . . Sometimes, people could only do their work effectively and exercise whatever competence gave them personal satisfaction if they knew how to

make their way through the more cumbersome and plodding official structure via the shadow political structure underneath.

Internal politics takes its toll on the entire organization. From an employee viewpoint, politicking destroys a sense of community, the sense that everybody is working together for a common cause. It also can destroy the organization itself, as Earl Shorris describes in his book *Scenes from Corporate Life: The Politics of Middle Management*:

> Within the layers and levels of a corporation, each competitor at an inner layer or higher level heightens competition among those below him to weaken them so that they are less able to compete with him. War inside the organization thus takes place vertically, horizontally, and tangentially. A view of the corporation from a great distance would reveal a war unlike the grand maneuvers of classic battles. It would appear far more like a riot spreading through the narrow maze of streets and steps of an ancient city.

One of the best recent examples of a company's being destoyed by internal politicking was described in Ken Auletta's best-selling book *Greed and Glory on Wall Street*, about the fall of Lehman Brothers. Auletta describes a company that typified Wall Street's reputation as a "jungle," where shouting insults and yelling were the order of the day. The politicking eventually reached the point where the company became polarized between the "bankers" and the "traders," which eventually paralyzed the entire firm and led to its being sold to Shearson/American Express.

That's just not the way things happen at Goldman Sachs. *Forbes* once remarked on Goldman's "minimum of infighting that afflicts most Wall Street firms. . . . Indeed, this unusual harmony is a major reason for the firm's unparalleled success." It's no accident that Goldman is different. As investment-banking partner Roy Smith says, "Totally losing your cool is considered a big no-no around here." Chairman John Weinberg says the firm tries to make internal politicking "unattractive." The company explicitly places its highest value on teamwork. Unlike other Wall Street firms, the firm specifically discourages "stars" and promotes employees on the basis of whether they are good "team players," on their ability to cooperate with others and contribute to the overall effort.

Good workplaces demonstrate that bad features of most workplaces, like destructive internal politicking, are not mere accidents of nature. They occur because people, especially those in charge, let them take place. And good workplaces, like Goldman Sachs, also show that a healthy workplace environment happens because of a determination to make things different.

You Get a Fair Shake

Management has few checks on its right to set wages, assign work, discipline, or terminate employees. The huge imbalance of power drives many conflicts underground.

It's no wonder that many people come into a job frightened. It starts when first applying for a job. Besides having to fill out endless forms and submit to questioning, many prospective employees are now required to pee into a jar. In this atmosphere, people say very little and don't talk frankly, fearing they won't be hired.

These feelings of powerlessness and intimidation usually carry over to the workplace. Many people do the job and pick up the paycheck. They know that the best thing is to keep their mouths shut when they disagree with the way things are run. They don't want to jeopardize their jobs.

Most companies offer little in the way of basic citizenship rights. If people are treated unfairly on the job, they often have no recourse. You can't make an issue of it the way you can if you receive a traffic ticket you think was undeserved.

Good workplaces offer a dramatic contrast to business as usual in America, where being fair to employees is considered optional. Few nonunionized firms, for instance, have even an elementary grievance procedure that offers any protections. And even strong union grievance procedures only seem to moderate the worst abuses. They don't create an atmosphere of fairness. It may be nice to run a company that values fairness, the argument goes, but what does it have to do with making money? Employees at good workplaces consistently, and often without being asked, make remarks like: "They treat us fairly here," or "The company doesn't take advantage of you," or "You get a fair shake around here."

Such statements must be taken seriously. It's extremely difficult to fool people into believing they are being treated fairly when they're not. Most of us, especially in workplace situations, have a highly trained sense of injustice. We carefully note examples of favoritism, bias, inequity, and abuse, even if we don't express our outrage. So we don't gratuitously say something is fair when we know it's not. We normally offer that judgment sparingly, and only when it's genuinely deserved.

Similarly, being fair is not something that happens automatically. Because the company holds most of the cards, the management has little incentive to assure fairness. In the short run, it's far easier for a company to ignore supervisors who abuse employees than to take them to task for such behavior. For one thing, there's often a long-standing us-versus-them mentality that may create a difficult political problem among middle managers if the company sides with an employee against a middle manager. And the company always faces a delicate problem of avoiding undermining managerial authority in the short run, even if being fair ultimately generates the kind of trust that enhances that authority. At any rate, it takes a lot of courage as well as energy to make sure employee complaints are heard impartially and fully. It requires a genuine commitment to justice to overrule a supervisor who has unfairly disciplined or fired a subordinate. And it becomes increasingly tougher to maintain standards of fairness as a company grows larger.

At several good workplaces, I heard company founders or presidents assert that being fair is always the right thing to do, regardless of whether it creates problems for the management. Jerry Sanders, founder of Advanced Micro Devices, a maker of silicon chips, says, "I am a nut when it comes to fair treatment" because "people go berserk when they are not fairly treated." Unfortunately, he says, most managements only give lip service to fair treatment because "they really want privilege."

More Than a Job

Work is one of the principal means through which life becomes
meaningful. We often define our personal identity by our work.
"I'm a secretary." "I'm a bricklayer." "I'm lawyer." This is
how we describe who we are. Merely having a job, though,
doesn't necessarily make the work meaningful. As Albert Ca-
mus once wrote: "Without work all life goes rotten. But when
work is soulless, life stifles and dies." It's depressingly common to feel that work is soulless. It occurs when people don't
perceive that they can make a difference—that they can have
any impact. The pride of authorship is missing.

Employees of good workplaces describe a refreshingly different attitude toward their work. While interviewing employees at Fisher-Price Toys headquarters near Buffalo, New
York, I met Denise Bowen-Fishback, who had been working
in Fisher-Price Toys' marketing department for five years.
Soon after joining the company, she suggested that any customer who bought two Fisher-Price toys be given free baby
blocks. To her amazement, the idea was accepted and implemented. Her comment was, "You can have an impact on things
here."

Bowen-Fishback's remark reflects a typical attitude found
at better workplaces. She's saying she feels her work has meaning. She's not just putting in her eight hours while going
through motions like an automaton. A number of employees
at a variety of workplaces make the same point by insisting
that they feel they have "more than a job."

Philosopher Hannah Arendt helps us understand what is
meant by this phrase in her book *The Human Condition*. In a
critique of Karl Marx, Arendt notes that all Western European
languages have separate words for *labor* and *work*. In Latin,
there are *laborare* and *facere*; in French, *travailler* and *ouvrer*;
and in German, *arbeiten* and *werken*. Though both terms relate
to similar activities, they are by no means synonymous. The
English philosopher John Locke makes this distinction when
he writes about "the labor of our body and the work of our
hands." Labor is seen as an inferior activity to work. Labor
often entails pain or trouble, sometimes without any obvious
purpose. Work suggests energy spent purposefully, to produce
something. Work has a definable end product; labor does not.

In German, *Arbeit* originally connoted only what serfs did, while *Werk* was what craftsmen produced.

Arendt's distinction helps evaluate differences among workplaces. In some of them, you feel like you're laboring. You are merely getting through the day. You may be active the entire time you're there, but you have a feeling that what you accomplish has little or no meaning. As Arendt explains, labor is often equated with subsistence. It's what you do to make enough money to feed yourself and your family. What you do isn't significant. It's the paycheck at the end of the week that's important. In the vernacular, you'd say: "It's just a job." For a job in this context has the same inferior status as the concept of labor. It has similar connotations of lacking any purpose other than sustenance.

When employees say, then, they feel their work is "more than a job," they are saying it has meaning. In Denise Bowen-Fishback's case, she suggests that her work means something because she can see what kind of effect it has. While this may be obvious to many workers, this is often not the case in large organizations. In some manufacturing enterprises, some workers don't understand how the widget they labor on relates to the finished product or how it is actually used. This is not true at Control Data and Tektronix, for instance, because groups of production employees regularly take field trips to other production plants to observe other stages of the manufacturing process or they visit customer facilities to see what happens to their product after it leaves their work area.

There's more to feeling your work has an impact than understanding how it fits into the whole picture. You also need to feel that your work is *your* work. You must feel *responsible* for it. So companies that want employees to understand more about the work, it's often because the firm wants them to assume an increasing share of responsibility. Earl Wantland, president of Tektronix, explains the rationale for encouraging more worker responsibility:

> I think it's impossible to define work in finite segments and lay it all out in a logical pattern that is going to be valid for any period of time. There's usually quite a lot of unforeseen dimensions to work. So it's very important that people don't get stuffed into a finite box, but that they enter the job in more of

an open manner. They should be told: "This is generally what we are trying to accomplish, here's some of the things we need to do, which you can advance by doing as much of that or learning to do as much of that as you can." People really ought to be involved in their work, not just in a kind of goody-goody sense, but in a more substantive way, of accepting the broader responsibility for work and improvement of work and, just as important, the future of that work.

It should not be surprising, then, that employees at good workplaces often remark that the company gives them a lot of responsibility. Those who have worked elsewhere often suggest that the greater level of responsibility they are given is the biggest change they notice. This is a key point because more responsibility implies more control over one's work. The issue of control over work strikes at the very core of what distinguishes good workplaces. Note, however, that we're not talking here of merely *feeling* like you have control over your work. Control is primarily a political issue, not a psychological one. Control relates to power. By definition, a powerless person has no control over his or her environment. So when people report that they have responsibility and control over their work, they mean that they have some power.

Like with the issue of fair treatment in the workplace, employees are highly aware of questions of power in the workplace. They can easily distinguish between jobs that give them control over their work and ones that only appear to do so. In recent years, there have been hundreds, if not thousands, of companies that have implemented job-enrichment or job-enlargement programs. These programs redesign jobs by, for instance, giving workers a greater variety of tasks. The industrial psychologists who conceive of such programs do so with the explicit objective of getting employees to *feel* more control over their work. As often as not, however, such programs don't change the real power relationships of the workplace. At good workplaces, when people talk about feeling control over their work, they usually can also point to ways in which they have a role in defining their own job, determining priorities and deadlines, and criticizing actions made by others (including supervisors or top management) without fear of retribution.

There's more to the idea of meaningful work than understanding its impact and having responsibility for what you do. There's also an important social dimension. Your work also has meaning when you feel it makes a valuable contribution to society. The nature of some occupations, like doctor or artist, offers this kind of meaning in abundance. And certain kinds of companies, like Fisher-Price or Apple Computer, make products that make people who work there proud to be associated with. But similar statements of pride can also be heard at companies that are not usually thought of as offering a distinctive product or service—like life-insurance companies. But at Northwestern Mutual Life, several employees mentioned that they feel a special pride when telling outsiders they work there. They are proud because they believe Northwestern is the best in its field, which makes them feel like winners. They also express pride that their company has taken the lead in many civic and humanitarian activities in Milwaukee. They feel the company's good-guy image in the community rubs off on them.

Northwestern's employees are saying, in effect, that they feel their company stands for something more than a business that makes a profit from selling certain products. John Siske, an employee at a Publix Super Markets store in Miami Beach, Florida, certainly has a similar view of his firm. He offered this view of his company: "Publix represents something. It's not like working for Kroger or Winn-Dixie or someplace like that. When you work for a company like Publix, you try to make sure to behave well even when you are off the job." Siske, like many other Publix employees, feels the company doesn't just offer groceries. It also offers a kind of socially beneficial experience ("Where Shopping Is a Pleasure" is the corporate slogan) that conveys a special aura to all who work there.

Workers at Hallmark Cards in Kansas City have a way of expressing that their company stands for more than making money from selling greeting cards. They talk proudly of being Hallmarkers. Being a Hallmarker is not merely being on the payroll there. It means that an employee has internalized the company's approach and commitment to producing a quality product. For example, press operators who refuse to print a greeting card because they don't think it meets the company's standards are applauded even when it costs the company money. They are exercising their prerogative as true Hallmarkers, guardians of the corporate ethos.

Feeling proud of what you do and who you do it with makes people at good workplaces say that they have "more than a job."

It's Just Like Family

At Delta Air Lines, people don't talk about being merely Delta employees. They prefer talking about being part of the Delta family. You hear the same expression at Federal Express, Hallmark Cards, IBM, Quad/Graphics, Gore, Publix Super Markets, and Northwestern Mutual Life. In fact, employees at such firms often speak about a family feeling.

Just what is meant by family? Of course, there are families and then there are families. Some have loving parents, while others have wife beaters and child abusers. So to suggest that a company is like a family may suggest widely different interpretations. Generally speaking, people who work for good employers mean something very positive when they say their workplaces have a familylike atmosphere. Among other things, they mean:

1. *A caring, nurturing environment:* Employees at good workplaces talk about how supervisors take an interest in their personal lives. People talk a lot about how they feel valued as individuals, not just as part of an undifferentiated mass that performs tasks for the organization. This also applies to the relationships between workers. There is a pervasive feeling that your personal concerns are important to others in the organization.

2. *A long-term commitment:* You're in a family for life. You can't leave at will. By the same token, people at good workplaces often remark that they feel they have made a lifelong career commitment to the organization. Good employers recognize and appreciate that commitment. As Don Hall, chairman of Hallmark Cards, explains: "Employees have literally thrown their lives in with you." Recognizing that fact means Hall sees the company as something different from a transient

economic association of individuals. To Hall: "Those that make up the corporation are indeed the corporation."

3. *We're all in it together*: One of the best things about being part of a family is that it's assumed that everyone can play a distinct and valuable role. Part of the reason for this attitude has been that families have historically been economic units in which members pool their resources to sustain one another. Within the family, there's a feeling that everybody is "in it together." Family members are supposed to unite when confronting outsiders. Within an organization, this feeling does more than engender camaraderie. It also helps the organization achieve its goals more effectively. This is one factor that explains why good employers tend to be more productive and profitable than their competitors.

Not everyone likes to be part of a family. To some, a suggestion that people are part of the same family implies limitations on personal freedom and independence and a lack of privacy. Family members are generally expected to participate, to be part of the group. People can't just do as they wish. They are part of something bigger than themselves. This is an aspect of many of the nation's best employers that turns off some people. Some avoid working at family-type companies even if such firms offer superior pay, benefits, more challenging work, and career opportunities. Such places can be too intense, perhaps a bit too socially demanding, for some people. Some good employers are especially sensitive to this issue. Don Hall, chairman of Hallmark, explains that despite the strong value placed on the company as family, the management tries to "make room for people who just want to put in their eight hours and go home." In other words, any good society must allow for loners.

There's another reason why the family metaphor fails to adequately express what is going on in good workplaces. Family carries with it the idea of hierarchical roles, such as parents and children, and of paternalism, which has negative connotations when applied to the workplace. As mentioned earlier, good workplaces are often characterized by a social egalitarianism that mitigates against the sort of rigid hierarchy suggested by the family metaphor. So, regarding the relationships between employees and management, it's common to hear people at good workplaces use the term *partnership*. As partners engaged in a common enterprise, everybody has something of value to contribute. What's more, the concept of the workplace as a partnership carries with it the element of mutual respect, which is a fundamental characteristic of a good workplace.

While the idea of partnership may more accurately describe some aspects of a good workplace, it does not adequately get across the feeling of a community. For a good workplace does offer a sense of community in a society that is increasingly becoming atomized. Few people feel much attachment to the town or city they live in. For many people, the work organization offers the only place to experience a feeling of belonging to something outside the family. Lewis Lehr, former head of 3M, explains that it's natural for a company to be a "social center" because "people spend more time with their compatriots at work than they do with their neighbors." It's a sad commentary on our society, however, that most workplaces only aggravate people's feelings of isolation. It may well be that the most important contribution of good workplaces is social: providing a harmonious community in a society where few such opportunities exist.

There are several other phrases that employees often use to characterize the working atmosphere of good workplaces. But continuing to reflect on these phrases would only give us more of an appreciation of why people like working for good employers. It wouldn't help us put our finger on what are the essential characteristics of a good workplace. To do that, we need to define the phenomenon we've been talking about.

2
IN SEARCH
OF A
DEFINITION

What Is a
Great Place to Work?

Most of us can, without hesitation, answer the question "Is your company a good place to work?" And we're used to hearing and passing along friends' assessments about life at other companies—that the one John works for is a terrific place to work, that Mary's is a miserable place, or that Bill's is so-so.

In making those judgments, we have an implicit notion about what is or is not a good workplace. But because the concept of a good workplace has not been considered in its own right, we don't have generally agreed upon ways to compare workplaces. Worse, we don't have an easy way of explaining *why* one is better than another.

Let's look at Delta Air Lines and Northwest Airlines. Both air carriers are about the same age and size and have about the same number of employees. Both have performed well financially over a long period of time. And both carriers offer comparable wage and benefits packages. But Northwest has had a long history of labor conflicts and Delta is widely acknowledged as a great place to work. Why?

The difficulty we have in explaining why one employer is better than another can be traced to the lack of a conceptual framework that lets us see how various policies and practices relate to each other. We don't understand the underlying principles of the workplace. We lack ready-made ideas that can help us get a handle on the nature of a workplace—ways to evaluate why a company like Delta is considered to be good and one like Northwest bad.

The absence of concepts to appraise companies as workplaces contrasts with the abundance of tools to assess companies as businesses. There's the notion of market share, which helps explain how well a company is doing relative to its competitors. There's the notion of sales growth, which helps explain whether a company is growing larger. And there's the notion of profitability, which is the basic barometer of an enterprise's financial health. In short, we're not stuck with merely saying a company is doing well or doing poorly and giving some random facts or anecdotes to support our opinion. We have a variety of well-established shorthand devices to pinpoint how a company is performing as a business enterprise.

Not so with workplaces. Our vocabulary is more limited. About all we usually say is that a company is a good or a bad or a so-so place to work. To analyze workplaces, then, we need some concepts comparable to those used to evaluate a business's financial well-being. Let's start with the concept of a great place to work.

How would we define a great place to work? Here are some possible definitions:

You're paid a lot of money.

You're treated like a human being.

You do interesting work.

You get good benefits.

You're not fired at the slightest downturn.

Our immediate responses may focus on one or possibly two issues. But if we were presented with a list like the one above and asked to define a great workplace, we'd probably say, "All of the above." On reflection, we might add a few more ideas to the list. Like working in a clean and safe environment. Or having all the tools to do the job right. Or being able to make suggestions or complaints without fear of reprisal.

We could easily expand our list into a hodgepodge of personnel policies, precepts about how managers should act, and descriptions of well-designed jobs. We could have listed *policies* and *practices* that we would expect to find in a great place to work. But we haven't answered the original question.

A better starting point would be to ascertain what a variety of real-life good workplaces have in common. Such an inquiry could begin by reexamining the data gathered in *The 100 Best Companies to Work for in America*. That book was, after all, the first systematic effort to describe the policies and practices of companies considered by their employees to be good places to work. Any careful reader would quickly discover, however, that there is no simple pattern uniting good workplaces.

Let me give some examples. Trammell Crow Company is a large real estate developer based in Dallas, Texas. *The 100 Best Companies to Work for in America* described the firm's exceptional profit-sharing program, which adds an extra 25 to 75 percent bonus to already substantial salaries. The offices don't have partitions, so even the top executives sit in the same bullpen area as the secretaries. That includes the founder of the firm, Trammell Crow, one of the three dozen richest men in America, worth more than $750 million, according to *Forbes*.

If we only consider Trammell Crow Company, we might conclude that these two policies—profit sharing and no executive office suites—might be two ingredients of a great place to work. Alas, it's not that simple. IBM, a company long considered a superlative employer, has no profit-sharing plan and its top executives sit in private offices. No bullpens for IBM's top brass. IBM, however, has had a no-layoff policy since before the Great Depression, while Trammell Crow Company has no such explicit policy and, in fact, has on occasion laid off some employees during real estate bust periods.

Perhaps we picked the wrong policies to compare. How about employee ownership? Admittedly, most of the companies on the *100 Best* list are *not* employee owned. But perhaps all employee-owned companies are good workplaces. Workers at Publix Super Markets, the largest grocery retail chain in Florida and an entirely employee-owned operation, express an almost evangelical love for Publix, often citing the fact that they own the company as the main reason.

You would hear a different story about employee ownership if you talked with some of the ex-workers of Hyatt Clark, a New Jersey maker of roller bearings for automobiles. The former General Motors subsidiary slid into bankruptcy after six years as an employee-owned company. The problem: conflicts between the employee-owners and the company's management exacerbated already difficult problems it was having in its competitive industry. A *New York Times* reporter noted that Hyatt Clark employees "discovered that no ownership plan can overcome deep-rooted rivalries and distrust between workers and management."

The fact that particular policies and practices fail to define a great workplace has also frustrated human-resource professionals. They tend to think something like this: General Electric has a nifty employee savings plan; let's see if we can't do the same thing here. Over the past decade, personnel fads have included: cafeteria benefit plans, quality circles (Japanese-style work teams), employee stock ownership plans (ESOPs), and 401(k) savings plans. Some have represented genuine improvements in income or benefits for millions of employees. But the piecemeal approach does not get at the essence of the great workplaces. The peculiar elan of such organizations—the excitement about the workplace that pervades these companies—is not so easily exportable. You can't suggest that an employer only needs to throw in a new pension plan and expect to come up with Delta Air Lines' well-publicized "family spirit." At good workplaces, the whole is greater than the sum of its policies and practices.

The question becomes, How do you explain the whole—the glue that seems to put policies together in a way that works? Why does one policy that seems so central in one great workplace not have any effect somewhere else?

I decided to revisit some of the *100 Best* companies to pursue that specific question. We had originally sought out lower-level employees to get their views on their employer.

As can be seen from the last chapter, you can learn much about the working atmosphere from talking with employees. But they generally don't have much of an overview to help explain why everything fits together. Now I found I wanted specifically to talk to the top executives and, when possible, to the founders. Because of their crucial roles in setting the direction for their own organizations, I hoped they could shed some light on my inquiry.

From these interviews, it became clear that the quality of the workplace was something they had thought about a great deal. Most explicitly stated that they saw creating a good workplace as one of the most important goals of the organization. They enjoyed talking at length about their notions of what makes for a great place to work. On one point they were united: If their companies are good workplaces, it is not because of any specific policies. Far more important than the specific policies is the nature of the *relationship* between the company and the employees.

Ewing Kauffman, chairman and founder of Kansas City-based Marion Laboratories, offers this example. During the drug firm's quarterly Marion on the Move meetings, he often hands out large bonus awards to various employees. At one meeting, for instance, he handed a production worker shares of Marion stock worth $8,000 for ten years of perfect attendance, and three other employees got stock worth $7,000, $12,000, and $15,000 for money-saving suggestions. Kauffman stresses that it's not just the fact that the company regularly gives such bonuses that is significant. Equally important is the spirit in which the bonuses are presented—that is, the attitude behind the bonuses. He says: "If you do it because you want to be a father and a giver, that's not good. You don't *give* anything. They *earn* it. Marion doesn't give anything." Kauffman realizes that handing out bonuses could be interpreted as a paternalistic act. But he is not interested in playing that role. He is not interested in having a father-child relationship with his employees.

Larry Quadracci, president and founder of Quad/Graphics, a Midwest printing company, makes the same point: "The systems are only as good as the attitude upon which the systems are operated." Quadracci says the fundamental attitude of his company toward employees is that "we're all in this thing together as partners for the same thing—and that is to make money. And we believe that together we're going to make more money than any of us individually can do."

It emerged that good employers give a lot of time, thought, and energy to developing a certain type of relationship with employees. Once I understood this point, I quickly recalled how often I'd heard employees of good workplaces talk about the quality of their relationships with their supervisors, the company, and even other employees. "Everybody gets along with each other around here" was one way this idea was often expressed. By "everybody" they clearly meant everybody, including management and employees.

Larry Quadracci offers the analogy of a marriage: "Marriages are not made in heaven, nor are jobs. Both are close, personal relationships that must be worked at daily." Quadracci's analogy makes good sense. We would not consider a good marriage to be synonymous with two people having a house, a car, two children, a dog, and three cats. We would say that a good marriage depends on how the two people relate to each other. And the very best marital relationships are characterized by mutual love and respect. In this vein, I could see that my initial impulse to define a good workplace was like trying to understand the quality of a marriage by looking only at externals.

Once I looked instead at the employee-employer relationship, I found it easy to characterize the essential quality of good workplaces. Just as love characterizes the attitude of both parties of a good marriage, trust characterizes the attitude of both sides of a good employment relationship.

Why trust? First, employees at good workplaces constantly speak about how they "believe," "have confidence in," "have faith in," or simply "trust" their employers. Similarly, managers at the same companies talked about how they "trust," "can rely on," and "can depend on" their employees. There's an atmosphere of mutual trust that permeates good workplaces. Second, trust is completely lacking in bad workplaces, and it appears only sporadically in workplaces considered mediocre. Based on my experience as a labor reporter, it is invariably true that union-organizing drives or strikes often occur when trust between employees and their employer breaks down. (That is not to say a unionized firm can't be a great workplace, as we will see later, in the chapters on Northwestern Mutual Life and Preston Trucking.)

When I considered trust as the defining characteristic of a good workplace, I found a straightforward handle with which to evaluate various policies and practices of a company, as well as the recurrent phrases used by the employees. Let's return to the earlier example of Trammell Crow sitting in the bullpen with the secretaries and lower-level employees. That practice could be interpreted in different ways. After all, employees could consider this a reflection of the boss's distrust of them, since in the bullpen, he would be able to watch and hear their every move. But that isn't how Mr. Crow's employees see it. On the contrary, they believe he sits in the bullpen because he respects their opinions and has nothing to hide from them. What's more, they think it shows he doesn't consider himself to be a separate breed despite his immense wealth.

A focus on the underlying relationships of a workplace does not mean that actual policies can be ignored. On the contrary, the policies are tangible manifestations of the relationships. To evaluate a workplace, we must consider what employees are paid, what benefits they receive, to what degree employees have a say over their own work, whether they have a grievance procedure, and so on. These are real issues.

To cultivate a specific employee-employer relationship is to build something that really exists. It is a much different matter from what some management gurus do when they talk about trying to induce a "feeling." Thus, Tom Peters devotes an entire chapter of *A Passion for Excellence* to describing how to get employees to *feel* like owners. Though the chapter is entitled "Ownership!" Peters barely mentions the issue of real dollars-and-cents employee ownership.

Techniques that manipulate people's feelings ultimately backfire unless there's a corresponding change in the reality of the power or economics of a relationship. Nothing destroys employee trust more quickly than management techniques designed to make people feel good about something that they know isn't based on reality. Trammell Crow's employees think he respects them because he *does* respect them, not because he sits in the bullpen with everybody else. The technique makes sense for Trammell Crow because it flows naturally from his basic attitude toward employees. Employees can spot phonies. Managers who adopt the same practice only because it works at Trammell Crow Company will find it self-defeating.

Where trust exists, the employer believes the workers want to be productive and participate fully in the enterprise; employees assume the employer has their interests at heart. This trust frees employees to get a deeper sense of fulfillment from their work.

A relationship of trust between the employer and employees is the foundation of a great place to work. But two other kinds of relationships turn out to be nearly as important. First, there is the employee's relationship to the job itself. You may consider the particular tasks you do at work to be boring or challenging, unimportant or socially significant, and so on. By contrast, in the best working situation, you feel pride in what you do. You feel as though you contribute something by performing the task. It has meaning to you far beyond the compensation you receive for the time you spend. It's what employees at good workplaces mean when they say, "It's more than a job."

The other primary relationship in the workplace is that among the employees, including managers. This determines the quality of the workplace community. Your relationships with other employees can vary from your feeling that they are part of your family to your seeing them as enemies with whom you're at war. You may look forward to seeing them every morning, or you may dread having to encounter them. In the best working situation, you enjoy being with your co-workers. It's not necessarily fun in the sense of a constant round of laughs, though that can happen. But there is a kind of camaraderie that makes a pleasant working environment a "friendly" place. You feel part of a harmonious community, lacking in "politics," where people help each other develop and grow personally and professionally. It may feel like "family."

Because the workplace is comprised of these three distinct relationships, it's possible for one to be good and the other two lousy or two to be good and the third to be terrible. For instance, it's easy to imagine places where employees feel terribly proud of what they do and enjoy the other employees they work with but still consider it an awful workplace because they hate the company or their boss. In fact, in some bad workplaces I've visited, employees report that half the fun they get from working there comes from the games they play with other employees to plague their bosses. In this same destructive environment, the supervisors may enjoy plotting various tactics to "get" individual employees.

Another frequent pattern occurs when employees say they don't like their particular job, but they still think the company is a good employer. They are personally dissatisfied with their current position, but they feel the company is not to blame, because for one reason or another, the employee isn't well suited to perform the assigned tasks.

The three relationships are to some extent independent, but one can affect the other two. If you don't enjoy the other people you work with (or your immediate boss), it's difficult to find satisfaction from your job. You may feel that you'd rather work alone. Or if the employer-employee relationship is an exploitative one, it can detract from your feelings of pride in your job. And it can upset your relationships with fellow employees, because the employer has you constantly pitted against them. Similarly, if you have a good relationship with the employer, it may facilitate your relationships with other employees and enhance job satisfaction.

Looking at the workplace as three distinct relationships reveals the shortcomings of management theories and techniques that focus on the employees' relationship to their jobs (or with their immediate supervisors) without simultaneously trying to affect the overall relationship with the employer. This myopic view has a long history, as will be discussed in more detail later. In Elton Mayo's Hawthorne experiments, for instance, the management consultants tried to figure out ways to improve job satisfaction while ignoring the Depression-induced layoffs occurring in the factory.

To sum up: From an employee viewpoint, a great workplace is one in which *you trust the people you work for, have pride in what you do, and enjoy the people you are working with.* This definition offers us a starting point for our inquiry. To get more of a flavor of good workplaces, we need to look more closely at each of the three primary workplace relationships.

PART TWO

DELIVERING ON WHAT THEY PROMISE

By looking at specific policies and practices of several good employers, we can examine how they approach the three distinct relationships that are part of any workplace.

3
SHOWING
GOOD
FAITH

New Lanark, Publix Super Markets,
Marion Labs

Robert Owen is best known as utopian because of the cooperative community he founded at New Harmony, Indiana, in the early nineteenth century. What is less known is that before setting out for America, Owen managed a textile mill in New Lanark, Scotland. At the time, it was one of the largest cotton-spinning mills in Britain, with about fifteen hundred employees.

When Owen took over the mill in 1800, he confronted a problem that has bedeviled anyone who has sought to improve the workplace. He discovered that the mill's workers were highly suspicious of their new employer's motives. As Owen put it in his autobiography: "The workpeople were systematically opposed to every change which I proposed, and did whatever they could to frustrate my object." The mill workers were convinced Owen only wanted "to squeeze as much gain out of them as possible."

No one should fault workers for assuming the worst. Since the early days of the Industrial Revolution, there have been dramatic examples of employers who have sought to "squeeze" as much as possible from the work force. For their part, workers often respond by doing only the minimum required, while demanding the maximum possible for their labor. It's a familiar game. Both sides try to obtain as much from the bargain as possible. But a good workplace is different.

Another dynamic operates in addition to that of everyone for himself or herself. As discussed earlier, there's a high degree of trust between the company and employees in good workplaces. At the very least, that means that both sides aren't always seeking to take advantage of the other. In a good workplace, the dynamic of relentless self-interest is supplanted by a different kind of relationship—where both sides find common ground to work together for their mutual benefit without compromising their separate interests.

Owen's tenure at New Lanark was notable because he overcame the workers' initial suspicions and forged a more harmonious relationship with his employees. Owen noted, however, that "it was long before the majority of the people could be convinced that I was earnestly engaged in measures to improve their permanent condition." To convince the workers, he needed to show them he was operating in good faith— that he had no secret agenda, that he was not trying to manipulate them or "squeeze" them. He needed to demonstrate that his actions were in accord with his avowed intentions.

Biographer Margaret Cole explains how Owen went about changing his relationship with the workers:

> Owen was in no hurry. He certainly intended to improve their discipline and their standards both of work and of living; he meant to make New Lanark into a model community. But he did not intend to thrust either his standards or his discipline down anybody's throat; he wanted the workers to see for themselves that his was the better way, and to take them along with him step by step.

Owen's patient spadework finally paid off. In 1806 the United States placed an embargo on cotton exports to Britain, creating a major crisis for the cotton industry. Most British mill owners simply shut down their factories and laid off the workers. But Owen believed that throwing the mill's employees out of work would have been "cruel and unjust." So he continued to pay the workers to keep the mill's machinery in good working order. Owen maintained this policy for the four months the embargo lasted "without a penny being deducted from the full wages of anyone." His action cost the company seven thousand pounds in the short run, but it had a big impact on the mill's employees. As Owen put it: "This proceeding won the confidence and the hearts of the whole population, and henceforward I had no obstructions from them in my progress of reform."

What's important to note here is the *process* through which Owen gained the confidence and trust of his work force. It reveals an *an open-ended time commitment.* There are no shortcuts to gaining people's trust and confidence. As Douglas Strain, founder of Electro Scientific Industries, puts it: "Trust isn't built up overnight. It takes a while to evolve."

Owen instituted many reforms during his quarter century in New Lanark. He forbade corporal punishment, stopped the hiring of pauper children, eliminated summary firings, reduced the working hours from fourteen hours to ten and a half hours a day, and provided a high-quality school for all children in the village. He also instituted the unheard-of practice of allowing workers the right to appeal supervisors' judgments about their job performance. One historian remarked that this novel procedure "contributed more than a little to the workers' willingness to cooperate with him." Owen had a reputation for fair-mindedness. A teacher at the New Lanark school reported: "I never knew, in a single instance, Mr. Owen ever to dismiss a worker for his having manfully and conscientiously objected to his measures." Near the end of his tenure, Owen apparently even proposed to transfer ownership of the mill to the workers to run for their own profit. Owen's business partners squelched this scheme, however.

Word of this model industrial community spread widely. Between 1815 and 1825, nearly twenty thousand people made the trek to the Scottish lowlands to see the mill. Included among the visitors were British nobility and politicians, ambassadors from many countries, even Grand Duke Nicholas of Russia. Many visitors remarked at the mill's unusual esprit. Economic historian Sidney Pollard insists that New Lanark's business success stemmed partly from Owen's "ability to win the cooperation of his workers."

It would be wrong to assume that after the 1806 embargo, working life at New Lanark resembled a fairy tale in which everyone lived happily ever after. By modern standards, Owen's New Lanark would hardly pass as an ideal workplace, if for no other reason than the presence of child workers (though he raised the minimum age from six to ten). Partly because many of the workers were children, there was a paternalistic air about the place. Owen made all decisions personally, without input from the workers.

Unfortunately, relations also began to slip during the final years of Owen's management. Owen's growing fame and involvement in various national social reform movements led him to take long trips away from the mill. As a result, he became an increasingly remote figure to his employees. One New Lanark visitor remarked in 1819: "[Owen] has as little direct intercourse with the inhabitants of his colony as a general has with his soldiers." A few years later, Owen sought to increase the workers' contribution to the employee sick fund, set up by Owen to cover illnesses but supposedly administered by the workers. Owen's actions became a public issue when a group of New Lanark workers wrote a letter to Owen's business partners, complaining:

> We view it as a grievance of considerable magnitude to be compelled by Mr. Owen to adopt what measures soever he may be pleased to suggest on matters that entirely belong to us. Such a course of procedure is most repugnant to our minds as men, and degrading to our characters as freeborn sons of a highly favoured Britain.

Of course, this may have been an isolated event. But the episode helps demonstrate a final important lesson that can be drawn from the story of this Scottish mill: Employment relationships involve *constant communication*. Owen's reforms may have broken down the initial hostility and generated a reservoir of goodwill among the workers. But such a reservoir inevitably runs dry if everyday human contact is neglected. In the sick-fund instance, Owen had a perfectly reasonable justification for augmenting the contributions as there had been an outbreak of typhus fever. But he apparently didn't approach the problem with the kind of tact and patience that characterized his earlier years there.

That this flare-up could happen to someone universally acclaimed in his day as a great employer should give pause to anyone who thinks that a few new benefits here or progressive personnel policies there will magically turn a company into a

great workplace. Progressive policies and enlightened workplace practices can provide a healthy foundation for a good
relationship. But the foundation should not be equated with
the entire relationship, any more than the skeleton of a body
is the same as a human being. Much of the quality of a human
relationship depends on the nature of the interactions between
people. At New Lanark, it appears that in the final years, Robert
Owen simply stopped communicating regularly with his employees. If true, the mill may have had the best policies in the
world, but the heart and soul of good workplace would have
been missing.

Publix Super Markets: "They Didn't Have to Do That"

Constant communication is the byword at Publix Super Markets, whose three hundred-plus stores are all located in Florida. The quality of the company's interaction with its fifty-one
thousand employees has impressed several outside observers.
Several years ago, for instance, respected industrial pollster
and social analyst Daniel Yankelovich interviewed scores of
Publix's employees. His conclusion:

> Publix Super Markets, Inc., is a remarkable operation. The
> people who work there are the most highly motivated people
> I have ever seen in a large organization. I admit I have seen
> people as highly motivated in a very small family organization.
> But . . . Publix is now a very large organization, and to see
> people with that quality of motivation is really outstanding.

You can get some flavor of how Publix relates to its employees from observing one of the banquets held the night
before a new store's opening. In early 1985, I attended the
banquet held at a hotel in Jacksonville celebrating the opening
of Publix's Store 263 and honoring the forty-seven new employees. As they do for every store's opening, the company's
top dozen corporate officers traveled to the banquet from the
Lakeland headquarters (two hundred miles away).

The banquet had the earmarks of an old-fashioned revival
meeting. Corporate executives and managers from other Publix
stores rose to give testimonials—all variations of the same gos-

pel: "I started with this company at the bottom, just like you, and after years of hard work, I've been able to get ahead in my career. You can, too, because Publix is a land of opportunity for anyone who works hard. This is a company that cares about you and your success." One Jacksonville store manager told of an incident early in his twenty-seven-year career in which another employee was hospitalized for surgery and the store manager stayed with the family at the hospital during the operation. "I felt like I was part of a family," he declared. "Publix people have a heart." His testimonial was met by a chorus of amens from several of the old-timers.

Between testimonials, the emcee for the banquet, a regional Publix executive, engaged the new employees in a trivia quiz: "How large is Store 263?" Someone answered, "Thirty-eight thousand square feet." "Where does the name Publix come from?" Another employee raised his hand and explained that it was the name of a now-defunct movie theater chain. After a few more similar questions, the emcee asked: "Who owns Publix?" Everyone in the crowd answered at once: "We do!" The emcee congratulated them and proceeded to explain that all Publix shareholders are employees, and that after one year's service, new employees would be granted stock and become eligible to buy more.

The high point of the evening came when George W. Jenkins stood up to speak. Wearing a bright green sports jacket emblazoned with Publix logos, the seventy-seven-year-old company founder sprinkled his talk with numerous anecdotes about the good old days, gave a sermonette on "getting along with other people," and at one point told an off-color story about a philandering husband. Referring to himself as "an old groceryman who loves to talk shop," Jenkins noted that Publix was now Florida's largest supermarket chain, selling more than $3 billion a year worth of groceries. But he also observed that "It's harder to stay on top than to get there because everyone's trying to pull you down. So we don't want to get complacent." He mentioned several grocery chains that had been unable to cope with success and had even been run out of business, throwing hundreds of employees out of work.

But Jenkins's talk wasn't meant to scare newcomers. He gave an upbeat assessment of the valuable contribution he expected from the new people. He asserted that Publix has always sought

to live up to its corporate slogan: "Where Shopping Is a Pleasure." He also noted that Publix has always tried to be a place
"Where Working Is a Pleasure." (That slogan adorned the cover
of the banquet's program brochure, which listed all of Store
263's employees.) He told the newcomers: "My wish for you
is that you have as much satisfaction working for Publix as
we did at the beginning, working seventy to eighty hours for
fifteen dollars a week." According to Jenkins, it was up to
them, as employees, to determine whether Publix achieved its
twin goals. He said: "Starting tomorrow, Publix will be a little
better or not quite as good, depending on you."

By the end of the evening, the energy and enthusiasm were
almost palpable. The excitement continued the next morning.
Long before Store 263 opened its doors at nine o'clock, the
chain's top executives (including Jenkins and company president Mark Hollis) were all there, helping in the bakery, ad-
justing rows of cans on the shelves, fixing meat-counter
displays. When the first customers came through the doors,
the executives were still there working alongside the newcomers, even doing such menial tasks as bagging groceries and
carrying them out to customers' cars.

At first glance, this banquet and store opening may appear
to be like a sports pep rally. From an employee viewpoint, it
is difficult to look at pep rally-style events without some cyn-
icism. For one thing, there is typically an air of unreality about
such gatherings. You hear "Our team is the best in the world"
even when the team has lost the last ten games. In a rah-rah
environment, the last thing you expect to be told is the truth.
For another, pep rallies appear to be a blatantly manipulative
technique. The principle ground rule seems to be: Tell people
whatever will make them feel good. Then they'll work harder
so we (the company) will make more money.

The opening-night banquet certainly had all the earmarks of
a typical pep rally. But much more was going on at the banquet.
We need also to consider the *context* of the banquet—in this
case, *the overall relationship between the company and the
employees.* Employees will usually pick up on the true intention of a technique. If a technique is actually meant to manipulate them into working harder, employees will eventually see
the ploy for what it is. Nobody likes being manipulated. Employees may work harder because the technique does "work,"

as management consultants would say. But such techniques may undermine efforts to develop a healthy employment relationship.

So let's consider the Publix banquet in terms of the effect it has on the workplace rather than its impact on productivity. On the one hand, the employees were certainly turned on by the event, judging from their comments afterward. It was pretty heady to have the founder, president, and other top executives of a large company welcome you in person to the enterprise and then work alongside you during your first day on the job. That kind of personal attention is bound to make people feel special.

But Publix officials also made a series of *promises* and *implied commitments* to new employees. They promised a "career, not just a job" in a "land of opportunity." They said the new employees would be "owners" of the company. And they said that the employees were now part of the "Publix family," where they would be cared for as people, not just as cashiers or meat cutters. Company president Mark Hollis dramatized this commitment by telling the newcomers: "If there is any way I can ever be of any help to any of you, I hope you will call on me." So it would be an error to conclude that employees were only turned on because executives made a two-hundred-mile trek from corporate headquarters, ate a chicken dinner with the troops, and then rolled up their sleeves to tidy up shelves, cut meat, and bag groceries. Employees were even more impressed by the implications for their own future. The company had, after all, gone out of its way to pledge an extraordinary relationship with them.

There is, of course, a down side to any promise or commitment. As any politician knows, you can win votes by making promises, but voters eventually expect you to deliver. By welcoming employees into the "Publix family" with open arms, the company was taking a risk. It was raising expectations about the employment relationship—far beyond what workers could hope for at most workplaces, let alone at most retailing establishments. On opening day, employees had no reason to question whether the company's leaders were sincere in their talk about "family" and "opportunity" and "your company." But the banquet's speeches and testimonials upped the stakes. If the reality of work life at Publix didn't match the eloquent talk, Store 263 might turn out to be an even worse place to work than had Publix's officials stayed away altogether. Employees might perceive Publix management as no more than hyped-up cheerleaders. The seeds of distrust would have taken firm root.

Publix's leaders have, of course, been around long enough to be fully aware of these dangers. Keeping commitments is serious business at Publix. Founder Jenkins, for instance, insists that he won't commit the company to a no-layoff policy in part because he's not sure the company can always provide jobs for people. He has seen too many big chains lose their shirts in Florida to think it can't happen to Publix.

Company president Mark Hollis offers another example. The company publishes a biweekly bulletin that lists all the births, deaths, marriages, and serious illnesses of employees and their families. For more than twenty years, the previous Publix president had sent personalized cards to the families of everyone listed in the bulletin. But when he became president in 1984, Hollis decided to discontinue sending cards for births, marriages, and illnesses, only keeping the practice of sending sympathy cards. He simply didn't think he would always be able to write the notes. He thinks that it is better *not* to do something than to commit yourself to something you may not be able to deliver.

Not only are Publix's leaders extremely careful about making commitments, they are also conscientious about keeping the ones they do make. Hollis speaks frankly about the problem: "I think [the relationship with employees] could change on us very quickly if we suddenly stopped visiting the stores so frequently. If corporate officers just sat up in their ivory tower, it could turn on us in just the matter of a couple of years." He admits that such a commitment means "you have to work hard to prove that you're worthy of their credibility." New store openings have averaged two a month for the past few years, and Jenkins, Hollis, and other senior executives personally attend every one, as they did Store 263's. What's more, all of them make it a point to visit every store in the chain once every two years. And these executive visits are not just token appearances, with a brief ceremonial walk through the store followed by a long, closed-door session in the store manager's office poring over the profit-and-loss statements. The executives make it a point to talk personally to employees. And several employees say it's not unusual for company executives to do tasks like bagging groceries if the store is busy.

I observed one example indicating that Hollis apparently does practice what he preaches. Soon after Store 263 opened its doors, I met an energetic young man named Mike Brown. He was busy greeting customers by handing them circulars with the advertised store specials as he wheeled them shopping carts. Brown had worked part time at another Publix supermarket for several years as he was completing college. He had transferred to Store 263 because it was closer to home. While we were talking, Hollis walked by and greeted Brown by his first name and asked him how his studies were coming. I later asked Brown whether he was surprised that Publix's president remembered his name. Brown just shrugged his shoulders and explained that Hollis and the manager of the other Publix store he had worked in had encouraged him to stay with Publix after college because they liked his work so much. Brown saw nothing extraordinary. He simply didn't realize how unusual a company he worked for, that presidents of firms with only a hundred employees often don't know the names of their part-time workers, let alone take an active interest in their careers.

Like the opening-night banquets, frequent executive visits to the stores could be construed as a great technique because it appears to lift employee morale. But again, to draw such a conclusion would be to view the technique outside the context of the company's relationship with employees. At Publix, the high visibility of executives also serves another function—that of delivering on their commitment to make employees part of the Publix "family."

One final point: When doing his study of Publix, Daniel Yankelovich found it significant that employees frequently stated: "They didn't have to do that." (It was a phrase, incidentally, I also heard repeatedly at Publix and at other good workplaces.) Yankelovich observed that employees typically made this statement after they remarked on an unusual benefit or an unexpected gesture by a manager. Yankelovich cited examples ranging from the free lunch offered at the warehouses to a manager who visited a new employee's family when her little daughter was hospitalized. Another example was an employee whose manager had thrown a Christmas party for the store's employees. She told the interviewer:

> He [the manager] is doing it on his own. Now, that is the sort of thing that makes you feel appreciated, and he really does notice that we do good work. He didn't have to do that.

In each of these instances, employees find it meaningful that the management goes out of its way to do something for them. More important, these voluntary acts also have the effect of personalizing the workplace. They indicate that the management recognizes the employees as unique human beings, not as easily replaceable cashiers and stock clerks. Indeed, Yankelovich reported that the most common single comment he heard from Publix employees was that they felt treated "like a person, not like a number."

As we have seen, Publix often goes beyond what is expected or customary. Publix's top executives don't have to appear in person at every store's opening. Publix's top executives don't have to show up and work alongside employees in the stores. Publix's managers don't have to take a personal interest in the careers of employees. But they do. And because they take the risk inherent in going beyond the traditional employee-employer relationship, they open the possibility of developing a fuller, more human, more trusting relationship.

Granted, a thin line separates this pattern of action from paternalistic acts that have the effect of stifling people. The paternalistic employer, as we shall discuss in a later chapter, often gives employees unexpected gifts, whether or not they are deserved. He does so as a gesture of power, making the person who receives the gift feel even more dependent. At Publix, the management gives no gifts. As in the instance of the manager's throwing a Christmas party, Publix managers invariably express explicit appreciation for something the employees have done. So rather than feeling suffocated by these gestures, employees generally feel that they are based on something that is genuinely deserved but not normally recognized. The focus is on the employees and their contribution, not on the management as giver.

Marion Labs: An "Uncommon Company"

At Marion Labs, employees refer to the company as "uncommon" and to those who work there as "uncommon people." The term uncommon is also applied to certain benefits. For instance, during the summer months, employees are permitted to take Friday afternoons off (with pay). So those days are called uncommon Fridays. If production meets certain specified goals, employees are given an additional week of paid vacation between Christmas and New Year's Day. That's called uncommon winter.

Headquartered in Kansas City, Marion Labs manufactures and sells prescription drugs. Marion's two thousand employees (who refer to each other as associates) have other reasons to consider Marion uncommon. Marion has a no-layoff policy. Marion has a generous suggestion-award program, distributing some ten thousand shares of stock annually among those with the best suggestions (one year it resulted in an average of $1,000 worth of stock apiece for the employees whose 237 suggestions were accepted). And Marion is one of the very few companies in America that offer stock options to all employees.

Typically reserved only for the top corporate officers, a stock option is the right to purchase shares of a company's stock at a guaranteed price. After being with Marion for one year, an associate can buy up to one hundred shares of Marion stock at any time during the next ten years at the same price the stock sold for on the associate's first anniversary with the company. Because Marion's stock has risen in value more than 1,000 percent over the past decade, many Marion associates have cashed in their options for a handsome profit. In fact, because of the stock-option plan and a generous profit-sharing plan, more than seventy Marion associates have become millionaires.

The stock-option and profit-sharing plans stem directly from a principle that is constantly repeated at Marion. It is: "Those who produce shall share in the results." This sounds like a reasonable principle for any organization to follow. But Ewing Kauffman, Marion's founder, knows from bitter personal experience how rarely it is practiced in corporate America. Kauffman (who is called Mr. K. by associates) is one of Kansas City's

most colorful characters, best known locally as co-owner of
the Kansas City Royals baseball team. He explains that he left
his previous company, where he was a drug salesman, precisely because that firm didn't share fairly:

> I worked for another pharmaceutical company and was paid
> no salary, no expenses, just straight commission. The second
> year, I made more money than the president. So they cut my
> commission rate. I stayed and built it back up so that I again
> made more money than the president. This time they cut up
> the territories to cut my income. So I quit and started Marion
> Laboratories [in 1950]. That experience left me with a firm
> resolve that I would never do that to my people. I was also
> smart enough to figure out from mathematical formulas that the
> more money they made, the more money the company would
> make. So we would share. They would share in the results. And
> we extended it to everybody—manufacturing, packaging—not
> only salesmen, but throughout the company.

Kauffman's experiences also led him to the second principle
that forms the basis for Marion's relationship with its associates. It is a secularized version of the Golden Rule: "Treat
others—whether customers, suppliers, or other Marion associates—the same as you would want to be treated . . . as an
individual, with integrity, trust, and honesty."

While the first principle can be seen clearly in various personnel policies, the second is translated into what Kauffman
calls the "little things"—the way everybody treats each other.
These little things, which might also be called managerial precepts, include such practices as:

• *Acceptance of honest mistakes*: One middle manager can
tell the story of how he made a serious error of business judgment that cost the company nearly a hundred thousand dollars.
At the time, he had only been with the company for a year.
He was called into a meeting with three senior executives to
discuss the error. At the beginning of the meeting, the manager
was "as nervous as a cat on a hot tin roof and as white as a
piece of paper." But the three executives kept telling him to
relax, and they spent the next hour going over the details of
the mistake. Finally Gerald Holder, a senior vice-president,
asked the manager, "Do you know how it happened? What

you would do different? How would you prevent it from happening again?" When the manager indicated that he understood, Holder told him, "Congratulations, the chances of that happening again are minimal, aren't they?" When they started to leave, the manager asked to meet Holder for a minute privately. The manager then said, "I just want you to know, that's the most unusual thing I ever saw. I thought I was going to get fired or something bad was going to happen to me. You guys actually do what you preach."

This does not mean that Marion never fires anyone. On the contrary, Marion executives insist they have very high standards and do not tolerate "mediocrity." But they make a sharp distinction between employees who consistently fail to meet agreed-upon expectations and employees who make honest errors of judgment. Fred Lyons, Marion's president, makes the point this way:

> We try to do the right things instead of trying to do all the things right. That means correct problems, don't go back and try to reconstruct them to nail somebody to the cross. Nothing is achieved by that. That doesn't mean you ignore accountability for problems, but you want people to learn from the mistakes. We tell people: "Feel free to make mistakes. If you're not making mistakes, you're not doing anything. Just don't make the same one twice."

• *Criticize up, praise down:* Ewing Kauffman says that he has long had a saying that he repeats to everybody, especially to managers: "Don't bitch, complain, or criticize on your same level or down because all it does is hurt morale and lower you in the estimation of your fellow people. Instead, make complaints up the ladder, because it's the only way to get action." By making his views known so widely, Kauffman effectively puts company managers on notice that they must always be willing to listen to complaints and take action to rectify problems. Otherwise, problems can fester, making everything even worse.

At the same time, Kauffman preaches that it's always important to give credit where it is due. He thinks this is particularly difficult for most middle managers to do. It often happens that when a subordinate comes up with a useful idea and tells it to his or her manager, the manager will pass the idea along to his superior without acknowledging the source. In the short run, the middle manager thinks he looks good in the eye of his superior. But in the long run, the subordinate will eventually stop passing along good ideas. Worse, this kind of behavior fosters backstabbing and unhealthy internal competition.

Kauffman explains that this is a difficult pattern to break since in our culture it is so common to act in our own short-run interest. So he encourages managers to acknowledge the contributions of others. When a manager presents an idea to Kauffman and credits it to a subordinate, Kauffman makes it a point to contact the subordinate directly to compliment him or her. Kauffman says the subordinate's first reaction is: Boy, the old man praised me. Then he or she thinks: My boss told Mr. K. that I thought it up. He didn't take credit for himself. Don't I have a wonderful boss!

• *Share information broadly*: Four times a year, the entire company attends the Marion on the Move meeting. Two things stick in my mind about the meeting I attended in the summer of 1985. First, the good-natured fun. One of the executives gave a sidesplitting account of how various associates worked hard to get approval of a new drug from a reluctant Dr. No-No at the Food and Drug Administration. Many of the jokes were at the expense of various company officials. Second, I was also struck with the candor with which executives spoke about the company's financial condition and the competitive problems they faced.

Company president Fred Lyons says the company regularly discloses crucial information to associates. He gave an example of how associates are told about plans for new products:

> We try to share with everybody what is going on. We feel that when people understand what it is we are trying to do and how we are coming at it, they can tie into it and grab hold of it faster without themselves having to be involved with the actual development [of new products], because not everybody can be involved with everything. We are pretty open. If we have a vulnerability, it's the fact that we're too open with each other.

But that's okay. We take that chance. But we keep a very open
communication and we share a lot of things that I think in many
companies would be considered confidential.

While Marion's distinctive personnel policies may be considered the flesh and bones of its relationship with employees,
these "little things" give lifeblood to the relationship. For it
is through the little things that the company's management
demonstrates its *respect for people as thinking, feeling human
beings*. Because management shows respect to associates, the
associates show respect toward both the management and each
other. The respect people feel toward each other is why the
term *associates* seems like an acccurate description of the relationship among people at Marion. It doesn't have the feel of
a label imposed by management to paper over an exploitative
or paternalistic setup.

Marion associates also have a phrase to describe the way in
which people treat each other within the organization. They
call it the Marion spirit. To outsiders, talk of the Marion spirit
may sound semimystical. But it refers to something very real
to the people working there. We can best understand what is
meant by the phrase by hearing how Marion associates themselves explain it. One issue of the company newspaper carried
an entire page full of quotes from associates attempting to
define the Marion spirit. Here are some excerpts:

A sales associate: " 'It's a good feeling. This is my company.
I want to do things the Marion way. The Marion spirit is great.
It is a good attitude. It is a friendly, family type feeling.' "

Another sales associate: " 'Here's an example: Everyone was
so nice and helpful in covering my desk during my recent
maternity leave so I could spend a little extra time with my
daughter before returning to work.' "

And finally, an associate who works in quality-assurance
inspection said the Marion spirit was " 'doing whatever it takes
to get the job done. Cooperation. Doing more than the job
requires.' "

In short, when Marion associates talk of the Marion spirit,
they are saying that people who work there trust each other.
The "little things"—which seem like commonsense notions of
how people should relate to each other in organizations—all
foster an environment where a more trusting relationship can

flourish. This relationship calls upon what is more distinctively human on both sides—appreciation, sharing, caring.

The Good-Faith Principle

Trust does not exist naturally in the workplace. Where it does take root and grow, it is a highly perishable commodity, requiring constant attention and care. Part of the reason for this difficulty in establishing trust is that human beings naturally question the motives and intentions of others. We are all afraid of being taken advantage of. So we are very careful about whom we trust. Managements of good workplaces seem to acknowledge the fact that everyone inevitably has doubts about the company's credibility and reliability. Rather than ignore this natural skepticism, they act in ways that allow employees to make up their own minds about the company's trustworthiness.

In this chapter, we've seen examples of companies that have shown the ability to gain and (at least for two of them) maintain the confidence of employees. How these managements demonstrate their trustworthiness can be summed up as follows:

• *Patience and consistency*: Developing confidence doesn't flow from the results-oriented approach that dominates much of American management thinking. Trust is not amenable to quick fixes that can be reflected on quarterly income statements. Managers at good workplaces avoid surprises. They implement and change their policies and practices with great care and deliberateness.

• *Openness and accessibility*: When there's a free flow of information, employees have plenty of opportunity to learn for themselves what the management is up to, and they can raise questions directly with those in authority.

• *Willingness to go beyond the conventional relationship with employees*: When a company does more than it has to do for employees, the employees feel free to do more than they have to for the company. This dynamic of the trust relationship is addressed more fully in a later chapter.

• *Delivering on promises*: While high-sounding promises may generate enthusiasm and excitement, they also increase people's expectations. People are extremely conscious when others don't do what they say they will. It undermines trust.

• *Sharing the rewards of mutual effort equitably*: A company's management can use very sophisticated human-relations-oriented techniques to obscure fundamental inequities in the sharing of rewards. For a while, these techniques may fool employees. But eventually, employees will become disillusioned if they aren't satisfied with how the profits, credit, and ownership of the company are distributed.

These five points have one quality in common. They all demonstrate that the company is acting in good faith. They are tangible indications of the company's integrity. Employees can look at these traits to assure themselves about the company's motives and intentions.

We are all familiar with how this works on a personal level. If someone hides information from us, we immediately suspect that person's motives. We might find it difficult to believe what that person does tell us, because we would be concerned about what that person is *not* disclosing and that person's reasons for withholding information. In other words, we would be questioning that person's credibility and wondering why that person is distrustful of us. By the same token, someone gains credibility in our eyes when he willingly provides complete information. By his doing so, we would say that the person shows us *respect*. He would be letting us make up our own mind about his truthfulness.

By being patient and consistent, open and accessible, a company's management makes it easy for employees to evaluate the company's actions for themselves. We might formulate this as the *good-faith principle*. It means earning trust by continually demonstrating respect for the employees' right to question the motives for the company's actions. By acting in good faith, the company can demonstrate that it is *not* trying to manipulate people into doing something against their own interest. This has an incalculable effect on how people relate to each other. My brother, who works at Armstrong (a *100 Best* company), puts it this way: "In our company, I know that if someone tells me something, I can believe it. There aren't any hidden agendas and such. This isn't necessarily the case everywhere."

One final point. Acting in *good faith* should not be confused with the similar-sounding notion of acting with *goodwill*, in the sense of benevolence, or acting with pure or disinterested motives. Employees aren't looking for benevolence; they are more interested in fairness. Employees are fully responsible and capable adults who work to provide for themselves and their families. They assume that the company exists for reasons other than their personal welfare. Instead of benevolence from the company, employees are more interested in being able to earn their living with integrity. Good faith enters the picture to make that possible, as that is how a company shows respect to employees as people.

4
REDESIGNING
JOBS
Northwestern Mutual Life

In 1910, a symbolic milestone
was passed when census data revealed that blue-collar workers
exceeded farm workers for the first time in U.S. history. But
the industrial age was short-lived, soon overshadowed by the
information age and an economy based on offering services
rather than manufacturing goods. As a result, the overwhelming majority of Americans now go to work at an office instead
of a factory. The 1970 census disclosed that clerical workers
(typists, secretaries, data-entry operators, etc.) had become the
largest single occupational group in the country. This group
is often referred to as pink-collar workers because it is so overwhelmingly female, accounting for one third of the women
but only 6 percent of the men in the work force. When female
college graduates are excluded, more than half of all remaining
women workers hold clerical jobs (one in six women college
graduates is a clerical).

This dramatic shift has not, however, been accompanied by
an equally dramatic change in management thinking about
work. In fact, many companies have simply applied Frederick
Taylor's scientific-management approach (the subject of a later
chapter), originally developed in a factory setting, to the office.
In adapting time-and-motion-study techniques, some zealous
adherents of the scientific-management gospel resorted to mechanical devices to monitor clerical work. Early examples in-

cluded typewriters with keystroke-counting attachments and clock-driven time stamps to record when clerks received and completed batches of work. Scientific managers could then use such information to divide and subdivide the work into discrete tasks and prescribe the "one best way" for clerical workers to do their jobs. The goal was to make the office as efficient as an assembly line.

Taylorism has been especially attractive to managements of large banks, insurance companies, and other financial-services firms. Their huge staffs of clerical workers spend their working hours manipulating bits of data, the building blocks of the information age. The 1960 Oscar Award-winning movie *The Apartment*, with Jack Lemmon and Shirley MacLaine, depicted an early version of the office as factory. Lemmon works for a big insurance company. His small office adjoins a large bullpen, where dozens of clerks busily operate their calculating machines to record figures in the stacks of paper sitting on their desks. The image is of a well-oiled paperwork factory.

Dividend Dotters and Computers

Like factory workers, many clerical workers are expected to repeat the same task all day long. Before computers were commonplace, for example, life-insurance companies had the job of dividend dotter. To determine the annual dividend, one worker performed a complicated calculation on a manual calculator and entered the figure for the dividend in pencil on a card. The card then went to another worker, the dividend dotter, who conducted the entire calculation again. If the dividend dotter arrived at the same answer, she or he would place a red dot next to the original dividend figure.

At one time, Northwestern Mutual Life Insurance Company had a dozen dividend dotters. Computers have made that job, as well as manual calculating machines, obsolete. But the introduction of computers did not eradicate the legacy of Frederick Taylor from Northwestern Mutual, or from many similar enterprises. At best, the computer has been a mixed blessing for clerical workers. Computers have enabled managements to be even more scientific about measuring and monitoring work than Frederick Taylor would have thought possible, provoking a national debate about whether they unfairly invade workers' rights to privacy. At the same time, the new technology has often meant more, not less, specialization and assembly-line-style working conditions. For instance, Northwestern Mutual once employed twenty clerical workers who did nothing but handle the six hundred thousand address changes the company receives each year. By 1982, however, that job specialty had been eliminated. How Northwestern Mutual reacted to the changes caused by computers and transformed its clerical work is the story to which we now turn.

The story begins in 1979, when company executives noticed an increase in complaints from both agents and policy owners about the quality and efficiency of service rendered by the Milwaukee home office. Officials first commissioned a management-consulting firm (Roy Walters & Associates) to study the problem. The study concluded that the solution lay in reorganizing the work flow rather than merely adding more staff, as had been done in the past. At this point, company officials made a crucial decision—to include the workers who were directly involved in all aspects of the reorganization.

The first step was to inform everyone of the problem. Executives conducted general meetings with the approximately 550 clerical workers in two departments, new business and policy owners services. They detailed the nature of the complaints and described the consultant's findings. At these meetings, they outlined the mechanism for change—task forces to look at every aspect of the work flow, including each job and each step in the process. Eighteen task forces were set up to survey issues like technology, training, communications, and systems. Each task force had a half dozen members, including upper management, middle management, and clerical staffers.

From the outset, company officials emphasized that the goals of the reorganization were to improve service and to increase productivity. But they explicitly assured everyone both in writing and verbally during the mass meetings that productivity improvements would not result in anyone's being laid off or fired. They also invited officials of the Office and Professional Employees Union to the first general meeting to hear firsthand the presentation made to employees. The union has represented clerical workers in Northwestern Mutual's home office since 1935. Robert Ninneman, the senior vice-president who oversaw the reorganization, says that inviting the union leaders to the initial meeting was important, "to give them a feeling for what we wanted to accomplish. They recognized that we were operating in good faith, and they went along with the change." As evidence of union support, he says not one union grievance was filed, though hundreds of jobs were affected.

The lack of union grievances is all the more remarkable when you consider how much the workers' jobs were changed in less than two years. In the policy owners services department, there were about sixty different, distinct job classifications for only two hundred workers. As on an assembly-line-production setup, each worker performed clearly defined tasks. In addition to the workers who only entered address changes, others only handled changes in the frequency of premium payments, while still others only made substitutions in policy beneficiaries, and so on. Under the old system, three different clerks had to handle a letter requesting three different changes in the policy, with each making the required computer entries before passing the file along.

There was a rationale for the old system: efficiency. Clerks who only entered address changes could become extremely fast at that operation, especially when they handled large numbers of them at a time. What's more, the company didn't have to spend much time in training, because each worker had to perform only one limited task. And workers could be easily replaced if they became sick or quit, because the tasks were highly specific. On the down side, the task forces discovered that many of the customers' complaints could be traced to the fact that several clerks handled the typical piece of correspondence, increasing the chances for delays. Worse, no one could be held accountable when delays occurred. For instance, if someone complained about the slow response to a specific letter, the address-change division might blame the beneficiary-change division, or vice versa. In a nutshell, nobody felt any overall responsibility for how quickly the letter was serviced. It's no wonder. After all, the Taylor-style system placed distinct limits on each worker's responsibility. The situation corresponded to a frequent criticism of conventionally orga-

nized auto-assembly plants. Individual workers don't assume
responsibility for the quality of the entire car because jobs are
sharply defined to preclude any sense of the whole.

One-Stop Service

The task forces met this problem head on. They suggested
overhauling the entire system by dramatically increasing the
scope of each clerk's job. After considerable study, the task
forces reduced the sixty different job classifications in the policy owners services department to six. The byword of the reorganization was one-stop service. As a result, only one clerk,
not three, was needed for a letter requesting changes in a
policy's premium-payments schedule, beneficiaries, and addresses. Greatly expanding the workers' jobs required extensive retraining. Each employee underwent an average of
over four weeks' training (35,000 classroom hours for the two
hundred employees in the policy owners services department).

The reorganization greatly expanded employees' responsibilities in another way. The task forces decided to divide the
country into four different geographic regions. Clerical workers, now called service representatives, were not only assigned
to a region, but to specific agencies within the region. They
were then responsible for all correspondence from those agencies. Service representatives, who previously only related to
stacks of paper and their computer terminals, began communicating directly with insurance agents and agency-office
staffs. The company also encouraged face-to-face meetings between the home-office clerks and their local counterparts,
often paying for service representatives to visit local offices.
Several service representatives once flew to New York on the
corporate airplane with the company president. While he met
with investment advisers, they visited local agency offices.

The reorganization accomplished the basic business goal of
improving service. Complaints were sharply reduced. Efficiency also improved markedly. In the new business department, 82 percent of applications for insurance were handled
within five working days as opposed to the previous 52 percent. And productivity increased, too. The company increased
the value of its insurance policies by 50 percent between 1982

and 1984 but only had to increase the new business staff by 7 percent.

On a personal level, most employees felt much better about their jobs. A year after the reorganization, I interviewed Kathy Mandella, a service representative in the new business department. She said:

> I think it is great. At first everybody had a scary feeling. But it's more interesting than just punching numbers on the screen. We are doing more than before, but I think it's beneficial to us because we are learning more about the underwriting aspects of the job. Now we can read the attending physician's statement. We never even looked at that before. There's a better opportunity to move up to underwriting.

Mandella's reaction may have been typical, but it was not universal. Some of the clerical workers simply didn't want the increased responsibility. Ninneman describes how the company dealt with this group:

> We had a handful, as might be expected, who were much more comfortable doing the relatively simple job, with a narrow dimension to it. In those cases, we literally tried to redesign something that would fit what they wanted to do and what they could feel comfortable with. A very small handful of them concluded that the whole reorganization had changed things so much that early retirement or something like that became more desirable than staying in a narrow job, so a couple of people left early. There was a little shuffling of personnel from department to department. We ended up with a little pool of people that didn't quite fit, but they eventually got placed somewhere in the company. So we kept our commitment, and everybody felt very good about it.

Employees also generally felt good that the company had gone to great lengths to express appreciation for the troops involved in the process. Northwestern held a series of thank-you luncheons for employees in the executive dining rooms. And about a third of the employees were promoted (with higher pay) because of the increased responsibilities they had assumed.

Enriching Jobs

People familiar with contemporary personnel trends might categorize the reorganization at Northwestern Mutual Life as job enrichment or job enlargement. This technique was popularized by Frederick Herzberg, a management theorist and consultant in the Elton Mayo human-relations tradition (discussed in a later chapter). Many of the technique's practitioners have been influenced by Herzberg's motivation-hygiene theory, first put forth in his 1959 book *The Motivation to Work*. In it, Herzberg identifies five factors that can make a job satisfying: achievement, recognition, the work itself, responsibility, and advancement. He asserts that the job satisfiers are "motivators." That is, people feel motivated to work harder when they can achieve something tangible in doing their job, get recognized for their work, feel the work itself is interesting, and so on. So instead of concentrating on factors—like pay and working conditions—that don't have much impact on motivating people, Herzberg argues that managers should focus on enriching workers' jobs (making the work more interesting, increasing workers' sense of responsibility and achievement, etc.). In that way, workers would both be happier and work harder.

The Northwestern Mutual clerical workers undeniably had their jobs enriched. But as we shall see, what happened at Northwestern Mutual differed in several important respects from the classic job-enrichment program. Fortunately, it is possible to compare the Northwestern Mutual experience with a job-enrichment program that occurred at nearly the same time at another midwestern insurance company. In her 1977 book, *Pink Collar Workers*, Louise Kapp Howe devotes a chapter to a large Chicago-based insurance company that had recently implemented a typical job-enrichment program.

The Chicago insurance company (which Howe does not identify) was considered an enlightened employer. It offered good benefits—medical and life insurance, a pension, a stock-investment plan, a tuition-refund program, and "the assorted we're-all-one-big-family activities: travel clubs, picnics, baseball games, bowling teams, holiday parties, a company newspaper." Like Northwestern Mutual, the Chicago insurer even provided employees a free lunch in the company cafeteria. In this environment, the company's job-enrichment program, which was then at the cutting edge of progressive personnel practices, fit in perfectly. It was aimed at making people's jobs "more interesting and challenging." According to the personnel officer in charge, the program was based on three principles: that workers "want to do a complete job and not an isolated task," that they need "regular feedback on their performance," and that "they want more control over their work, they want to participate in decisions about how the work is done, instead of simply being ordered from above." The personnel officer described to Howe how the company implemented a "job-enrichment" program in one department:

> In group claims we took a large office of eighty clerical workers and broke them into smaller units of ten each. Now each clerk is handling the records of individual customers from beginning to end, instead of just fragmented pieces of the job. We think that's much better.

At first glance, the personnel officer's description may make it appear that what happened at the Chicago company was identical to the reorganization at Northwestern Mutual. At both companies, for instance, there had previously been clerks who only performed address changes. After the reorganizations, those same workers handled a variety of items in addition to address changes. At both companies, the employees' jobs were expanded to give them greater responsibility.

But the similarities stop there. According to Howe, the clerical workers in the Chicago company felt that at best, their jobs had improved only marginally as a result of the job-enrichment program. She interviewed employees who thought there was no improvement, and some thought it made their jobs worse than ever before. And it made no dents whatsoever in the underlying suspicions of people toward the company, which they referred to as Big Daddy.

Even the personnel officer responsible for implementing the job-enrichment program admitted that it had not succeeded, using his own four objectives for the program: to increase worker happiness, reduce absenteeism, decrease turnover, and increase productivity. He explained that he could not give any evidence whatsoever of improvements in any of the four areas:

We're really still in the experimental state. Elsewhere in our
different regional headquarters they seem to be having varying
results, some good, some not so good. It seems to depend quite
a bit on the attitudes of supervisors, but none of the evidence
is very conclusive yet. Here or at other corporations. Let's face
it. Job enrichment is still more of an art than a science.

To account for the resounding success of the Northwestern
Mutual reorganization and the apparent failure of the job-enrichment program at Howe's Chicago insurance company, we
have to explore the basic differences between the two stories.
For one thing, we should recall the assurances Northwestern
Mutual made at the outset both to the union and to the individual clerical workers that nobody would lose her job as a
result of the reorganization. By contrast, the workers at the
Chicago insurer had been hearing rumors for months that
the company was thinking of moving to the suburbs. One of
the workers told Howe: "Everybody's afraid Big Daddy's going
to abandon them." (Several months after Howe's initial interviews, she reported that the rumors were well founded, as the
insurer had indeed decided to move its headquarters to a small
suburban community in Indiana, more than an hour away from
Chicago, forcing many of the clerical workers to leave the company.) In this atmosphere, it is easy to see why workers would
not see the point in enriching a job that might soon be
eliminated.

Northwestern Mutual was unionized, and the Chicago firm
was not. Whatever else is true about unions, they do provide
a mechanism for protecting individual employees' rights. That
Northwestern Mutual went to such lengths to involve the
union in the reorganization process was a powerful statement
to employees that the company had no intention of upsetting
either the established process for settling disputes or the basic
wage-and-working-conditions structure that had been negoti-
ated between the parties. The Chicago firm was not only not
unionized, but at least a handful of the employees were trying
to organize a union there. In this context, some workers perceived the job-enrichment program as a thinly veiled effort to
keep the union at bay.

Parts Versus the Whole

Another significant difference was that Northwestern Mutual gave promotions and pay increases to at least a third of the workers. At the Chicago company, the clerical workers may have had their jobs "enriched," but not their pocketbooks. When Howe asked the personnel officer whether workers got any more money or promotions from the job-enrichment program, he answered: "No, those are separate issues; important issues to be sure, but separate from what we're talking about here—which is improving the job itself."

The personnel officer revealed an assumption common throughout the business world, the notion that the workplace is made up of several distinct and separable parts and that employee morale can be improved by simply tinkering with each part individually. Managements install progressive-sounding programs like job enrichment or work teams, believing that they will make employees happy and increase productivity. It's a mechanistic approach. Employees are treated like automobiles that require periodic repairs to run properly. Sometimes employees need more pay; other times, a new pension plan or health-care benefit; still other times, enriched jobs. Like the personnel officer quoted above, they are surprised when their solutions have little or no impact on either morale or productivity. The irony is that many well-meaning executives, including otherwise enlightened personnel officers who are committed to ridding the last vestiges of scientific management from the workplace, also adhere to this workplace-as-machine view. They believe that you can "enrich" a job without dealing with issues of job security, pay, and advancement.

What's rarely recognized is that the workplace is a *system of interdependent relationships*. The quality of a workplace involves three distinct but overlapping relationships—with the company, with the job, and with other employees. How people feel about the workplace depends on all three of those relationships. In the case of the Chicago insurer, the employee's relationship with his or her job may have improved somewhat because of the job-enrichment program. But because the company did nothing to assure people about their job security, the gnawing distrust of the company's intentions continued to fester (and for good reason). In fact, the company's efforts to make jobs more interesting and challenging also had the effect of raising workers' suspicions even more. They wondered what the real reason was behind the company's doing something nice.

It's noteworthy that Northwestern Mutual employees did not have this distrust of the company's motives. It wasn't just because of the assurances of job security, either. The company demonstrated its good faith by involving employees in the reorganization process itself. Their presence on the task forces was not token. According to all involved, many of the changes derived directly from suggestions made by the clerical workers themselves. The reorganization was not imposed from above. Northwestern Mutual's employees talk proudly about being responsible for the changes. And company official Robert Ninneman repeatedly emphasizes the value of that contribution:

> The people on the job really had a lot of ideas about how their jobs could be done better. And if you create an atmosphere under which you let them know that you will listen to them, it explodes.

This contrasts sharply with what took place in Chicago. In the first place, despite the rhetoric about giving workers more "control" over their work and the right to "participate in decisions," the Chicago company was offering only token control and a phony form of participation. The company had already decided the parameters of the changes. The major limitation was that changes were not to affect adversely the level of productivity. Howe interviewed one employee who sat before a computer terminal all day and said that the best way to enrich her job would be to let her get up and move around more often, "but since they're mainly interested in more production that's the last thing they'd allow." It's not that the employee was unwilling to help figure out ways to increase her output. She simply didn't want to stare at the computer screen for hours at a stretch. But that never occurred to management, nor did it ask employees for their opinions.

The Chicago firm had already decided that an enriched job was one where workers did "a complete job and not an isolated task." Like a doctor who prescribes a pill whether or not you need it, the company decided that people were going to do more fulfilling, self-actualizing jobs because that was going to make them happier.

The Happiness Paradox

The problem is that not everyone fits the Herzberg (or any other) psychological model. Howe interviewed one employee who complained that the job-enrichment staff treated employees as if they were "all alike," not allowing for the fact that some like to work at a different pace and in different ways.

As we saw from the Northwestern Mutual story, some clerical workers preferred the old system, where they typed address changes all day long. And some couldn't make the adjustment and left the department. Others took early retirement. And even Kathy Mandella, who ultimately loved the new system, acknowledged that she initially found the prospect of changing her job "scary." Because of the enormity of the changes, the firm made an effort to reach all the employees, building up their confidence as well as their skills. Northwestern didn't proceed from a single model of human nature. Rather, it assumed that people *have* individual differences and did its best to accommodate those differences. It's important to remember that theoretically, at least, the task forces involved in the reorganization could have concluded that even more, not less, specialization was needed.

This *recognition of individual differences*, a belief that everybody doesn't fit into the same mold and that the organization has to make allowances for those differences, is one of the key reasons why the Northwestern Mutual experience worked for employees. During the task-force process, the company respected what individual workers had to offer. And when the changes were ultimately implemented, the company tried to do everything possible to help each individual fit in.

This leads us to the final—and most fundamental—contrast between the two episodes. The Chicago insurer claimed that the principal objective of the job-enrichment program was to increase worker happiness. The company assumed that if the employees were happier with their jobs, they would be absent less often, stay with the company longer, and work harder. At Northwestern Mutual, worker happiness was not on the agenda. Improved service was the primary objective, and increased productivity was secondary. The irony is that Northwestern Mutual was more successful at achieving worker happiness than was the Chicago insurance company, whose specific aim was to make the workers happy. How can we explain this paradox?

In the first place, it wasn't really true that the primary objective of the Chicago job-enrichment effort was worker happiness, despite the claims made. Only a naïve fool would believe that a big company would spend thousands of dollars merely to help workers feel better about their jobs. The top management presumably bought the underlying thesis of all motivational management techniques—that self-actualized workers will be more highly motivated workers and will work harder. So job enrichment is a means to higher productivity; it is not an end in and of itself. As Howe discovered, workers at the Chicago company were neither naïve nor fools. They immediately saw through the rhetoric and understood the real goals of job enrichment. So the dishonesty of the company's presentation destroyed its credibility. It polluted the relationship between the company and employees. It meant the company was operating manipulatively, by using subterfuge to get people to work harder.

Northwestern Mutual, on the other hand, told people honestly from the outset what it intended to do—and why. It wanted people to work smarter, if not harder. It wanted them to engage their minds and share their knowledge and experience to help improve service. This straightforward approach helps explain why employees there felt better about the changes in their jobs. Employees could concentrate on their jobs and not worry about the machinations of company higher-ups.

That's not all. Northwestern Mutual employees participated in redesigning their jobs. According to some management theorists, the fact that they participated is why they felt so good about their jobs. These theorists argue that employees will feel more committed to a change if they are allowed to participate in the process. That may be true psychologically, for some people. But again, this idea assumes that the goal is to make employees happy—and ultimately more productive. That's why these theorists advocate participation.

Unfortunately, these management theorists miss the whole point. Northwestern Mutual did not involve employees in redesigning their own jobs to raise their morale and level of motivation. They did it because it made sense. The company genuinely believed employees had significant contributions to make. And the employees' ideas did make a difference. First, their insights helped improve service. At the same time, the employees helped to design jobs for themselves that, for the most part, made the best use of their aptitudes, skills, and interests. In other words, employee participation may have helped morale, but it wasn't the higher morale that led to more satisfying jobs. It was the substance of employee participation—their suggestions and ideas—that led to the creation of more challenging and satisfying jobs. Because much management literature is fixated on the psychological impact of worker involvement, it tends to ignore the actual content of that involvement. So given the opportunity, workers will redesign their jobs, not only to make them more productive, but more interesting and satisfying as well. At least that's what happened at Northwestern Mutual Life.

There's another way of viewing this point. Northwestern Mutual's management acknowledged from the outset that the employees individually and collectively could help solve a problem. So it treated the employees as partners. And it did so in a democratic fashion—giving employees full information and the ability to have an impact on issues that directly affected them. It was through a democratic partnership that Northwestern Mutual reorganized its clerical work.

Had Northwestern Mutual gone the path of the Chicago firm and tried to create a bunch of happy workers, it's doubtful it would have either solved its service problems or had a happy workforce. Honesty goes a long way.

5
PROMOTING
FAIRNESS

Federal Express,
Pitney Bowes, Tektronix

We generally accept as a given the contrast between our time at work and the rest of our lives. Once you enter the office or factory, you lose many of the rights you enjoy as a citizen. There's no process for challenging—or changing—bad decisions made by the authorities. There's no mechanism to vote for people to represent you in decision-making bodies. There's no Freedom of Information Act to help you discover what is going on behind closed doors. There's no presumption of innocence or trial by peers.

We take for granted that such rights and protections don't apply to the workplace partly because most of us have never seen examples to the contrary. There are, however, some remarkable companies that have long made a serious attempt to incorporate some of the ideals of political democracy to promote fairness in the workplace. What follows are portraits of three such companies.

Trial by One's Peers

"COMPANY POLICY PROHIBITS INTIMIDATION." So read the headline in an issue of Federal Express's monthly newspaper, distributed to all of the overnight-delivery company's fifty thousand employees. What followed was this story:

Jason Alan had been called into a meeting with two supervisors. One proceeded to berate Alan for poor work performance. The discussion became heated. Alan stood up and said
he was going to talk with his personnel representative. One of
the supervisors told him to sit down and finish the discussion.
Alan refused and left the office. The next day Alan's supervisor
gave him a warning letter for insubordination and put a copy
in Alan's personnel file.

The story may sound typical of what happens every day in
companies throughout the land. An employee refuses to follow
an order and gets reprimanded. No big deal, right? Not at Federal Express. The story had a happy ending for the employee
(whose name was changed for the article). Alan filed a complaint through the company's grievance machinery, and a
board of review overturned the management decision. According to the article: "The board's rationale was that Alan
had been put in an intimidating environment—two managers
against one employee." Ted Sartoian, the executive who oversees the grievance process, was quoted as saying: " 'Federal
Express employees have the right to work in an environment
free of intimidation. The autocratic manager who rides rough-
shod over employees is not tolerated at Federal Express.' "
The article concluded with a list of guidelines for employees
to follow if they feel they are being intimidated:

Don't ignore the intimidation.
Trust your instincts.
Seek advice and counsel from your personnel representative
or the employee relations department.
Assess your options: Keep a log or diary in a secure place,
not your desk.
Put your complaint in writing.
Find out if other people (past or present employees) in your
area have been intimidated. If they have, you'll get support and
credibility.

The newspaper article is just the tip of the iceberg at Federal
Express. The company has what is probably the most fully
developed system for handling employee grievances. Its Guaranteed Fair Treatment (GFT) procedure has received rave no-
tices from Alan Westin, senior professor of law at Columbia

University and nationally recognized expert in constitutional
law. The GFT evolved out of an earlier open-door policy, where
employees who had conflicts with their supervisors were encouraged to complain to managers higher up the hierarchy.
(The term *Guaranteed Fair Treatment* was taken from Mar-
riott's policy of the same name, but Federal Express executives
insist their GFT is a *procedure*, not just a *policy*.) Federal
Express's GFT procedure consists of five steps:

1. Discussion of the problem with immediate supervisor.
2. Review by the supervisor's manager.
3. Review by the senior vice-president of the division. He
or she can uphold or overturn the previous management decision or initiate a board of review.
4. Establishment of a board of review consisting of five vot-
ing members. A majority of members of the board are actually
selected by the employee who files the GFT complaint. The
nonvoting chairman of the board picks three members from a
list of six nominated by the employee. The employee selects
the other two members from a list of four employees nominated
by the chairman. Decisions of the board of review are final and
binding on the company as well as on the employee.
5. Review by the appeals board, made up of the firm's chief
executive officer, chief operating officer, and senior vice-president of personnel. It decides whether to grant a board of
review if it was denied in Step 3 by the division's senior vice-
president.

Note that the employee making the complaint can nominate
people from his or her own work area. So the majority of the
board of review can literally be friends of the person bringing
the complaint. Based on his experiences in the marine corps
in Vietnam, Federal Express's founder, Fred Smith, argues that
an employee's peers don't automatically vote for their co-workers. He explains: "People who are professional and do their
job well don't brook laggards. Contrary to the great myth that
the work ethic is dead, people are very anxious to do a good
job."

Professor Westin finds the peer-review aspect of the GFT
process important for two reasons: First, "employee participation helps achieve better results over the long course by

building employee experiences and attitudes into the decision-making process." At the same time, "having employee participation usually makes rules unfavorable to the complainant more acceptable, and earns more general employee trust in the system than one entirely presided over by management members." According to Westin's in-depth study of the system, the overwhelming majority of employees rated the system as fair. In fact, more than 80 percent of the employees rated it as fair as or fairer than the criminal and civil courts or a union grievance system.

It's not just the employee involvement that makes this system work. The review by the appeals board—Step 5 in the GFT process—symbolizes the top management's commitment to the process. Every Tuesday morning, Fred Smith, Federal Express's founder and chief executive officer, Jim Barksdale, the executive vice-president, and Jim Perkins, the top personnel officer, sit down in corporate headquarters in Memphis to review between three and a dozen GFTs that have worked their way up the system. They usually spend a full morning on the cases, and it is not uncommon to devote the entire day to grievances.

According to Professor Westin, this commitment is crucial. He writes:

> Given the inevitable conflicts between employee fair treatment and hard-driving managers and executives "getting things done," it will always take the prestige of the CEO—or a top executive enjoying the CEO's full confidence—and occasional intervention by that executive, to protect the system from favoritism or the "management-team instinct." Also, only the CEO or other top executive can insure that the visible and invisible reward system that spurs managers on is geared to recognize allegiance to the fair procedure system, and to punish the occasional abuse of it by managers.

When Federal Express instituted GFT in 1982, company founder Smith wanted to make sure employees understood that the company was serious about it. Smith insisted that plaques outlining the GFT procedure be placed in all work areas throughout the company—some eight hundred plaques. The plaques are made of metal and wood, costing nearly a hundred dollars apiece. And Sartoian remembers the final touch—four metal rivets: "Fred Smith told me, 'I want rivets put in there so that people think that this is solid, in the wall, that it ain't going anywhere.' " And the company backs up the GFT process with money—an estimated $2 million a year to administer the GFT. That is about seventy dollars per employee per year for a system to ensure fair treatment.

The rivets in the wall are only symbols, as Sartoian is the first to admit. He insists that the Guaranteed Fair Treatment policy is ultimately only a "technique":

> If there's not some underlying reality that the technique arises naturally out of, it's going to fail. You can't build that underlying reality by piling techniques, one on top of the other.

The GFT is only one part of Federal Express's people philosophy, and the structure of GFT is applicable to every organization. It is tailored to Federal Express, whose business, like its famous TV ads of the fast-talking businessman, relies on speed. Federal Express employees often find themselves in conflict because their jobs involve making important decisions under time pressure. But GFT operates with several assumptions that have broader applicability. Federal Express managers talk of the importance of ensuring that GFT decisions be both fair and consistent. It's essential, for instance, that a courier in Atlanta not be fired for failing to report a vehicle accident while a courier in Peoria is only given a warning letter for the identical offense. Fred Smith talks of the need to have written rules and precedents: "One of the good things about the United States system of law is that although sometimes you win, sometimes you lose, but at least there is a body of law that you are dealing with. I'd hate to be in some sort of Solomonic role where there wasn't any law and you decide every case on the way you feel that day."

To make sure Federal Express managers know the sort of precedents being established by GFT decisions, the company sends out summaries of important cases in a monthly package. Other employees can read of significant cases, like the intimidation case, in the employee newspaper. The company also maintains a library of all cases heard by the appeals board or a board of review. The library is open for any manager to peruse.

The company makes an effort to keep managers informed about GFT precedents for another reason. Since the process typically involves challenges of managerial decisions, some managers have seen the GFT as a threat to their authority. Federal Express copes with this problem in two ways. First, management-training courses include instruction in the GFT. In the company's week-long training program for new supervisors, for instance, a full day is spent on GFT.

The company also makes clear to managers that they are covered by the GFT. They are employees, too. In one case, a middle manager filed a GFT because she thought she had been wrongly denied a promotion. A board of review found in her favor and ordered that she be given a comparable promotion. Far from being penalized for using the GFT, two years later she was given a $5,000 award for outstanding service in her new management position.

Fred Smith once told a group of Federal Express managers that he considers the GFT "the glue that holds this company together." Smith's metaphor has wider applicability. In a profound sense, fairness is the glue that holds a good workplace together. When employees perceive that the management makes a sincere effort to be fair to employees in compensation, in benefits, in handling promotions, and in coping with disputes with supervisors, they are more likely to extend their trust in other areas. An atmosphere of fair treatment affects every aspect of the workplace.

By the same token, without the glue of fairness, an organization falls apart internally. If you don't feel you are getting a fair shake, you may turn to backstabbing, politicking, sabotaging, or opting out. Unfairness increases everyone's feeling of alienation with the system. The late Bill Gore, founder of W. L. Gore & Associates, makers of Gore-tex, emphasized this when he said:

> The most destructive thing that I know about in enterprises is unfairness—perceived unfairness. People can forgive mistakes if there's a sincere effort to try to be fair. But deliberate unfairness destroys the communication, the cooperation, and all of the things that are necessary for successful teamwork.

Town Meeting

The scene is a church social hall a few blocks from the Pitney Bowes corporate headquarters and main factory in Stamford, Connecticut. On a stage are two long tables with nameplates. A half dozen employee representatives are seated at the table on the left; at one on the right are an equal number of company executives. About two hundred office employees are seated in rows of folding chairs.

Welcome to a Pitney Bowes jobholders' meeting, held every year since 1945. Patterned on annual stockholders' meetings, the jobholders' meetings are held with groups of two to three hundred employees each spring. Before the meetings, the twenty thousand Pitney Bowes employees are sent the annual jobholders' report, which recounts activities of the previous year and includes charts detailing the minimum, average, and maximum pay received by all company employees in categories ranging from hourly factory employees to top corporate executives. Like a typical shareholders' meeting—or a New England town meeting, for that matter—any employee may stand and ask top management any question of concern. Employees can also submit questions in writing (management is not allowed to see the written questions in advance). Employees who submit the best written and the best oral questions are given fifty-dollar savings bonds.

After a round of introductions and a brief film about retraining at a nearby plant, one of the employee representatives begins the questioning. Chairing the question-and-answer half of the meeting is Al Salvino, an offset-press operator elected several years earlier to the office of cochairman of the company-wide council of personnel relations (CPR). The CPR is a unique in-house mechanism for airing employee concerns. His counterpart on the management side is Thomas Loemker, a thirty-year company employee who recently assumed the position of president of Pitney Bowes Business Systems, the company's main operating division. The first dozen questions were submitted beforehand. Employee representatives ask the written questions. Then the chair opens the meeting to questions from the floor. During the next hour or so, about twenty different employees stand to raise their concerns. Division president Loemker either answers the queries himself or refers them to one of the other executives.

A surprising number of questions revolve around business issues: Have the Japanese come out with a mailing machine meter (Pitney Bowes's principal product)? Answer: Not yet. What is the company doing to get back a certain big account that it recently lost to a competitor? The answer reassures everyone that the management is equally concerned and is working hard on it but has not yet made any progress. Is Pitney Bowes planning any more acquisitions? (A few years earlier, it had bought Dictaphone.) The answer indicates that no plans are in the works, but if an opportunity arises, the company will pursue it. There are a few softball questions, like: How does the stock-purchase plan work? But most strike closer to home and are stated bluntly: Why are prices skyrocketing in the cafeteria? One employee gets up to complain that there are only three personal computers in his department when others seem to have no trouble getting more. Another asks (apparently seriously) why all the employees in a certain department are so arrogant.

The way the questions are handled reveals the seriousness with which everyone takes the meeting. When an employee asks why he didn't receive a bonus for referring a new professional employee, a personnel manager apologizes and suggests it must have been a mistake. At that point, CPR employee cochairman Salvino interjects that this problem has been raised before but nothing seems to have happened. The manager counters that it may have happened once or twice, but he doesn't think the problem is widespread. Sensing dissatisfaction with the manager's response, division president Loemker asks for a show of hands to see how many people have had the same problem. Five raise their hands. Loemker then asserts that it's obvious something is clearly wrong, winning a few points with the crowd by taking the employees' side against the personnel manager. Loemker wins a few more points later when somebody asks him how to pronounce his last name. His response: "I do answer to Tom. I would just as soon that you call me that."

The meeting is not, however, a love feast for a new division president. The appreciation of Loemker stems from his forthrightness and apparent concern to do what's right. But there's an underlying tension at the meeting—a constant testing to see if the company really does care about its employees. Questions are asked without hostility, but there's a sense that the management has to prove itself. On this day at least, the employees assume that the management is working for them and not the other way around.

The sense that management is accountable to employees, just as it is to stockholders, is deeply ingrained at Pitney Bowes. Bill Redgate, a company vice-president, explains that "at Pitney Bowes, managers are always aware that their decisions can be challenged." This makes it difficult for new managers who are not used to being questioned, especially by subordinates. Some can't make the adjustment.

Accountability to employees is not a one-day phenomenon, either, as evidenced by the presence onstage of CPR cochairman Salvino and the other CPR employee representatives. As the interchange over the referral bonus illustrates, the CPR is a kind of watchdog, making sure that the management does indeed follow through with its promises.

The CPR's structure parallels the organizational structure of the company. Employees elect representatives at the section, department, division, and company levels. Once a month, all employees meet for about half an hour in groups of about fifty employees and their supervisors. The first half of the section CPR meeting is chaired by the foreman (or office equivalent), who reports how the company is doing and any problems the work unit has been having. An elected employee CPR co-chairman chairs the second half, during which employees raise questions, concerns, and problems. Any issues that can be resolved are done so at that time. A week later, the section CPR representatives and their management counterparts have a division meeting to discuss issues arising from the section meetings. The next week, a similar meeting takes place at the department level, followed a week later by a meeting of the main CPR council, with departmental CPR employee representatives and their management counterparts. The president of Pitney Bowes sits as cochairman of the main CPR; the other cochairman is an employee (the office held by Al Salvino at the time of the jobholders' meeting). Minutes from the main

CPR meetings are the most widely read document in the company.

At the lowest level, the CPR representative functions somewhat like a shop steward in a unionized plant. (The only serious unionizing drive at the company was resoundingly defeated in 1947.) Employees often bring personal problems directly to the CPR representative, who tries to resolve the matter informally with the supervisor. And the CPR acts as a constant pressure to upgrade benefits. In a recent jobholders' report, the CPR took credit for getting the company to implement "a general wage adjustment, an increase in pension benefits to past retirees, coordination of benefits for two married Pitney Bowes employees, an increase in allowance for orthodontia, and an eleventh paid holiday."

At the same time, everyone sees the CPR as a mechanism for two-way communication. The management uses the various CPR meetings to give reports on how the business is going and to explain new business plans. Walter H. Wheeler, Jr., the longtime company president who set up the CPR, saw this as one of the main purposes of the system. He told a management association in 1950:

> Most employees have only the vaguest notion about what management does. It's hard to get understanding of the fact that the more we trust employees with all the facts of our business, the more they are inclined to accept our judgment and decisions concerning those facts; that by consulting with employees on all our problems we don't risk losing management's prerogatives, but actually restore their faith in them.

The idea of two-way communications extends beyond the workings of the CPR. It's basic to the way Pitney Bowes conducts its business, according to company president James Harvey. He says employees should be listened to for the simple and obvious reason that they have an important contribution to make:

> When you do something foolish or wrong, you want your employees to be able to tell you that what is happening is wrong, that your quality is suffering, that there's a better way to do

things. You need to have their feedback and be able to listen to those things because those are the people who are meeting our customers directly, the people who are on the production line, the people who are involved in the everyday events of what we are doing. If you don't have their feedback, the management can go right along dreaming that everything is great when all of a sudden it finds out that maybe it wasn't so good. You have to have that openness.

Maintaining that "openness" is precisely what such devices as the jobholders' meetings and the CPR structure accomplish. These practices show employees that the management is not only open to criticism, but it is also open to taking their ideas seriously. By making management accountable to employees, the company implicitly subscribes to the democratic principle of equality. There are no second-class citizens if everybody is given the opportunity to make an important contribution—mental as well as physical—to the working community. And there are no first-class citizens if no one is above questioning, above reproach.

Freedom of Speech, Freedom of Press

Tektronix publishes one of the few weekly newspapers for employees in corporate America. But it's not the weekly frequency that makes *Tekweek* so unusual. It's published without any censorship from the management. As the paper's masthead says proudly: "*Tekweek* is published by and for employees of Tektronix, Inc."

Anyone familiar with company newsletters or magazines can immediately see the difference. Most are bland and unrelentingly promotional. Not so with *Tekweek*, where employees often directly challenge management decisions. For instance, there's a regular feature entitled "Employees Are Asking." The questions are followed by responses from management. One *Tekweek* column in 1987 had the following question: "When things are as tight as they seem to be, why is [the instrument division] spending $100,000 to move a group or groups to a new location in the same building? . . . Will this add more profit share to our bottom line?" The vice-president of the division gave a detailed response, arguing that the move would reduce leasing costs by $39,000 to $52,000 a year, make the work areas more efficient, and improve the appearance for visiting customers. "As a result," the vice-president wrote, "yes, we do expect more profit to our bottom line."

This kind of exchange is commonplace at Tek, as the company is universally called. Managers know that they are living in a goldfish bowl. Even relatively minor acts, like moving office space, can be challenged by any employee, forcing the manager to justify a decision publicly to all employees. And if employees don't like the response, you can be certain that the manager will hear about it in the next issue of Tekweek.

Tekweek also has a letters-to-the-editor column. Tekweek's first editor, Joe Floren, recalls that when it was initiated, he thought that employees should be permitted to withhold their names in case they feared punishment for speaking out. An executive vice-president disagreed with Floren and argued that people should be willing to speak up for what they believe in. The issue was eventually debated in a executive meeting, and Floren's position won out. The next week the vice-president wrote a letter protesting the policy, and Tekweek published it. According to Floren, "After all, these are employee publications that are open to all employees, including management people as employees."

This openness at Tek can be traced to its history. Founded in Portland, Oregon, in 1946, Tek is the world's largest manufacturer of oscillosopes used for measuring electronic instruments, making it a Fortune 500 company, with some twenty-thousand employees. Its founders, Jack Murdock and Howard Vollum, were intrigued with the concept of industrial democracy and were influenced by the example of an early electronics company called General Radio, which was 100 percent employee-owned, with a generous profit-sharing plan. Tek instituted its first profit-sharing plan during its second year of business and still pays out 35 percent of its net profits to employees. Murdock was also impressed with a participatory-management system, called multiple management, at McCormick Company, the Baltimore spice company. At Tek, the idea of employee participation has been translated into what is known as the area-rep program.

The area-rep activitity is similar to what goes on in the coun-

cil on personnel relations at Pitney Bowes. Employees elect a
representative from their work groups (one area rep for about
every forty employees). Once a month, each work group is
granted forty minutes of paid company time for the area-rep
activity (excluding travel time), which the area rep organizes.
Generally speaking, area reps use the time to learn more about
different aspects of the company. They may visit another Tek
facility. They may visit a customer. They may visit a supplier.
They may invite a senior official to talk about a specific subject.
On a monthly basis, the approximately three hundred area reps
get together for a forum on a topic of interest, such as compensation. Employees throughout the company give questions
for their area reps to ask the executives who speak at such
forums. The highlight of the year is the area-rep meeting addressed by the president. He delivers a State of Tektronix
speech and then opens himself to questions from the area reps.
As might be expected, the kid gloves are off during the question-and-answer period. The tougher questions and the president's answers are reported in full in the next issue of
Tekweek.

Tek's president, Earl Wantland, acknowledges that the free-
wheeling and critical atmosphere can be uncomfortable for
management:

> Anxiety is a natural part of the human creature. But it's im-
> portant to deal with people honestly and openly about issues
> and give them some opportunity to express their positions. It's
> also important to give people a chance to adapt to whatever the
> new norms are likely to be rather than for changes to come in
> as completely arbitrary actions, with no common courtesy at
> all in terms of the impact on the individual.

Wantland points out, however, that management is uncomfortable with the free flow of ideas for another reason:

> A lot of people, especially folks that aren't very secure, have
> a tendency to restrict the flow of knowledge, because it is a
> power source. And if you keep the people uninformed, you
> keep them vulnerable and insecure and therefore not very ag-
> gressive, and with an unwillingness to question what's going
> on.

Information, in other words, is a source of power in any organization. When managers restrict its flow, they may further their own personal goals. It enlarges their power at the expense of those under them. However, this strategy creates serious problems for the organization because people need information in order to make intelligent decisions about what to do. Unless you prefer an organization of automatons, the more knowledge people have, the better will be their individual work and the more productive will be their collective efforts.

At the same time, restricting information goes hand in hand with a more rigid, hierarchical approach to doing business. People in the hierarchy jealously guard their information and only apportion it a little at a time. They think that to give up more information than absolutely essential decreases their power. They may also feel that nobody down the line can be trusted to make the right decision because truth resides only among those in the loftier ranks. Such thinking is dangerously self-defeating, according to Wantland:

> In general, the highly planned, highly structured, hierarchical approach to business doesn't work. Each person, no matter where they are in the hierarchy, only knows so much, and that's not near enough. If you push everything through a hierarchy, you're going to be missing important elements of what it is that you're dealing with, because of the natural filtering process that goes on whenever information is passed along. Some people have skills in management, but that doesn't make them the most knowledgeable person about any particular issue that comes up. So it's very important that we have an open enough atmosphere here so that we can bring knowledge to whatever issues we are dealing with—and to let the information flow in a fairly free and fluid form.

Wantland is arguing here that the free flow makes sense strictly on business grounds. But it also makes sense in terms of workplace relationships. The way information is handled affects any community. If you don't know what's going on, rumors can fly. When information gets restricted, power structures get created. If you don't understand something, it's hard to contribute fully and enthusiastically. When information gets distorted, people begin to mistrust each other. Once credibility is undermined, cooperation suffers. In short, without the free flow of information, the workplace community can't work together as well as when everyone has the chance to make an informed contribution.

Ultimately, the value of democratic forms like freedom of speech (or trial by one's peers or town meetings) is that they make for a better community. Free speech is not something that we advocate merely because it sounds good or is in accord with the ideals of the eighteenth-century Enlightenment. Democratic forms make sense because a democratic society makes for a better way to live.

Robert Dahl, the respected political scientist, recently wrote a book arguing that the disparity between an undemocratic workplace and a democratic society is no longer tenable. He writes:

> If democracy is justified in governing the state, then it must also be justified in governing economic enterprises; and to say that it is not justified in governing economic enterprises is to imply that it is not justified in governing the state. [Emphasis in original.]

The crux of Dahl's argument is that if nobody should be treated as a second-class citizen in society at large, why should the same people be accorded second-class status during a large part of their waking hours? A good workplace takes this argument to heart.

PART THREE

HOW MANAGEMENT GETS IN THE WAY

The main obstruction to the kind of workplace described in the previous chapters is the thinking inherited by conventional management. By analyzing from an employee viewpoint the ideas of four management gurus, each of whom represents a popular style of management, we can appreciate why most workplaces are so bad.

6
SCIENTIFIC
MANAGER
Frederick Winslow Taylor

Most of us have worked in places where the boss contends that it's his job to do the mental work while the employees do the physical or routine work. Gordon Forward, the president of Chaparral Steel, once summed up the idea perfectly: "Most companies assume you should check your brains every morning at the factory door."

If you've ever wondered where that idea came from, meet Frederick Winslow Taylor, the father of scientific management. Other Taylor legacies include efficiency experts, time-and-motion studies, standardized work procedures, planning departments, and the piece-rate wage based on established standards—"paying men, not positions."

Taylor's techniques were ideally suited to mass production. Taylor made several visits to the infant automobile industry in Detroit. In 1909, for instance, he delivered a four-hour lecture to Packard's management, which soon proclaimed itself "Taylorized." And Henry Ford's right-hand man, James Couzens, came under Taylor's influence. He helped put the principles of scientific management into practice at the world's first moving assembly line, which opened in Highland Park, Michigan, in 1913, two years before Taylor's death. Taylor also served as a consultant to other major companies, including Du Pont and General Electric, which helped spread the gospel of scientific management throughout American industry. Time-

and-motion studies continue to be used widely. United Parcel
Service, for instance, employs over a thousand efficiency experts who track UPS drivers' movements with stopwatches.

More than specific Taylor techniques have filtered through
to the present day. Taylor's philosophy is almost universally
accepted in practice, if not in theory, by managers throughout
the world. Indeed, as Peter F. Drucker once wrote: "[Scientific
management] may well be the most powerful as well as the
most lasting contribution America has made to Western
thought since the Federalist Papers." Taylor's contribution has
not been limited to capitalist countries, either. Lenin urged
Soviet industrial managers to study scientific management:

> The possibility of building socialism depends exactly upon
> our success in combining the Soviet power and Soviet orga-
> nization of administration with the up-to-date achievements of
> capitalism. We must organize in Russia the study and teaching
> of the Taylor system and systematically try it out and adapt it
> to our ends.

Most people who've written about management have been
consultants or business-school professors. Few of them have
actually been workers or managers. Frederick Taylor was both.
Born in 1858 into a middle-class family in Philadelphia, Taylor
passed up a chance to attend Harvard and went directly to
work as an apprentice to a patternmaker in a machine shop.
He rose through the ranks from day laborer to journeyman
machinist to gang boss to foreman and finally to chief engineer
of the Midvale Steel Company. In his managerial positions,
Taylor began his experiments to bolster efficiency and for-
mulated principles of the "task system," later known as "scientific management."

Taylor had two distinct sides to his personality. On the one
hand, he had a wide range of interests outside of work. He
was a terrific tennis player. Taylor and the son of the co-owner
of Midvale Steel won the 1881 equivalent of the U.S. Open
tennis doubles championship. He had a good sense of humor.
In Frank Barkley Copley's definitive biography, there's a price-
less photo of Taylor in the costume of a woman; he played her
part in an amateur play. This engaging, social side of Taylor

helps explain how he spread his ideas so effectively and acquired so many disciples, including Frank and Lillian Gilbreth. (The home life of this husband-and-wife team of efficiency experts was popularized in the 1959 movie *Cheaper by the Dozen*, starring Clifton Webb and Myrna Loy.)

But Frederick Taylor also hated imprecision. A childhood friend, who later became an artist, recalled:

> Fred was always a bit of a crank in the opinion of our boyhood band, and we were inclined to rebel sometimes from the strict rules and exact formulas to which he insisted that all our games must be subjected. To the future artist, for example, it did not seem absolutely necessary that the rectangle of our rounders' court should be scientifically accurate, and that the whole of a fine sunny morning should be wasted in measuring it off by feet and inches. . . . Even a game of croquet was a source of study and careful analysis with Fred, who worked out carefully the angles of the various strokes, the force of impact and the advantages and disadvantages of the understroke, the overstroke, etc.

Biographer Copley traces this aspect of Taylor's personality to his Puritan and Quaker forebears. Wherever it came from, Taylor always strove for perfection. Above all, he couldn't stand to waste time or energy, and he thought it unforgivable for anyone else to do so, either. Loafing on the job, or soldiering, as it was then known, was to Taylor "the greatest evil with which the working-people of both England and America are now afflicted." His entire career was devoted to rooting out soldiering from the industrial scene.

Why do people loaf on the job? Taylor believed it stemmed from "the natural instinct and tendency of men to take it easy." This inherent laziness is compounded when you get a group of workers together. They invariably pressure more energetic workers to slow down. What's worse, they engage in "systematic soldiering . . . with the deliberate object of keeping their employers ignorant of how fast work can be done. So universal is soldiering for this purpose that hardly a competent workman can be found in a large establishment . . . who does not devote a considerable part of his time to studying just how slow he can work and still convince his employer that he is going at a good pace." Taylor spoke from experience. He had worked alongside other machinists at Midvale for a number of years.

How do you get people to work harder? When first promoted to management as a gang boss, Taylor thought he could easily induce his former associates to move faster. He estimated that his fellow workmen had set the machines to produce only one third of their potential. So he tried a variety of tactics—from verbal persuasion to "discharging or lowering the wages of the more stubborn men." After three years, output increased; it even doubled in some instances. But Taylor's hard-nosed techniques had provoked a "war" between the workers and the management. This was altogether unsatisfactory. As Taylor later wrote: "For any right-minded man, this success is in no sense a recompense for the bitter relations which [a manager] is forced to maintain with all those around him. Life which is one continuous struggle with other men is hardly worth living."

Taylor sought another approach. He wanted a method that would both increase output *and* lead to the "harmonious co-operation between the workmen and the management." That goal is worth noting because it has often been under the guise of bettering the conditions of workers that some of the worst abuses have been perpetuated.

Taylor's system had several features. First, management must analyze each task. Taylor knew that when a manager tells someone he is working too slowly, the worker is likely to retort, "No, I'm working as fast as I can." How can management counter that response? Science. The scientific manager subjects every task in the workplace to dispassionate scientific inquiry to eliminate any dispute about whether someone is goofing off. "Every single act of the workman can be reduced to a science," Taylor insisted.

One of Taylor's examples was shoveling coal. Based on his studies at Bethlehem Steel, Taylor concluded that "a first-class man would do his biggest day's work with a shovel load of about 21 pounds." Not 18 or 24 pounds per shovelful, but 21 pounds, Taylor pronounced. That was only part of "the science of shoveling." To arrive at conclusions about shoveling, Taylor's people "conducted thousands of stopwatch observations . . . to study just how quickly a laborer . . . can push his shovel into the pile of materials then draw it out properly." These time-and-motion studies determine the "one best way" to shovel coal or perform any other task, thereby "substituting exact scientific knowledge for opinions or the old rule-of-thumb of individual knowledge."

With this information, the entire workplace could be organized scientifically. Many new management positions were created. The planning department, as the "brains" of the operation, directed every aspect of the work. Workers, who previously had nearly total responsibility for their own jobs, were now taught how to do their work scientifically. A single foreman was replaced by a half dozen or more managers, whom Taylor called "teachers." In one machine shop, Taylor created seven different slots to oversee the workers. In this scheme, the "inspector" explains the quality that is expected; the "gang boss" elucidates on the quickest motions; the "speed boss" makes sure the machine runs at the proper rate; the "repair boss" takes care of the machine; the "time clerk" keeps track of output for piece-rate payments; the "route clerk" coordinates the flow of materials to and from the worker; and finally, "in case a workman gets into any trouble with any of his various bosses, the 'disciplinarian' interviews him."

To hear Taylor, or any of his army of disciples, talk about its virtues, scientific management was the best friend the American industrial worker ever had. The scientific organization of the workplace frees the worker to concentrate on improving his efficiency. To overcome any worker resistance to the system, Taylor preached that new piece-rate standards must be set so that workers would be paid substantially *higher wages* than before, even double or triple their previous earnings. The company could afford paying more because the improved efficiency from Taylor's methods meant it would incur much *lower total labor costs.* Besides getting more money, workers in a Taylor-run plant received elaborate training, the proper tools to do their job right, and the best possible physical working conditions. What more could anybody ask?

If the work relationship was merely a one-for-one market exchange, like buying a loaf of bread, scientific management would have made a nirvana out of thousands of American workplaces. Instead, its impact has been disastrous. Scientific management is rooted in distrust. Taylorism assumes that workers are naturally lazy and that they will sabotage efforts

to increase productivity. Taylor designed his system to make
that impossible. It makes a frontal assault on the worker's main
source of power—his knowledge. Without scientific management, Taylor explains, employees know more about the details
of work than management. As Taylor wrote in his classic essay
The Principles of Scientific Management:

> . . . traditional knowledge may be said to be the principal
> asset or possession of every tradesman. . . . Foremen and su-
> perintendents know, better than any one else, that their own
> knowledge and personal skills fall far short of the combined
> knowledge and dexterity of all the workmen under them.

Because the workers can't be trusted, scientific management
tries to wrest control of their knowledge. The industrial engineers don't use stopwatches and other techniques merely to
establish an objective scientific standard. These agents of management aim to steal what Taylor frankly acknowledges as the
employee's "principal asset." Once it possesses enough know-
how about the specifics of each task, the management can exert
absolute control over the workplace. Taylor summed it up
clearly in this passage from *The Principles of Scientific
Management*:

> It is only through *enforced* standardization of methods, *en-
> forced* adoption of the best implements and working conditions,
> and *enforced* cooperation that his faster work can be assured.
> And the duty of enforcing the adoption of standards and of
> enforcing this cooperation rests with the *management* alone.
> [Emphasis in original.]

All of Taylor's talk about creating a "harmonious" relationship between management and the employees aside, scientific
managers may have to bare their fists if they don't get voluntary
cooperation. Once cooperation has been "enforced," the division between planners and doers can be made permanent.
As Taylor put it: "One type of man is needed to plan ahead
and an entirely different type to execute the work." In short,
the manager provides the brains, the worker provides the
brawn. This conception of management has dominated the
workplace since Taylor's day. As William Batten, former pres-

ident of the New York Stock Exchange, said in 1979: "Work today is still rooted in scientific-management theories. The approach has been softened, but management [still] identifies and monitors all aspects of the workday, sometimes down to the exact number of minutes employees may spend at the water cooler."

Over the years, Frederick Taylor and scientific management have had their share of critics. Some have singled out several of Taylor's anecdotes in which he refers to workers as "mentally sluggish," "stupid," or like an "ox." Though Taylor did indeed use those phrases, the critics have ignored the context of such phrases and the politics of scientific management. Taylor did not say that workers were inherently stupid. Quite the reverse. As we've seen, Taylor realized that workers had brains and a considerable amount of knowledge. He objected to workers' using their intelligence against management instead of for it. So Taylor devised a system to neutralize the power of employee intelligence and make it irrelevant to how work was accomplished. In other words, under scientific management an employee not only doesn't have to think—he's not supposed to. His thinking is to be done by the new cadre of managers ("teachers"). Under scientific management, the stupider and more docile the person, the better the worker. The replaceable worker—comparable to a machine part—is what scientific management attempted to achieve.

Scientific management had an especially devastating impact on employee pride. Pride implies a feeling of control over your work. Without a sense of control, it's almost impossible to take much satisfaction in what you do. Taylor's system took away more than the employee's knowledge ("his principal asset") about how to do a job. With its focus on productivity, scientific management took away pride of workmanship.

This point can best be illustrated by listening to comments from workers with some firsthand experience of Taylorism. The year was 1911. The place was the Watertown Arsenal near Boston. Not long after some Taylor-trained industrial engineers armed with stopwatches came into the arsenal, the machine-shop molders staged a wildcat walkout. The molders returned to work after a week, and Taylor's disciples continued their time-and-motion analysis. In itself, the event was insignificant. But because it occurred at a federal installation, the government sent investigators to study the situation. As a result, we have transcripts of interviews done at the time with the molders. A central complaint revolved around the destruction of self-esteem.

A molder named Isaac Goosetray told investigators: "It will make an inferior class of workmen, for the simple reason that when a man is speeded up too much he will slight his work and the consequence will be in a short time from now that . . . we will have an inferior class of workmen."

James A. Mackean, who worked in the arsenal's machine shop, echoed this concern: "They can give us certain speeds and feeds in figures; but they cannot show us how to do the work better by any system than we know now. They can show us how to do it faster, but not better."

Mackean's remark sums up another key problem with scientific management. It does offer the possibility of improving productivity—how fast some procedure is accomplished. But what about quality? Since workers are distrusted, more agents of management have to be hired—in this case, quality inspectors. One industry that has taken scientific management to heart is the American auto industry. Problems with poor quality in American automobiles can be traced at least in part to this Taylor legacy of removing the responsibility for quality from the worker. The Japanese car makers, by contrast, have long placed responsibility for quality in the hands of the workers through the mechanism of work teams or quality circles.

Some Japanese even blame Taylorism more generally for America's industrial problems. Japan's management guru Konosuke Matsushita, founder of that country's largest electronics firm, Panasonic, once told a group of Western industrialists:

> We Japanese are going to win and the industrial West is going to lose out. There is nothing much you can do about it because the reasons for failure are within yourselves. Your firms are built on the Frederick Taylor model where the bosses do the thinking and the workers wield the screwdrivers. You are convinced deep down that this is the right way to run a business.

Matsushita's observation has merit. The Taylor system has had an enormous appeal to managers the world over. It gives them a superior status in the workplace. At the same time,

Taylorism itself has helped create many of the managerial positions. After all, more managers—a lot more managers—were needed to operate a plant scientifically. The scientific managers were extremely proud of their position in the plant. In his book *Taylorism at Watertown Arsenal*, Hugh G. J. Aitken made this observation about the managers:

> They felt that they, and not the workmen, were really managing the arsenal for the first time. To an appreciable degree one of the side effects of Taylorism was to make persons of executive and supervisory rank regard themselves as more important people, with greater control over what happened in the plant, than before. Taylorism not only involved certain new managerial functions; it also involved having them performed by new classes of people with new titles and more clearly specified responsibilities.

Since this new class of managers benefited from this system, it follows that they would be threatened by a system that trusts the employees. That is precisely what has happened. In the late 1970s and early 1980s, a number of American companies instituted quality circles and other participatory-management techniques, largely in response to the desire to emulate the successful Japanese. In 1986, *Fortune* published an article about the experience:

> It was really beautiful. Hourlies and supervisors, pencil pushers and clock punchers, all gathered around the corporate foundry to forge a new relationship based on the idea that workers could play an active part in management. . . . The new way entailed asking employees how their work might be improved and then letting them improve it, often in work teams or so-called quality circles. The initial results were [impressive]: A study of 101 industrial companies found that the participatively managed among them outscored the others on 13 of 14 financial measures.

Based on such results, we should have expected that every company in the land would have eagerly signed up. Here was the obvious answer to boosting America's competitive edge. But no, just the opposite occurred. *Fortune* quoted one business-school dean as saying, "The problem with participative management is that it works." About 75 percent of the programs installed during the early 1980s were scratched by 1986. Why? According to *Fortune*, the opposition came not from the workers but from:

> ... management, upper, middle, and lower. The concept was banished to the shop floor and, even if it flourished there, was never permitted to creep higher. Jump on the quality circle bandwagon? Sure. Takers were everywhere. But change the behavior of managers or the organizational structure? Not this decade, thanks.

As the *Fortune* article demonstrates, you can't de-Taylorize a workplace without displacing the people whose jobs depend on acting as the employees' "brains." Chapter 10, on Preston Trucking, shows how one company rooted out the scientific-management thinking and replaced it with a philosophy based on the assumption that the individual employee knows how to do his or her job best. Fully one quarter of the managers left the company as a direct result of that transformation. (Preston has meanwhile performed better than many of its competitors.) Theories of management have serious political implications within a company; they are not merely abstract philosophies.

One final point. Taylor argued that soldiering stems from natural laziness. Yet his own account contradicts that analysis. Consider the machinists at Midvale Steel Company before Taylor instituted his task system of management. Taylor freely acknowledged that the machinists didn't just sit around all day doing nothing. They spent time and energy figuring out how to keep production levels down. Taylor's rhetoric places the blame on worker laziness, but the intent of his system is to redirect the energies of the workers—to get them to cooperate with management rather than to subvert production. Taylor the manager didn't try to figure out how to "motivate" his workers. That concept didn't come into vogue until later, with Elton Mayo and the psychological managers. Taylor assumed that workers were already motivated, but that they were motivated toward the wrong goals.

If laziness doesn't explain soldiering, what does? A more likely cause can be found in numerous accounts of working conditions since the onset of the Industrial Revolution. Workers lost the feeling of being connected to the product they made or the service they rendered. As skilled craftsmen or farmers, workers had a direct relationship with their own work. They used their tools to create something. In the factory setting, and especially under scientific management, the worker became a tool in the hands of others. As Taylor himself stated so clearly: "In the past man has been first; in the future the system must be first." If loafing on the job is seen in this light, its solutions lie in removing the sources of the alienation. Instead of having their brainpower neutralized, employees must be given the respect of being consulted about issues that directly affect them.

Taylorism undermines every aspect of a great workplace. It's antithetical to building trust, it's fatal to employees' feeling pride in their own work, and it's destructive to creating genuine harmony in the organization. His successors have been unable to root out Taylor's legacy in the workplace because, as we shall see, they share some of his assumptions about the relationship between manager and employee even as they have abhorred some of Taylorism's excesses.

7
PSYCHOLOGICAL
MANAGER

Elton Mayo

Police investigators often work in pairs. One adopts the tough-guy stance while the other plays the part of the nice guy. One relentlessly hammers away at his quarry; the other offers understanding and consideration.

This same duality can be seen in many organizations. Most companies not only have nice guys; they have an entire department in which they reside—the personnel department, now often called the human-resources department. This nice-guy approach to management didn't just happen accidentally. Its roots can be traced to the 1930s and an industrial psychologist named Elton Mayo. How Mayo's human-relations movement came to occupy such a prominent place in American management is an ironical story of the tough guys creating the nice guys.

The story starts with Frederick Taylor, who represents the tough-guy approach to management. Though he called his system scientific management, it should more accurately have been called engineering management. Frederick Taylor himself was a mechanical engineer, as were most of his early disciples. Taylor first made public his task system at a meeting of the American Society of Mechanical Engineers—the principal forum of the era for discussing ideas about management. And when universities decided to teach management in the early part of this century, they opened departments of industrial engineering.

The connection between management and engineering was natural. The Industrial Revolution was fueled by technological advances. Engineers figured out how to apply technology to industry. They designed products as well as the machines that produced them. The early factories existed because of these machines and were laid out to accommodate them, with little or no consideration for the people who operated them.

That machines came first was an unchallenged assumption of the Industrial Revolution. This perspective had a tremendous impact on the workplace, long before Frederick Taylor's day. In describing the English cotton mills of the 1830s, E. G. Hobsbawm, an eminent British economic historian, wrote the following:

> The "factory" with its logical flow of processes . . . all linked together by the inhuman and constant pace of the "engine" and the discipline of mechanization, gas-lit, iron-ribbed and smoking, was a revolutionary form of work. Though factory wages tended to be higher than those in domestic industries . . . workers were reluctant to enter them, because in doing so men lost their birthright, independence. Indeed this is one reason why they were filled, where possible with the more tractable women and children: in 1838 only twenty-three percent of textile factory workers were adult men.

The Luddites symbolized the early rejection of the machine age. They went around the English countryside between 1811 and 1813, broke into small textile-manufacturing establishments, and smashed the looms. Three decades later, Karl Marx and Friedrich Engels penned the famous *Communist Manifesto*, which decries the inhumanity of the factory system. The British trade-union movement also started during this period. It was the first effective organized reaction to industrial conditions, and helped form the pattern of labor movements in the United States and other countries. There was, however, a far more common reaction to the machine age than joining unions or becoming communists: Workers simply didn't give their all. They loafed on the job. They engaged in soldiering.

To attempt to solve soldiering, then, was to confront the

ultimate engineering problem—people, the problem that had perplexed industrial managers since the beginning of the machine age. This is why Frederick Taylor's scientific-management system has had such a profound impact on work throughout the world. It suggested an engineering solution to the people problem of industry. Management need only conduct detailed analyses of tasks to eliminate the troublesome "human element" from the workplace. Employees could then be manipulated with the proper mixture of wages and discipline, just as their machines could be adjusted to deliver peak performance. In effect, Taylor's system promised that management could deal with the workers as if they were machines.

What about fatigue? What about monotony? Even well-organized and well-intentioned employees get tired. They get bored. Their minds wander from their work, and productivity suffers. Ironically, fatigue and monotony became a greater problem with the spread of the scientific-management system. A factory embracing the Taylor system subdivided work, giving individual workers discrete tasks. The assembly line, where workers might perform only one task all day long, epitomized scientific management. But the repetitive nature of such tasks obviously made the jobs more boring, causing people to work less efficiently.

Since the engineering approach had offered a solution to soldiering, surely it could solve these new "human" problems, too. At least that's what Taylor's disciples and other engineer-managers believed. So starting around the turn of the century, factory managers sponsored numerous studies to figure out how to solve the problems of fatigue and monotony in the workplace. One of these studies had the surprising result of challenging scientific management itself.

The Hawthorne Discoveries

The top research engineers of Western Electric Company (AT&T) launched the study in question in 1923 at its sprawling Hawthorne Works plant near Chicago. They initially wanted to know whether worker productivity would be affected by changes in lighting. So they increased or decreased the lighting in several different departments. After months of study, they found no obvious correlation between lighting and work output. Sometimes people worked better when the room was dimly lit, sometimes worse. Changes in lighting alone didn't seem to have any significant impact on productivity.

The engineers then turned their attention to other factors, such as the effect of rest breaks and changes in piece rates. They picked five young women and built a special test room adjacent to a large work area for the experiment. By isolating the workers, they sought to minimize other variables and make the study more scientifically valid. The women performed their usual job—assembling telephone relays that consisted of thirty-five separate pieces secured by four machine screws. It generally took about one minute to assemble each relay. The women normally worked a forty-eight-hour week, including a half day on Saturday, without any rest breaks during the working day. The researchers wanted to know about fatigue. For instance, did rest periods in the morning and afternoon make the workers feel less tired and improve their output? Every few weeks for the next two years (1927–1929), they made changes in the women's work day and piece rates, and studied the effects of those variations in both worker morale and productivity.

No one anticipated the results: The workers' productivity improved almost regardless of which changes were instituted.

How could such results be explained? Baffled, the research engineers turned to Elton Mayo, head of Harvard Business School's new industrial research department.

The Australian "Doctor"

Mayo came from a family of doctors in South Australia. His grandfather was a famous doctor-settler in Adelaide, and everyone assumed that Elton would continue the tradition. But Mayo flunked or dropped out of three different medical schools before finally getting a degree in philosophy in 1904 at the age of twenty-four. The degree enabled him to teach, and he spent the rest of his career affiliated with universities, first in Australia, later at the Wharton School of Business at the University of Pennsylvania, and then at Harvard. Yet Mayo never fit comfortably into the narrow specialization of the academic world and never got a Ph.D.

Harvard Business School Professor Abraham Zaleznik, who joined the school as a research assistant in 1947, Mayo's last year there, wrote that Mayo had "a bit of the juvenile delinquent in him." According to Zaleznik:

> Everyone, with the exception of Mayo, showed up at the office early in the morning. Mayo arrived at mid-morning, worked a few hours conducting interviews with his assistants, in which he mixed therapy and work (for him the two were the same). He would then repair to St. Clair's restaurant in Harvard Square where he would take lunch and sherry late in the afternoon. Whether Mayo enjoyed this routine as much as he did flouting the culture of the Harvard Business School is an open question. . . .
>
> What he did with his time was a matter of conjecture. Perhaps the simple answer is that Mayo was fundamentally a lazy man who managed to dodge the pressures of the Protestant work ethic.

Mayo, nevertheless, had enormous personal effect on people. He had style. His biographer, Richard C. S. Trahair, writes: "When he entered a room he gave the impression that an important person had arrived. On the street in good weather he wore a brimmed hat with a colorful band, carried a cane, sported a handkerchief up his sleeve, and walked with a jaunty swagger that used the full length of his slim body." Mayo seemed like a witty character out of a play by Noël Coward, his favorite playwright. A brilliant conversationalist and a lecturer who could spellbind audiences, Mayo loved theorizing on a wide variety of topics. He was even more powerful when talking with people individually. He saw himself as a healer and a therapist. Despite the fact he never completed medical school or received certification, people assumed that he was a medical doctor and he was always referred to as "Dr. Mayo." Mayo never did anything to disabuse people of the notion and even had a set of doctor's scales in his business school office.

Mayo had a knack for captivating people who could forward his career. Shortly after arriving in America in 1922, almost broke and looking for work, he got himself an invitation to speak on medical psychology—a hot lecture-circuit topic of the day. His talk impressed an associate of John D. Rockefeller, Jr.'s. Interested in seeing whether Mayo's ideas about medical psychology could be applied to industry, Rockefeller agreed to fund studies of workers Mayo proposed to undertake at some factories in Philadelphia. Rockefeller continued to subsidize Mayo's work for a number of years after he joined Harvard's faculty in 1926.

It was through his association with Rockefeller that Mayo became known to Western Electric executives. They invited Mayo to come to Chicago and consult with them about their studies. Never at a loss for a theory, Mayo offered a radical interpretation. He contended that the changes that had been introduced—the variations in rest pauses and piece rates—were only "minor matters" compared with the profound change in the work environment brought about by isolating the women in the test room. In particular, Mayo singled out the role of the sympathetic and concerned "observer," who didn't act like a typical plant "supervisor." This is what is often referred to as the Hawthorne effect, a familiar term in the lexicon of social science. It means that behavior may improve because of the attention people receive from being singled out for study rather than because of the test changes themselves. More important, Mayo stressed that the test room was not merely six individual workers. They constituted a social grouping with a life of its own that needed to be studied as a social unit. So, to Mayo, the test room itself was "a new industrial milieu, a milieu in which [the workers'] own self-determination and their social well-being ranked first and the work was incidental."

Mayo suggested that the discovery of the social milieu in the workplace should be studied further. With Mayo's assistance, Western Electric launched what may well be the largest industrial study in history. To learn more about supervisory practices and improve the quality of supervision, Western Electric interviewed more than twenty-one thousand Hawthorne workers between 1928 and 1930. Thirty full-time researchers were employed. Mayo helped orient them in nondirective interview techniques, which are somewhat similar to the Jungian style of free association. Interviewers let the workers talk freely about whatever subjects interested them. (Psychologist Carl Rogers credited this interview experiment as the inspiration for his popular nondirective counseling style.) The interviews typically lasted one and a half hours.

The extensive interviewing project prompted one last experiment. This time the researchers decided simply to observe the social dynamics of the bank-wiring department, where fourteen men assembled telephone terminals. Unlike the procedure followed in studying the five women relay-assembly workers, researchers did not alter the bank-wiring workers' normal routine. The only difference was the existence of an observer. He mostly sat in a corner and took notes of the men's habits and conversations. Though the men initially viewed him with suspicion, the observer was soon accepted. The study lasted for six months, until May 1932, when the men were laid off because of the Depression.

What the Hawthorne researchers discovered would not have surprised Frederick Taylor. They saw that the bank-wiring workers intentionally restricted their output; that is, engaged in soldiering. The work group had an elaborate social dynamics. A worker who produced more than the group's informal standard of a day's work was called a rate buster and was subject to severe social pressures from his peers. Anyone who produced less, a chiseler. The workers also singled out as a squealer anyone who told a supervisor anything that could reflect badly on a co-worker. In short, the bank-wiring room was a sociologist's dream—and an industrial supervisor's nightmare.

The results of all three phases of the Hawthorne experiment also created a nightmare for the theory of scientific management. According to Mayo and his disciples, the Hawthorne study proved conclusively that merely changing the physical conditions of work won't even touch the underlying psychological and social problems that cause people to be less than fully productive. The workplace is much more complicated. Any effort to improve productivity had to start with an understanding of both human nature and the nature of social organizations. According to Mayo, the workplace is full of human beings, not machines, as Frederick Taylor would lead us to believe. The approach of the cold-hearted rationalist is doomed. It takes the sensibility of a humanist to understand and to deal with workers.

The Hawthorne experiments shook up the engineering-management establishment of the day. As historian David F. Noble wrote:

> The discoveries of Mayo and his colleagues were startling and constituted a revolution in management thought; needless to say, the engineers who had conceived the original project had hardly suspected anything of the kind. . . . The Hawthorne experience called into question many of the basic assumptions of scientific management, gave impetus to the infant applied sciences of industrial psychology and sociology, ushered in the new field of "human relations," and provided management educators with a wealth of case-study material.

Engineer-managers found the Hawthorne critique so persuasive because it was cloaked in scientific garb. The books detailing the results of the Hawthorne experiments have every appearance of works of science. Minutiae of every stage of the experiments are presented: records of the daily production output, what the workers ate for lunch, hourly blood-pressure readings, hundreds of direct quotations from formal and informal interviews, dozens of charts and photographs, and so on. Though many social scientists subsequently criticized many of the Hawthorne researchers' techniques as sloppy and unscientific, the immense scope and details of the study were hard to ignore. The Hawthorne studies appear to be as scientific as, say, Taylor's own stopwatch studies of shoveling. Mayo chided his detractors:

> It is amusing that certain industrialists, rigidly disciplined in economic theory, attempt to shrug off the Hawthorne studies as "theoretic." Actually the shoe is on the other foot; Hawthorne has restudied the facts without prejudice, whereas the critics have unquestioningly accepted the theory of man which had its vogue in the nineteenth century and has already outlived its usefulness.

As could have been expected, Elton Mayo left the laborious task of writing up details of the experiments entirely in the hands of his protégés Fritz Roethlisberger and Thomas North Whitehead (son of Alfred, the famous philosopher). Instead, Mayo applied his skills as an orator and writer to preach the Hawthorne gospel. He lectured widely and wrote two short volumes (*The Human Problems of an Industrial Civilization* and *The Social Problems of an Industrial Civilization*) to put forth his interpretations of Hawthorne to a wider audience.

What Mayo actually says in those books defies easy categorization. He was an eclectic thinker who drew freely from various fields—anthropology, psychology, sociology, political science, and philosophy. His analysis of the Hawthorne interview program, for instance, provoked a lengthy discussion of psychologist Pierre Janet's theory about obsessives (somewhat similar to Freud's theories of hysteria). Or Mayo's ruminations about the cause of poor morale in the workplace led him to write for pages about sociologist Emile Durkheim's concept of anomie (which has some similarities to Marx's theory of alienation). Mayo's protégé Fritz Roethlisberger explains:

> Mayo was not a systematic thinker. Although he stated his ideas vigorously, he never stated them rigorously. His accomplishments are best seen in the context of face-to-face relationships. His chief products were the people that he influenced and helped to develop. Even the ideas that he developed in books were more often in the nature of seeds to be cultivated in the field than of rigorous hypotheses to be tested in the laboratory.

The seeds Elton Mayo planted have borne fruit in the form of a wide variety of management practices from psychological testing and attitude surveys of employees to job-enrichment programs and management training in human-relations skills. More important than the specific human-relations techniques, however, has been the widespread managerial acceptance of Mayo's basic humanistic premises. For instance, managers commonly assume the need to apply psychological techniques to get employees to perform more efficiently.

At first glance, Mayo's message may appear like one that should be applauded by employees. Mayo's humanism certainly offers a welcome antidote to Taylor's lack of compassion. It's also hard to argue with someone who recognizes your *human* qualities rather than only your skills. Unfortunately, the human-relations approach to the workplace also contains some serious flaws. From the human-relations perspective, workers are patients and managers are therapists. Both perceptions undermine the building of a great workplace.

Workers as Patients

Richard C. S. Trahair writes that Mayo saw himself as "a healer of disease in industrial society." Of course, the main sufferers from the disease are industrial workers. Mayo states this explicitly in his books. Using data from the Hawthorne interviews, Mayo wrote that the workers' statements about their working conditions and their supervisors were totally unreliable. Two workers with identical jobs under the same supervisor could give wildly different descriptions of their work situation. Mayo considered this as "a tendency to exaggeration and distortion in statements made by sufficiently normal people." Citing the theories of various psychologists, particularly Pierre Janet, Mayo speculated that the workers exhibited an "obsessive response" to their work environment. Mayo did not believe that all workers were crazy and would be better off in asylums. He explicitly wrote that of the more than twenty-thousand employees interviewed, "not more than a round dozen revealed themselves as unmistakable candidates for the psychiatrist." But he did believe the workers clearly suffered from a mild form of mental illness that affected their productivity. That's why they gave such distorted accounts of their work and were often unhappy with their jobs.

According to Mayo, talking out problems through a nondirective counseling session called an interview helped workers overcome their obsessions. Mayo provided examples of the efficacy of this technique from Hawthorne. He writes:

> One woman worker, for example, discovered for herself during an interview that her dislike of a certain supervisor was based upon a fancied resemblance to a detested stepfather. Small wonder that the same supervisor had warned the interviewer that she was "difficult to handle." But the discovery by the worker that her dislike was wholly irrational eased the situation considerably.

According to the researchers: "It was evident that the complaints of this type of person could not be taken seriously as criticisms of company policies or conditions." On the contrary, such problems should not be pinned on the company. In Mayo's opinion, Western Electric was "a Company definitely committed to justice and humanity in its dealings with workers."

What we see here is a clear example of the human-relations approach in action. Viewing the workplace through the prism of a therapist, the industrial manager tends to see all problems as personal problems. The appropriate solution invariably requires the individual worker to adjust to the company. But how accurate is Mayo's view of the workplace? We need look no further than the case Mayo himself cites. The full transcript of the interview with the worker is still available, and a reading of that transcript reveals that the woman might not have been so irrational after all.

In the transcript the worker contrasts the disliked supervisor with her previous one, who "says little jokes and makes you feel good." Her current boss, on the other hand, is "kind of mean like. He's so mean-looking. . . . He talks [mean] too." According to the worker, the supervisor criticizes employees harshly whenever a mistake is made, and he often harasses the employees with petty demands. She claims that other supervisors aren't so abusive. Most important, she insists that her feelings about the supervisor are shared by all the other workers: "They all feel the same; they haven't much use for him. It seems like he just likes to hurt people. He just wants you to know that he's the boss."

On the basis of the interview itself, the worker appears to have had lots of sound, rational reasons for disliking her supervisor. If anything, there appear to be ample grounds for arguing that her supervisor needed to change his behavior toward his subordinates. But that wasn't even considered an option. Mayo's interview technique places the entire burden on the employee, and the employee alone, to adjust to what appears to be a pretty bad situation.

The supervisor clearly believed that the interview would straighten out the worker. The technique, in other words, might have been portrayed to the workers as a purely neutral one, but the management wanted the workers interviewed because it might help them with their problem cases.

This example illustrates the deception at the core of the human-relations approach. Beneath the guise of making people feel better lurks the real goal: increasing productivity. Daniel Bell, a Harvard sociology professor, reviewed the work of Elton Mayo and the subsequent human-relations movement in his 1956 essay "Work and Its Discontents." According to Bell:

> The ends of the enterprise remain, but the methods have shifted, and the older modes of overt coercion are now replaced by psychological persuasion. The tough brutal foreman, raucously giving orders, gives way to the mellowed voice of the "human relations oriented" supervisor.

Certainly improving productivity is a desirable goal for an industrial enterprise. And anyone would prefer a mellow-voiced supervisor to a brutal boss. But there are serious problems for the workplace when matters are not communicated in an above-board way. It undermines trust. We saw an example of this subtle deceptiveness of a human-relations-style technique in an earlier chapter when discussing how a job-enrichment program was instituted at a Chicago insurance company. Although the real goal of the program was productivity, employees were told that the objective was to improve their well-being. Such tactics qualify under a definition of manipulation offered by Doug Strain, founder of Electro Scientific Industries. He says that "being manipulative means you are not dealing with your cards face up. You are having somebody do something without their understanding why they want to do it or should do it."

While Elton Mayo himself didn't come up with other techniques besides the interview, the human-relations movement he spawned continues to develop and expand on them: psychological testing, sensitivity training, job-enrichment programs, to name just a few. These management styles all view the workplace from a psychologist's perspective. Subsequent management theorists have had more sophisticated and refined theories of human nature than Mayo's rather crude view of obsessives and industrial maladjustment. For instance, one of those who have followed the trail originally blazed by Mayo is Abraham Maslow, a popular humanistic psychologist. Maslow developed a sophisticated model of human nature called the hierarchy of needs. Maslow argued that once people meet their basic survival needs they have a need for self-actualization. Two popular management styles are explicitly grounded in Maslow's model—Frederick Herzberg's job-enrichment program (discussed in an earlier chapter) and Douglas McGregor's Theory Y (which was the basis for sensitivity training and organizational development). A more recent exponent of the psychological approach to management is Tom Peters, whom we will discuss shortly.

Spontaneous Cooperation Without Conflict

Advocates of the human-relations approach invariably suggest that reliance on humanistic managerial techniques eliminates conflicts between management and labor. Instead of two warring factions, Mayo envisioned a workplace characterized by "spontaneous cooperation," where everybody would work together harmoniously. He saw this as the natural outcome as humanistic managers help the worker-patients overcome their psychological or motivational problems.

The vision of a workplace of cooperative workers has great appeal. But it assumes a fundamental unity of interest between the individual and the organization. What happens, however, if you think your supervisor is treating you unfairly? Or if you don't agree with your humane supervisor about how to do a task? Or if you think the company is paying you too little money? By trying to reduce such complaints to individual psychological problems, the human-relations approach implies that it's possible to achieve cooperation merely by making changes in the minds of the employees rather than in the policies and practices of the company. In this sense, Mayo's concept of spontaneous cooperation echoes that of Frederick Taylor's call for cooperation. Both assume that management alone will dictate the terms. That employees might have legitimate interests is simply not part of Mayo's theory. He was silent, for instance, on the subject of unions. A remarkable omission, considering that the 1930s was an era of aggressive union-organizing efforts throughout American industry. Mayo has nothing to say about unions because, like Taylor, he didn't believe they had a place in industry. He was convinced that adopting his humanistic approach would make unions unnecessary.

Perhaps more humanistic supervisors could keep unions out of some establishments, but Mayo's view ignores something more basic. It lacks a theory for handling *conflicts* in the workplace. The human-relations specialists who've followed in Mayo's footsteps have discovered that they simply have to step aside when major conflicts develop. That's one explanation for why personnel (or human-resource) departments usually get relegated to the background in organizations. The human-relations movement can make people feel better in organizations, but it doesn't offer much besides psychological persuasion and exhortation if the employees aren't responsive. It's small wonder that those who must deal with serious workplace conflicts often place little faith in the human-relations approach. For all its shortcomings, scientific management provides specific suggestions about how to deal with uncooperative (soldiering) employees. Taylor's approach sets standards and has mechanisms for enforcement—or, as Taylor put it, "enforced cooperation."

Perhaps the deficiencies in the human-relations approach could be overlooked if that approach was shown to be a powerful tool in raising productivity. But there is another, even more practical, critique of the human-relations approach that also explains why scientific management still retains the upper hand in so many workplaces. There's strong evidence from studies of worker performance that refute the underlying assumption of the human-relations movement that happier workers are more productive. As the eminent industrial psychologist Victor Vroom writes in his classic book *Work and Motivation:* "It was typically assumed by most people connected with the human relations movement that job satisfaction was positively associated with job performance. In fact human relations might be described as an attempt to increase productivity by satisfying the needs of employees." Vroom surveyed twenty different studies that attempted to see what relationship, if any, existed between job satisfaction and work performance. His conclusion: "There is no simple relationship between job satisfaction and job performance." Sometimes happier workers produced more; sometimes they didn't. Vroom could perceive no empirical evidence to support the assumption that increasing job satisfaction works.

How do we explain this finding? One explanation is that many of the human-relations-style techniques don't effect structural changes in the workplace. They often concern only how immediate supervisors relate to their subordinates. For that reason, workers often consider these techniques to be mere window dressing, if not by-products of a manipulative management. Thus, employees may appreciate being treated better and state that they are more satisfied than before, but it may not result in work getting done more efficiently.

Does that mean that productivity requires an authoritarian management style like Frederick Taylor's? Not if we look closely at the research Vroom and others have conducted. Vroom, for instance, has noted that when employees have more say over their jobs, they are often more productive. As Vroom puts it: ". . . we find substantial basis for the belief that participation in decision making increases productivity. There is experimental and correlational evidence indicating that higher levels of influence by workers in making decisions that they are to carry out results in higher productivity than lower levels of influence." In other words, when employees are accepted as full partners in the work process, as we saw in the chapter on Northwestern Mutual Life, they often work more efficiently. And as we saw in the same chapter, they may also be happier than if they are subjected to human-relations-style managers who view them as needing therapy or motivation.

It is ironic that Vroom's conclusion was entirely consistent with Elton Mayo's research at Hawthorne. In explaining the change in the environment of the test room of the relay-assembly workers, Mayo wrote what could have been used as a terrific example of building trust in the workplace:

> There had been a remarkable change of mental attitude in the group. . . . At first shy and uneasy, silent and perhaps somewhat suspicious of the Company's intention, later their attitude is marked by confidence and candor. Before every change of programme, the group is consulted. Their comments are listened to and discussed; sometimes their objections are

allowed to negative [overrule] a suggestion. The group un-
questionably develops a sense of participation in the critical
determination and becomes something of a social unit. This
developing social unity is illustrated by the entertainment of
each other in their respective homes.

Mayo could have used such examples from the Hawthorne
experiments to argue for greater employee democracy and participation in decision making. It could have led another researcher to assert the need to change the way the work was
organized—that is, challenge scientific management's implicit
distrust of employees. But that someone wasn't Elton Mayo.
Mayo had a lifelong aversion to worker participation. It had
overtones of socialism and of the trade unionism he'd opposed
in Australia. According to Richard C. S. Trahair: "Mayo preferred the American approach, which did not allow economic
areas to be debased by the modern developments in
democracy."

Instead of advocating a greater degree of democracy in the
workplace, Mayo placed his hope in a managerial elite.
Throughout his career, Elton Mayo voiced the highest regard
for industrial managers, but he held that they needed training.
One of the biggest contributions of Mayo's and his followers'
was the field of management training, especially in the area
of human relations—how to understand human nature to manage people more effectively. Mayo saw it as crucial that managers develop a clinical approach toward workers. Unlike the
"irrational" employees he oversees, "the administrator of the
future must be able to understand the human-social facts for
what they actually are, unfettered by his own emotion or prejudice." They just needed a little education in progressive ideas
from the social sciences. "We do not lack an able administrative elite, but the elite of the several civilized powers is at
present insufficiently posted in the biological and social facts
involved in social organization and control."

The key word to note here is *elite*. Like Taylor before him
and Peter Drucker to follow, Mayo helped provide the vision
for a distinct managerial class. This enlightened managerial
elite would have two sets of skills. One involves the finely
honed administrative skills allowing managers to make all necessary business decisions on their own without input from

employees. This is the Taylor legacy. The second encompasses the human-relations skills necessary to induce the "irrational" employees to go along with management's decisions—and feel satisfied with the arrangement to boot. This is Mayo's contribution. What comes through loud and clear from an employee viewpoint is the idea that management is an elite, whether the individual managers portray themselves as tough guys or nice guys.

8
PROFESSIONAL MANAGER

Peter F. Drucker

It's not unusual to hear a young person say that his or her vocational goal is to be a manager. We take that idea for granted largely because we generally consider management to be a profession, somewhat like medicine or law. As for other professions, you can go to a professional-training school where the discipline of management is taught and degrees are offered. In that sense, an MBA (master's of business administration) is similar to a medical doctor's M.D. or a lawyer's J.D. degree. About fifty thousand people a year receive an MBA in the United States. Of course, you don't need an MBA to practice management, nor do states license managers as they do doctors or lawyers. But still, we accept as commonplace the notion that someone can be a professional manager.

If any one person can be said to be responsible for the wide acceptance of the professional manager it's Peter F. Drucker. Born in Vienna in 1909, Drucker is the son of a former high government official in Austria who founded the prestigious Salzburg international music festival. Educated in Germany, Peter Drucker fled the Nazis in 1933 and settled in the United States in 1937. Two years later, his first book appeared, *The End of Economic Man*. Since then he has written almost two dozen books (including two novels) and hundreds of articles on economics, politics, social trends, and management. He also taught management at New York University for more than twenty years and, since 1971, has taught at the Claremont Graduate School in California. Writing and teaching are only sidelines, though. Drucker insists his real work has been as a management consultant to dozens of major corporations throughout the world.

In assessing his own influence, Drucker can't be accused of modesty. He calls himself the "man who *discovered* management." By that, Drucker says, "I first presented [management] as an organized body of knowledge and as a discipline. And this made possible—perhaps a dubious achievement—the teaching of management in schools." Drucker credits the acceptance of his ideas with saving "a dying Ford Motor Company"; with revitalizing Sears, Roebuck after the Second World War; and with getting General Electric to adopt a "decentralization policy"—a policy that, in Drucker's words, "probably had more impact on industrial structure around the world than any other move by a major company in the post-World War II period." Then, of course, there are the Japanese, whose success in the postwar years can be traced to their adoption of Drucker's ideas—at least according to Drucker. In Japan, Drucker writes, "I am credited with substantial responsibility for the emergence of the country as a major economic power and for the performance and productivity of its industry . . ."

Whether one completely accepts Drucker's self-assessment, he is certainly the ultimate management guru. He's been called "the management equivalent of Karl Marx," the "grand old man of management theory and literature," and "one of the last encyclopaedics"—a reference to his tendency to pepper his writings with wide-ranging references to literature, history, and music. At the very minimum, many of Drucker's ideas about management are taken as gospel and practiced by many of the ten million Americans who call themselves managers.

One of Drucker's most widely accepted notions is management by objectives, commonly referred to as MBO. In its simplest form, it means that managers ought to define goals and base their activities on them. According to Drucker:

> Each manager, from the "big boss" down to the production foreman or the chief clerk, needs clearly spelled-out objectives.

These objectives should lay out what performance the man's own managerial unit is supposed to produce. They should lay out what contribution he and his unit are expected to make to help other units obtain their objectives. Finally, they should spell out what contribution the manager can expect from other units toward the attainment of his own objectives.

When Drucker penned those words in 1954 in his popular book *The Practice of Management,* he thought American managers were overly concerned with process. Auto-company managers, for instance, got so involved in the process of making cars—in the details of design and workmanship—that they lost sight of the overall objectives of the corporation. Such managers might build great cars, but the company itself could go out of business because the managers ignored other goals, like making a profit.

Considered in isolation, it's hard to fault the management-by-objectives idea. It sounds like good, commonsense advice. What it has come to mean when put into effect is another matter. As John J. Tarrant points out in his biography of Drucker:

> In practice . . . we often see the concept of management by objectives translated totally into a formulation that might be called "bottom-line management," or management by results. More and more an upper-echelon executive holds himself aloof from what is going on beneath him. He figures that his responsibility lies in hiring somebody to do a job, telling him the "bottom-line" results that are expected, and then rewarding the subordinate if he delivers or firing him if he does not deliver.

This translates into a lot of personal pressure on lower-level managers. And it's not difficult to see how other employees can also get chewed up by an obsession with objectives. If all that matters are results, who is going to be concerned with the quality of the workplace? It's doubtful that the harried supervisor trying to attain his objectives is going to worry much about gaining the trust and confidence of individual employees. In other words, Drucker's management by objectives also tends to promote a philosophy of whatever works—the ends justify the means. Financial goals or production targets can easily be reduced to objectives. The quality of relationships is beyond the scope of reductionist thinking.

In *The Practice of Management*, Drucker writes: "It is not the business of the enterprise to create happiness but to sell and make shoes. Nor can the worker be happy in the abstract." The implication Drucker leaves us with is that the effective executive shouldn't bother trying to "create happiness." It's not his job. The manager is to focus on the economic objectives of the organization. If people happen to enjoy their work, good for them. But it certainly isn't the executive's task to create a good workplace. To Drucker, the main purpose of a business enterprise is "to create a customer." For that reason, he writes, employees "must be definitely subordinate to the claim of economic performance: profitability and productivity."

It would be misleading to imply that Drucker himself urged managers to devote themselves so ruthlessly to their objectives that they grind up employees. He writes persuasively in many books and articles about the importance of treating workers as "resources," not merely as "costs." An inescapable feature about Drucker as a thinker is that there are few Druckerisms that aren't diluted or flatly contradicted by other Druckerisms. Drucker addresses many issues and has opinions on everything. It would be fairer to join biographer Tarrant in calling many applications of management by objectives a "bastardization" of Drucker's thought. Nevertheless, even casual readers of Drucker's works can easily see how the hard-nosed, bottom-line, results-only managers draw much inspiration from Drucker.

On the other hand, there's a lot of good, even brilliant, insights in Drucker's thinking. His critique of Elton Mayo and the human-relations movement is devastating. In his book *Management: Tasks, Responsibilities, Practices*, Drucker blasts the movement as "psychological despotism" and a "gross misuse of psychology." He continues:

> They use terms like "self-fulfillment," "creativity," and "the whole man." But what they talk and write about is control through psychological manipulation. . . . Psychological despotism should have tremendous attraction for managers. It promises them that they can continue to behave as they have always done. All they need is to acquire a new vocabulary.

And he suggests that the key issue overlooked by human-relations managers is that the "work relationship has to be based on mutual respect. . . ." What makes Drucker frustrating, however, is that such insights aren't coupled with any understanding of the workplace from the employee viewpoint. For instance, a common Druckerism is: "The basic task of management is to make people productive." Workers aren't to be coddled into productivity à la Mayo and his cohorts, or exhorted into it à la Tom Peters; managers are to *make* them productive.

Drucker's lack of sympathy was shown, interestingly enough, in a meeting with Elton Mayo. The scene for the encounter between these two giants of management thought was a conference in honor of Mayo held at Harvard University in 1947. After Mayo had given his address, Drucker rose and made a number of comments. According to Richard C. S. Trahair:

> Drucker had failed to appreciate Mayo's main point. . . . Mayo was upset by hearing the conclusion he had reached in his study of situations in industry distorted in these ways, and took the floor to poke fun at Drucker's ideas. To show what a subordinate thinks about a manipulative boss, Mayo put his thumb to his nose and looking at Drucker, asked: "You know what this means?" Drucker did not. "Then you should," replied Mayo. The audience could see that Mayo's gesture signified not only the attitude of a subordinate who was willing to consent to directives from a domineering boss but also Mayo's view of the ideas that Drucker had expressed.

As this anecdote reveals, Peter Drucker lacks the common touch, a gut-level empathy with what workers actually feel about their jobs and their bosses. Indeed, Drucker's sympathies and concerns are totally with the manager in the employee-manager equation. And the thrust of his work has been to create a managerial elite capable of running business enterprises effectively. In the Drucker universe—reflected in practice by thousands of organizations throughout the land—employees are definitely second-class citizens. Drucker's devotees may protest such a harsh judgment, since he has written countless perceptive comments about avoidable problems created by authoritarian managers. And he has written approvingly for years of such managerial techniques as IBM's job-enlargement and job-security policies. Yet Drucker insists managers must always make clear who is boss.

Drucker makes explicit his top-down bias in his one and only utopian book, *The New Society*, published in 1950. In it Drucker spells out his ideal industrial order. He opposes profit sharing and employee ownership. He also advances the idea of a "self-governing plant community." It is to be a democratically elected body, composed of workers and managers alike, to govern areas related to the social life of the plant. For instance, it would oversee such areas as "transportation to and from work, parking, the cafeteria, recreation activities such as sports clubs, hobby clubs, picnics and parties, and educational activities." Through participation in such a body, workers would gain more of a "managerial attitude" and become increasingly "responsible workers."

Thirty years later, Drucker wrote: "I have always considered the responsible worker with his managerial attitude and the self-governing plant community as my most important and most original ideas and my greatest contributions." But he noted that the ideas have been rejected or ignored by American management, which "I consider my greatest and most galling failure."

Yet it's no wonder Drucker's idea of the self-governing plant community hasn't caught on and is unlikely ever to do so. Such ideas invariably met resistance or indifference by employees and employee unions. Employees are not interested in learning about being responsible second-class citizens. But Drucker apparently was oblivious to this concern. In explaining why worker participation had to be limited to such areas as the plant's social life, Drucker wrote:

> The rank-and-file job holders—whether of production, technical or clerical jobs—obviously cannot be given authority and responsibility for decisions regarding the enterprise's business. . . . The very definition of these jobs is that they take orders rather than give them.

Compare that vintage Drucker assertion with the following statement:

The person doing the job knows more about it than anybody else. It is the responsibility of managers to ask for suggestions, to listen to possible solutions to specific problems, and to help implement productive change. Each employee has unlimited possibilities.

That statement is contained in Preston Trucking's 1982 annual report to shareholders. In Drucker's top-down world view, it's "obvious" that ordinary employees cannot be given authority and responsibility. At Preston—and at other great workplaces—employees are trusted. They are to be brought into running the enterprise as much as possible. They are assumed to be responsible. They don't have to prove their "managerial attitude" first.

That's not to say that there isn't a distinct role for managers in companies like Preston Trucking. Managers are needed to coordinate the work flow with other aspects of the business, if nothing else. But managers don't have to operate as know-it-alls.

Part of the reason for the tendency of the Drucker-style professional managers to operate in a hierarchical fashion can be traced to Drucker's basic political outlook. He genuinely believes that society needs a managerial elite—a distinct class of people to run a complex society of organizations. A reading of Drucker's earliest books shows that Drucker has always posited a much higher mission for corporate executives: They are the torchbearers of a Western civilization almost destroyed by the nightmare of Nazism and what he sees as the scourge of Marxism. As Drucker once put it: "Management, its competence, its integrity and its performance will be decisive both to the United States and to the free world in the decades ahead."

In many ways, Drucker's managerial elite has indeed come into being. It isn't perfect, as Drucker would be the first to point out, and he often does in his caustic commentaries about the state of management. But an identifiable group of professional managers does indeed exist, many of whom have read and continue to read the words of wisdom from the master.

A problem with this managerial elite is that Drucker's professional managers have become all-purpose managers. In Drucker's view, there isn't much difference between the manager of a commercial airline, the manager of a bank, the manager of an automobile plant, the manager of a hospital, or the manager of a computer manufacturer. Drucker sees common threads in any and all of these positions. The logical extension of this has been the army of MBAs that graduate each year from business schools. Here is the corps of all-purpose professional managers ready to take over and run Company A, Company B, or Company C. It matters little the business's product or service. The professional manager is ready and willing to run it.

The economy is suffering from all-purpose managers jumping from industry to industry, according to several contemporary observers. Improving the quality of automobiles isn't something we can expect from a job-hopping MBA spending a few years in the auto industry before taking a better-paying job with a computer firm. The corps of all-purpose professional managers also has a deleterious effect on employee morale. As a breed apart, the professional managers not only block off possibilities for advancement for the nonprofessionals below, but they often tend to act like know-it-alls in areas where they are in fact know-nothings.

One further note. It's consistent with Drucker's goal-oriented approach that contemporary business-management schools are increasingly churning out specialists in finance. Finance is, after all, the ultimate managerial abstraction. All businesses can be reduced to numbers. So, as Robert B. Reich points out, "America's professional managers have become paper entrepreneurs." These managers don't have to know anything about particular industries. They merely need to know how to manipulate a business in such a way that the numbers look good in the short run.

In contrast to drawing from a pool of interchangeable managers, a good employer places a high priority on promotion from within, on the company's being run and managed by people who grew up in the business. At many of these companies, we even noticed that the line between management and nonmanagement is much fuzzier than that espoused by Drucker and the tradition he represents. At Delta Air Lines, for instance, it's possible to ask three people working in identical supervisory positions whether they are managers and have one say yes, another say no, and a third say he doesn't know. That's not to say that everybody at Delta is unclear about who's in management and who isn't. It's just that the distinction between management and nonmanagement doesn't seem to be as crucial as Drucker would have us believe. As the late Jan Erteszek, founder of Olga (a 100 Best company), said, "Management is a function, not a class."

9
EVANGELICAL
MANAGER
Tom Peters

A few years ago *Business Week*
published a chart listing twenty different crazes that have cap-
tivated American managers since the Second World War. A
few, like matrix management and zero-based budgeting, have
little direct bearing on the workplace. But most of them are
largely or entirely devoted to improving employee productivity, such as one-minute managing, Theory Y (participative
management), Theory Z (quality circles), and management by
walking around (excellence). Some of these managerial panaceas have probably "worked" in the sense of raising productivity at specific companies. Others have undoubtedly
enriched no one but the management consultants who helped
implement them.

Yet a failed program never seems to kill the managerial ap-
petite for new productivity gimmicks. And there are always
lots of management consultants who claim to have the answer.
Because management fads appear as frequently as food diets,
it is difficult to look at any popular managerial doctrine without considerable skepticism or even a slight feeling of cyni-
cism. Still, the latest managerial fashion often becomes the
enduring reality in the workplace, deserving of closer inspection.

Most business fads on the *Business Week* list have come and
gone without attracting the notice of the general public. Not

so with excellence, first promulgated in the 1982 book *In Search of Excellence*, which has sold more than five million copies. Besides making the book's coauthor, Tom Peters, a millionaire at age forty, the book helped catapult Peters to a celebrity status rarely associated with management consultants. Peters is a perpetual motion machine, on the road over forty weeks a year making some two hundred fifty speeches, sometimes as many as three in one day. He writes a weekly nationally syndicated newspaper column and has appeared on several nationally televised public-television specials. We would have to go back a half century to find a comparable management superstar. Dale Carnegie's 1936 book, *How to Win Friends and Influence People*, sold nearly nine million copies and sat on *The New York Times* best-seller list for ten straight years (an all-time record), and hundreds of thousands of managers have taken Dale Carnegie training courses in public speaking and managing.

But there is a vast difference in personalities between the low-key Dale Carnegie and Tom Peters. Peters earned a reputation for flamboyance at the staid management-consulting firm of McKinsey & Company. He occasionally showed up for work in khaki shorts and a T-shirt at the San Francisco office, where he met his coauthor Robert H. Waterman, Jr. This behavior is unheard of for a $250,000-a-year McKinsey consultant. It is also not what one would expect from someone with a civil engineering degree from an Ivy League university (Cornell) and both an MBA and a Ph.D. in business from Stanford University. But such eccentricities would not surprise anyone who has ever seen Tom Peters speak. He peppers his sermons with dozens of anecdotes, works up a sweat stalking back and forth across the stage like TV evangelist Jimmy Swaggart, and often shouts himself hoarse. Peters charges $15,000 for a two-hour speech and is reportedly the world's most highly paid speaker, earning about $1.5 million annually in fees, plus expenses.

Despite Peters's show-biz antics on stage, he is quite capable of holding his own with the sharpest of business-school academics. He has taught at the Stanford Business School and authored obscure articles in academic journals, such as a 1979 article in *Organizational Dynamics* entitled "Symbols, Patterns and Settings." But Tom Peters doesn't pretend to be a seminal thinker like Frederick Taylor, Elton Mayo, or Peter F. Drucker. He calls himself an interpreter, a popularizer of management thinking. Peters once declared: "There's absolutely nothing new whatsoever between [*In Search of Excellence's*] covers. It was a translation of ideas and material that had been around for up to fifty years. All it added was brilliant timing and packaging."

Good News from America

The timing was indeed perfect. In 1982 the country was in the midst of a recession, with unemployment hovering around 10 percent. Many of the unemployed were auto, steel, and textile workers recently displaced because of imports from Japan and other foreign countries. There was a widespread feeling, based on considerable evidence, that we were beginning to see the end of the decades-long American industrial dominance. Many people also believed that American corporations had become overly bureaucratic, stodgy, and out of touch. A sign of the times was the previous year's most discussed business book, William Ouchi's *Theory Z*, which advocated that American business adopt Japanese management practices. As Tom Peters later said: "American industry was ready for a little positive news." Peters and Waterman had just the ticket, an uplifting gospel. In some ways, their "upbeat message" paralleled the optimistic 1980 campaign oratory of Ronald Reagan, who promised to restore pride to the country after its international political humiliations. Both proclaimed solutions to America's problems through a return to basic American values. In the book's introduction, Peters and Waterman declare:

> There is good news from America. Good management practice today is not resident only in Japan. But, more important, the good news comes from treating people decently and asking them to shine, and from producing things that work. . . . Hierarchy and three-piece suits give way to first names, shirtsleeves, hoopla, and project-based flexibility. . . . Even management's job becomes more fun. Instead of brain games in the sterile ivory tower, it's shaping values and reinforcing

through coaching and evangelism in the field—with the workers and in support of the cherished product.

Peters and Waterman based their "good news" on what they found at America's most successful companies. They picked forty-three companies that were both innovative and had performed well financially over the previous two decades: ". . . the companies were not truly excellent unless their financial performance supported their halo of esteem." Peters and Waterman used six technical financial measurements (three related to "growth and long-term wealth creation," and three related to "return on capital and sales"). Incidentally, fifteen of the forty-three excellent companies also appeared on our roster of The 100 Best Companies to Work for in America (Dana, Delta Air Lines, Digital Equipment, Du Pont, Eastman Kodak, Hewlett-Packard, Intel, IBM, Johnson & Johnson, Levi Strauss, Maytag, 3M, Procter & Gamble, Raychem, and Wal-Mart Stores).

According to Peters and Waterman, the forty-three excellent companies had eight attributes in common, spelled out in chapter titles that have since become part of the American management lexicon: "A Bias for Action"; "Close to the Customer"; "Autonomy and Entrepreneurship"; "Productivity Through People"; "Hands On"; "Value-Driven"; "Stick to the Knitting"; "Simple Form"; "Lean Staff"; and "Simultaneous Loose-Tight Properties." Excellent management means staying in close touch with employees and customers. The shorthand name for the style they advocated was "management by wandering around."

Not ones to shy away from hyperbole, Peters and Waterman insisted that "the management practices in the excellent companies aren't just different. They set conventional management wisdom on its ear." Peters and Waterman claim that conventional management has been hostage to the "rational model," which the authors see as "a direct descendant of Frederick Taylor's school of scientific management." Peters and Waterman's theories can save managers from falling into the rationalist trap:

What our framework has really done is to remind the world of professional managers that "soft is hard." It has enabled us to say, in effect, "All that stuff you have been dismissing for so long as the intractable, irrational, intuitive, informal organization *can* be managed."

In Search of Excellence does not directly attack Peter Drucker, but in an article in New Management, a University of Southern California business-school journal, Peters takes some swipes at him: "It has become clear to me that the managerial pendulum has swung too far toward Druckerian rationality. . . . By over-listening to Drucker (and more significantly—his army of simplistic interpreters), we've arrived at a world of management by abstract analysis."

Peters prefers to emphasize the sunny side. In the same article, for instance, he paid tribute to Drucker, saying, "Our debt to Peter Drucker knows no limit." He later told a Wall Street Journal reporter that he always refers to Drucker "as His Eminence. I would never criticize Drucker in a setting with corporate managers. It would be pretty dumb to tick off 90 percent of your audience in one sitting. A lot of people think he speaks nothing but the truth." For his part, Drucker has dismissed In Search of Excellence as "a book for juveniles."

It's worth noting this somewhat muted controversy between Peters and Drucker because it helps place Peters in an historical context. When Tom Peters rails against the rationalists, he represents one of the cyclical swings away from the Taylor-Drucker rationalist model of management and back to the Mayo–Maslow–McGregor human-relations model. During the 1960s and early 1970s, the human-relations school was in its heyday. Job-enrichment schemes were popular. So was a discipline called organization development, which uses sensitivity training to help managers learn how to handle their feelings. But a decade later the human-relations movement was largely in disrepute, relegated to the personnel or training departments of large companies. Instead, there was considerably more emphasis being placed on a more hardheaded, analytical approach to business, especially in business schools.

While the rationalists seek greater productivity through planning and resource reallocation, the human-relations movement sees worker motivation as the key. But motivating people is very complicated, as Mayo and his followers have pointed out. It requires insight into human nature. In this regard, Tom Peters, who is referred to as a "motivational" speaker on the lecture circuit, follows the convention employed not only by management theorists like Elton Mayo and Douglas McGregor, but also by popularizers like Dale Carnegie. Peters and Waterman start with a theory of human nature and then show its application for managers.

Man as Irrational

Like Elton Mayo, the starting point for the Peters and Waterman view of human nature is that "people are not very rational." From their readings of recent studies in psychology, they conclude that "man is the ultimate study in conflict and paradox." First on their list of inherent contradictions is that "all of us are self-centered, suckers for a bit of praise, and generally like to think of ourselves as winners." At the same time, "none of us is really as good as he or she would like to think, but rubbing our noses daily in that reality doesn't do us a bit of good."

Superficially, this statement sounds a bit like Dale Carnegie's homespun observation that people like to feel important and respond favorably to a bit of sincere praise. But Peters and Waterman see this insight as the basis for organizational strategy:

> We all think we're tops. We're exuberantly, wildly irrational about ourselves. And that has sweeping implications for organizing. . . .
>
> The lesson the excellent companies have to teach is that there is no reason why we can't design systems that continually reinforce this notion; most of their people are made to feel that they are winners. . . . Their systems make extraordinary use of nonmonetary incentives. They are full of hoopla. . . .
>
> Researchers studying motivation find that the prime factor is simply the self-perception among motivated subjects that they are in fact doing well. Whether they are or not by any absolute standard doesn't seem to matter much.

Step back and reflect for a moment about what's being said here. People are irrational "suckers" who don't want to face reality. So organizations ought to develop policies that make them feel like winners even if they aren't. All that's important is how people *feel* about themselves. So companies should have frequent celebratory events full of "hoopla" and "razzle-dazzle."

Another example. According to Peters and Waterman:

> . . . the excellent companies appear to take advantage of yet another very human need—the need one has to control one's destiny. At the same time that we are almost too willing to yield to institutions that give us meaning and thus a sense of security, we also want self-determination. With equal vehemence, *we simultaneously seek self-determination and security.* That is certainly irrational. [Emphasis in original.]

Peters and Waterman have raised here a fundamental workplace issue—perhaps the most important one from the standpoint of employees. It's the intrinsic and ongoing conflict between the individual and the organization. Individuals always give up some control over their lives when working in an organization. At the very minimum, organizations require that people's efforts be coordinated. Employees can never be entirely free to do what they want to do, since no organization can afford a do-your-own-thing approach. This is a genuine and ongoing problem, not one that any organization (or society) has ever solved once and for all.

Because Peters and Waterman see this issue in strictly psychological terms, we should not be surprised that they offer a psychological solution:

> Psychologists study the need for self-determination in a field called "illusion of control." Stated simply, its findings indicate that if people think they have even modest personal control over their destinies, they will persist at tasks. . . . They will do better at them. They will become more committed to them. . . . The fact, again, that we *think* we have a *bit* more discretion leads to *much* greater commitment. [Emphasis in original.]

According to Peters and Waterman, this is why the excellent companies "push authority far down the line" and give people the "opportunity to stick out."

Giving lower echelons in the organization more responsibility is certainly laudable, as we saw in the story about North-western Mutual Life. This is an important part of a great workplace. So are a lot of other policies shared by good work-places that Peters advocates—"treating people decently," re-ducing hierarchy, and involving everyone in a team effort. But before jumping on the excellence bandwagon, we should ex-amine closely the context in which these techniques are being advocated. When we look more closely at what's behind the Peters-Waterman push-authority-far-down-the-line prescrip-tion, we discover that there's a catch. Based on psychological principles, they are saying that if you give people a little con-trol over their job, they will become more committed to the organization. The tension between the organization and the individual—between "self-determination and security"—can thus be eradicated. Whether the increased control people are given over their job is real or merely illusory doesn't matter. By ignoring this principle, the old-fashioned rational managers have, according to Peters and Waterman, missed the oppor-tunity to take advantage of "the emotional, more primitive side (good and bad) of human nature."

Motivation or Manipulation?

For the moment, let's assume that a company's management can successfully motivate workers by pursuing policies based on these psychological insights and theories. Peters and Water-man seem to think that's true, and they claim to have discov-ered forty-three companies that do so. They're not alone. Management consultants and business-school professors have been preaching variations of the same gospel for a half century now. And for almost a half century, the philosophy of moti-vational management has had its critics, mostly those who charge it with being manipulative.

As we observed in our chapter on Elton Mayo, management based on psychology has frequently been called manipulative. That's, of course, a weighty charge, as it implies there's some-thing unethical about it. Before leaping to the same assessment of the management style advocated by Tom Peters and his coauthors, we should examine what is meant by the term *ma-nipulative*. On this point, we might usefully refer to a recent article by moral philosopher Raymond S. Pfeiffer, "Is Motivation Management Manipulative?" Pfeiffer offers a definition of *manipulation* based on the work of various psychologists, social critics, sociologists, and social and political philosophers since the Second World War. Pfeiffer's definition is as follows:

> To manipulate someone, such writers broadly agree, involves a subtle influence on that person's actions, beliefs, desires, feeling, or values, which in turn inhibits rational deliberation. It may involve the falsification or omission of information, or it may involve a play on one's nonrational impulses. But it is widely characterized by an element of subtle and often deceptive persuasiveness.

Using that definition, excellence management appears to qualify. Peters and his coauthors seem to revel in what Pfeiffer would call "a play on one's nonrational impulses." As we've seen, Peters and Waterman argue at length that people are fundamentally irrational. Their entire theory of motivation flows from that assumption. To them, motivation means finding the right irrational buttons to push. Techniques that play on people's psychological needs (such as their need to be winners, or need to feel control over their destiny) create a subtle yet irresistible pressure on people to do as the management wants—to work harder than they might do otherwise.

Excellence management may also qualify as manipulative on the basis of what Pfeiffer calls deceptive persuasiveness. Consider the actual meaning of some of the terms Peters and Waterman use approvingly in their book. My dictionary defines *hoopla* as "something—as utterances—designed to bewilder or confuse"; *razzle-dazzle*, as "something that induces or is intended to induce a state of confusion"; and *sucker* as "a person easily cheated or deceived." Or we could note their sympathetic discussion of *illusion of control*. Peters and Waterman make no attempt to disguise the use of deceptive techniques. They celebrate it.

Integrity Versus Democracy

In fairness to Peters and his coauthors, they do recognize the problem of manipulation, so they stress the importance of "integrity." For instance, in *A Passion for Excellence*, Peters and coauthor Nancy Austin devote a chapter called "Applause-Applause" to celebrations. At one point, they talk about the "technology of enthusiasm" and compare getting people in a company enthusiastic to what management has been doing for years in marketing:

> What we're suggesting is that you can be just as thoughtful, just as meticulous and systematic in developing programs that substantially boost the enthusiasm in your organization, as you are when you test-market your new widget.

At the end of the chapter devoted to such observations, Peters and Austin have two paragraphs on integrity. Acknowledging that some of their "quieter friends" might view their advice with "alarm," they warn managers that:

> You can't fake this stuff. People have great built-in BS meters, they've been through the mill before. If you don't believe it, if you're behaving in an even slightly manipulative fashion, they'll see through you in a flash.

They then cite two corporate managers who apparently don't have this problem because both "really care" about employees: "They celebrate because they genuinely appreciate what their people have accomplished. It's plain as day from the gleam in their eye and the genuineness of their greeting."

It may well be true that these corporate leaders do care about their people. And it may be true that we can accurately judge someone's sincerity only by the look in her eyes or the quality of her handshake. But manipulation is not overcome merely by Peters's version of personal integrity. We can believe sincerely in what we're doing while taking advantage of others. The real problem with deceptiveness and playing on an employee's irrationality is that it clouds rational thinking. As Pfeiffer puts it, "Motivation management does not assist workers to arrive at a motivated state as the result of a wholly free, fully informed, open, rational, analytic, or critical approach to the issues."

Personal integrity is a good thing in all circumstances, but the antidote to manipulation is democracy. Democracy in this context does not mean that everybody in a company should have an equal vote on whether to buy more pencils. Rather, it's the notion that people should have some say in issues that directly affect them, like the process to redesign work at Northwestern Mutual Life. It means they should have forums for the free exchange of information, ideas, opinions (and criticisms), like the Pitney Bowes jobholders' meetings or the employee newspaper at Tektronix. It means they should have mechanisms that assure due process in cases where they feel their individual rights have been violated, such as the Guaranteed Fair Treatment procedure at Federal Express. Such companies have explicit policies and procedures that speak to the employee concern about manipulation in the workplace. Peters offers managers countless anecdotes and illustrations of progressive policies, but he's strangely silent about something as crucial to a good workplace as a viable grievance procedure. Without democratic institutions, citizens have no legitimate process to fight tyrants. By the same token, without democratic institutions in the workplace, employees have no recourse against being manipulated by well-meaning managers.

Organizations have every right to want their employees to be motivated. But employees have every right to make up their own minds about the level of commitment they wish to make to their organizations (over and above the minimal requirements of a job). The rights of the two parties are not necessarily inconsistent, but they do need to be balanced.

A Peters disciple (of which there are many) could, of course, challenge this whole line of argument. Even if there are potentially manipulative aspects of the excellence concepts, the little deceptions and tricks played on employees to get them motivated aren't exactly major transgressions. It could be compared to TV advertising. Everybody assumes that ads exaggerate and play on our emotions. It shouldn't be considered a big deal when managers resort to a bit of hucksterism to sell their product—productivity. Besides, the intentions of the Peters-style managers are good. These people do have integrity. If there is a little unavoidable manipulation involved, it's for a wholly justifiable cause—one that benefits both employees and the company.

This justification assumes that the interests of the employee and the company are the same. That is, after all, the biggest selling point of the whole idea of excellence. It proclaims that excellent companies are not only successful financially but offer consumers high-quality products and employees a good working environment. If true, there is no need to worry about manipulation, since employees benefit when the company succeeds. So everybody should happily pitch in together.

The Bottom Line

But is this claim valid? Do the employees' interests and the company's interests always coincide? One way to assess this claim is to look at how Peters defines the company's interests. On this point, Peters and his coauthors have been absolutely crystal clear. The bottom line of excellence *is* the conventional bottom line—profitability. An excellent company excels at making money. The excellent companies weren't picked because of the quality of their products. Nor were the excellent companies picked because they were good workplaces (as were, say, the *100 Best*). It was only *after* the authors had selected companies that demonstrated financial prowess that they then looked for common attributes, including workplace practices. In a review of *In Search of Excellence* in the *Harvard Business Review*, Daniel Carroll noted that it was ironic that the same "authors, who leave no doubt about their abhorrence of the rational model, with its numerative determinism, seem to use exactly that to select excellent companies." Carroll wondered "why they could find no substitute for that heritage when it came to screening companies for excellence."

To point this out is not to suggest that making money is inherently a bad objective. Nor is it to suggest that seeking profitability is inconsistent with a good workplace. Indeed, as we argue later in the book, companies that are good workplaces often are much more profitable than their competitors. But the relationship between workplace practices and a firm's financial performance is extremely complicated and usually must be examined on a company-by-company basis. (Carroll's *Har-*

vard *Business Review* article pointed out that Peters and Waterman failed to acknowledge that technology, finances, government policy, raw materials, and other factors can also affect a company's financial viability.)

What's important to note here is that if your eyes are fixed on one goal—in this case, profitability—it colors everything else you observe. For one thing, looking at everything through the lens of productivity/profitability blinds you to the employee viewpoint.

Consider McDonald's, the world's biggest fast-food chain. McDonald's has consistently grown larger and more profitable over the past three decades. That's why it was cited repeatedly in *In Search of Excellence* and singled out as one of the dozen or so most admired of the forty-three excellent companies. Not only that, Peters and Waterman single out McDonald's as one of seven firms to profile in their chapter on people management. The authors quote a former McKinsey colleague: " 'You know, one of the things that strikes me most about McDonald's is their people orientation. During the seven years I was at McKinsey, I never saw a client that seemed to care so much about its people.' "

You won't, however, hear such rave reviews of McDonald's by talking to those working behind the counters or in the kitchens—McDonald's entry-level employees, who often earn the minimum wage. They express their feelings about their employer by leaving it in droves. One hundred-percent-a-year turnover rates are common at McDonald's restaurants throughout the land. When my coauthor, Milton Moskowitz, interviewed young McDonald's employees in California, he heard comments like these:

"McDonald's is a place where you work hard for little money. The one I worked at would only allow you a small french fries, a small drink, and large hamburger for six hours of work."

"People leave all the time because the pay is low and lousy for the amount of work they put you through."

The employee perspective is simply ignored by most people writing about business, including Peters and his coauthors. They talk about employees a lot and create elaborate psychological theories about what makes them tick—or tick faster. But rarely do they consider the world from the employees' viewpoint. Everything gets reduced to the issue of productivity, including the problem of employee morale. So it ultimately matters little *how* a company's managers make things work faster. The objective is productivity. At McDonald's, the company creates a team spirit among its crew members through "hoopla" and "razzle-dazzle" to exhort everyone on. Founder Ray Kroc, one of Peters's often-referred-to corporate heroes, is quoted admiringly as saying: " 'A well-run restaurant is like a winning baseball team, it makes the most of every crew member's talent and takes advantage of every split-second opportunity to speed up service.' " The dreaded rationalist Frederick Taylor would have loved Ray Kroc.

As the example of McDonald's illustrates dramatically, a successful company is not necessarily a good workplace. That also matches most people's everyday experiences. We can all think of examples of companies like McDonald's. In fact, we can point to companies that appear to be financially successful precisely *because* they take advantage of their employees.

People First

What about companies that are both financially successful *and* good workplaces? Are the interests of the company and the employees identical in those places? Let's take a look at IBM, a company that has been both highly successful and generally thought of as a good workplace, especially by the overwhelming majority of people working there. It's one of the excellent companies. At one point Peters and Waterman introduce a passage about IBM with the following exhortation:

> Treat people as adults. Treat them as partners; treat them with dignity; treat them with respect. Treat them—not capital spending and automation—as the primary source of productivity gains. These are fundamental lessons from the excellent companies research. In other words, *if you want productivity and the financial reward that goes with it, you must treat your workers as your most important asset.* [Emphasis added.]

The authors then go on to quote Thomas J. Watson, Jr., who once wrote that IBM considers "respect for the individual" the most important single belief to the company and how that belief was "bone-deep" in his father. Both Watson and his father had been chairman of IBM.

Peters and Waterman did not, however, continue to quote Watson who, in the same book, stated explicitly: "As businessmen we think in terms of profits, but people continue to rank first." That Watson asserts that people "rank first" demonstrates something that distinguishes good workplaces. Put simply, what makes for a good workplace is the explicit recognition that people do matter *as* people. Some policies and practices of good workplaces are in place to assure that people are not trampled over in the demands to achieve ever higher productivity. It's only when organizations have to choose between "people" and profitability that we discover whether beliefs are "bone-deep" or merely suntan lotion for balmy days. It doesn't have any meaning to say that you "respect the individual" if you do so only at your convenience. To respect employees because you see that as a way to achieve "productivity and the financial reward that goes with it" has nothing to do with respect of people as people.

This may sound like mere quibbling over words. But it is an absolutely crucial distinction in understanding what makes for a good workplace. IBM, for instance, has on several occasions in its long history refused to lay people off in difficult times. But it did so because it really does put people first, even when it may mean some short-term financial problems. IBM executives who pay close attention to the bottom line might argue that in the long run, the no-layoff policy has potential financial benefit by maintaining employee morale. But that's beside the point to those whose vision is fixated on profits and productivity. The fact that the company sticks by its people in hard times invariably occasions a rash of articles in the business press quoting various Wall Street pundits about how much wiser the company would be to lop off thousands of employees as General Motors and Ford do.

Wall Street pundits are not alone in decrying the short-term effects of IBM's no-layoff policy. So, ironically, is Tom Peters. In his third book, published five years after the first, he proclaims an "end of the era of sustainable excellence." Because the world·is changing so rapidly, "There are no excellent companies. . . . No company is safe. IBM is declared dead in 1979, the best of the best in 1982, and dead again in 1986."

It appears that the fixation with the bottom line has actually led Peters to a betrayal of what a lot of people thought excellence was all about in the first place. Many people undoubtedly bought In Search of Excellence and its sequels because they thought they were going to hear some enduring truths. Among those truths appeared to be the notion that a company should stay close to its customers and treat its employees well. There was something about excellence that had a commonsense ring of commitment to some other ideals than merely transitory ones.

But no. Excellence, at least to the originators of the craze, meant exactly what they said it meant: financial success. The idea may have been trumpeted as iconoclastic, populist, and revolutionary. But it ultimately appears to embrace (or co-opt) precisely the sort of thinking it claimed to be rejecting.

IBM hasn't changed. Its performance may have slipped compared with what some of the Wall Street analysts would like to see. And if some Wall Street analysts were to be believed, it would have performed much better if it had laid off several thousand workers. But the company was willing to absorb some short-term problems because it places a value on something besides the bottom line. Peters, however, has apparently given up on IBM. It's not that IBM has abandoned its own principles—or even the Peters-Waterman eight attributes of excellent companies. IBM is no longer excellent because it only made $4.8 billion in net profits in 1986, down from $6.5 billion the previous year, thereby being only the second most profitable company in America instead of number one.

Sure times are tough today. But they've been tough before and will be tough as long as people try to make a buck in business. What Peters actually appears to be saying is that because times are tough, there are no lasting principles that anyone can perceive. There are no enduring ideas to stick to —only techniques that may work (which he calls "prescriptions") for those facing troubled times.

Many of Tom Peters's style techniques may be terrific ideas. Many of them, looked at in isolation, may represent substantial improvements in the workplace. But if the only techniques that are implemented are ones aimed at increasing efficiency, the heart and soul of a good workplace is still missing. As suggested throughout this book, a good workplace is not merely a collection of progressive workplace practices and policies. A good workplace is defined by the type of *relationship* that grows from a company's policies and practices. So how everything fits together is as important, if not more so, than the specific policies themselves.

The bottom-line-is-all-that-matters approach is also a self-fulfilling prophecy. A company willing to make any kind of change in order to keep the bottom line looking good creates the kind of chaotic world described by Peters. For example, if costs need to be cut and if the work force is considered just another cost, layoffs may seem logical and orderly from the perspective of the boardroom. But for employees, the disruption is chaotic.

Not only does having your eye fixed on one objective color how you see the rest of the world, it also makes the world seem more chaotic than it really is. Everything is up for grabs when everything gets reduced to one variable. The world simply looks much less chaotic when people—and companies— stick to their principles. This is especially true in tough times. One of the things we can learn about companies that are good workplaces is that they don't vary in their commitment to their people when times get tough. In the search for ways of making changes to meet new circumstances, variables covered by the commitment to their people are only changed as a last resort. If companies offer good workplaces, they are good precisely because they show some character under stress.

Evangelistic Management

One final point. Whenever assessing a management theory's impact on the workplace, it's always a good idea to look at the nature of the relationship between the manager and employee that is projected. In Taylor's case, we could say the relationship could be compared to that of thinker and doer. In Mayo's, doctor and patient. In Drucker's, superior and subordinate. In the case of Tom Peters, a close approximation would be that of evangelist and convert.

This analogy seems appropriate for several reasons. Tom Peters not only talks explicitly of the need for "evangelism" in relations with workers, but it's part and parcel of his speaking and writing styles. His second book, *A Passion for Excellence*, even concludes with what sounds like an altar call:

> When you have a true passion for excellence, and when you act on it, you will stand straighter. You will look people in the eye. You will see things happen. You will see heroes created, watch ideas unfold and take shape. You'll walk with a springier step. You'll have something to fight for, to care about, to share, scary as it is, with other people. There will be times when you swing from dedicated to obsessed. We don't pretend that it's easy. It takes real courage to step out and stake your claim. But we think the renewed sense of purpose, of making a difference, of recovered self-respect, is well worth the price of admission.

The manager with this "passion for excellence" is, above all, supposed to instill the same sense of purpose and, as Peters puts it repeatedly, "meaning" in the lives of the employees. The theoretical basis for this, according to Peters and Waterman, is the concept of a "transforming" leader, a concept developed by political scientist James MacGregor Burns. Unlike the rational and bureaucratic "transactional" leader, the "transforming" leader is charismatic. According to Peters, "He is concerned with the tricks of the pedagogue, the mentor, the linguist—the more successfully to become the value shaper, the exemplar, the maker of meanings. . . . He is both calling forth and exemplifying the urge for transcendence that unites us all."

Like the evangelist, the transforming leader has a gospel to preach—a "cherished product," in this case—and he seeks to convert the uncommitted, to motivate employees to higher and higher levels of productivity. It's a heavy burden indeed for the leader to bear. He not only has to get employees to do their work, but he has to help them in the spiritual quest for meaning in their lives. This burden takes its toll. And Tom Peters and Nancy Austin are the first to acknowledge it:

> We are frequently asked if it is possible to "have it all"—a full and satisfying personal life and a full and satisfying, hard-working professional one. Our answer is: No. The price of ex-

cellence is time, energy, attention and focus, at the very same time that energy, attention and focus could have gone toward enjoying your daughter's soccer game. Excellence is a high-cost item.

Since the excellent manager is constantly trying to instill the same "passion" in employees, they too may discover that the "meaning" they have achieved for their lives is also a "high-cost item." Once this is understood, we can see that in the end, an excellent workplace is a workplace of workaholics. This is precisely what happened at People Express, a role model cited repeatedly in *A Passion for Excellence*.

As an heir to the Elton Mayo human-relations school, Peters holds out the possibility that the underlying conflict between the individual and the organization can be overcome through the use of various motivational techniques. Because the interests of the organization are paramount, there is no provision for the individual who won't give his or her all to the company. There is, of course, nothing wrong with individuals *willingly* and *rationally* agreeing to work as hard as possible. But employees' rights as individuals must be protected to make sure that people don't get trampled over by the organization—or by charismatic leaders. Without strong mechanisms to make management accountable to employees, it's difficult to build the kind of trust inherent in a good workplace.

Like other management gurus of this century, Peters ultimately promotes a managerial elite. It is not the kind of elite suggested by Frederick Taylor or Peter Drucker, who saw a distinct class running organizations. Peters's manager is a modern-day variation of Mayo's "administrator of the future," who was to apply the skills of a social scientist to the organization. For the Peters transforming leader uses the "tricks of the pedagogue, the mentor, the linguist" to become the "value shaper, the exemplar, the maker of meanings." But where Mayo's administrator was detached and "unfettered by his own emotion or prejudice," the Peters's style leader is himself emotional, prone to work in shirtsleeves while wandering around inspiring the troops. As with the Taylor–Drucker/rationalist-style managerial class, the Mayo–Peters/human relations-style managerial class sets itself apart as the embodiment of the will of the organization.

There's no room for a genuine partnership with employees in either school of management thinking. Neither vision provides a way to overcome the latent distrust of the individual toward the organization, because neither is founded on a basic respect for individual rights out of which a partnership of shared interests can be forged. Great workplaces suggest that such a partnership is possible.

P A R T   F O U R

TWO CASE STUDIES

A workplace is more than the sum of its policies and practices. It involves a complicated interplay of various workplace relationships, as the following two case studies illustrate.

10
CAN A
BAD WORKPLACE
BECOME GOOD?

Preston Trucking

Good workplaces are typically new companies. Employees of newly formed companies frequently describe a "familylike" atmosphere and say that they feel genuinely appreciated by the bosses. They often talk about their experiences in glowing terms. They not only talk about the thrill of building a company from scratch; they also say they feel they are treated like human beings. They get deep satisfaction from their work because they are building something from scratch, and they enjoy the people they work with.

After the honeymoon phase, however, employees ordinarily view the situation in a new light. The feeling that nobody cares replaces a new company's family feeling. The attitude that it's just a job replaces the perception that people are working together toward some important goals. Office politics replaces the feeling that everybody is in the same boat and having fun.

Size is a common culprit. When more employees are taken on, the personal touch gets lost. The founder, who used to know the names of each employee's children, doesn't even recognize the newest employees, let alone know their names. As the company grows more, newer employees often understand neither the company's goals nor the importance of their role in the enterprise. The company issues ID cards; the employee's identity becomes a number. As the operation becomes more complex, professional managers appear on the scene with their bags of human-relations techniques that supplant the informal ways of doing things. Bureaucratic structures appear; memos replace personal conversations. This pattern occurs so predictably that an astute observer might be able to cite stages of the erosion of workplace morale. This pattern was repeated, with some unusual twists, at People Express, as we shall see in the next chapter.

There are exceptions to this model. *The 100 Best Companies to Work for in America* disproves the proposition that size and age necessarily doom a workplace. Firms on that list have been in business an average of about fifty years and employ about twenty thousand people. Most of the *100 Best* companies have long since passed through the start-up or entrepreneurial stage. Yet in almost every instance, the founder instilled into the fabric of the organization strong precepts about how people are to be treated. Adherence to the founders' principles about people have helped keep these firms from the pitfalls that usually come from growth and age. To take a well-known example, Tom Watson insisted that IBM make "respect for the individual" a cornerstone of its business, and he set up numerous policies and programs (open-door, no-layoff policies, etc.) that helped realize that principle. Generations of IBM executives have, to a large extent, followed Watson's philosophy.

The typical good workplace, in other words, is good because the basic bond of trust with employees that was established when the organization was founded has never been broken. The relationship may have had its ups and downs over the years. But in general, these firms at least had the advantage of starting off on the right foot.

Such cannot be said of Preston Trucking. After an initial start-up phase, the firm lost its family feeling. The founder, A. T. Blades, was well respected personally, but he had not set forth any distinctive personnel policies or principles. By the time the Teamsters and International Longshoremen's Association organized the drivers and warehouse workers, Preston resembled most other medium-sized truckers. At least, that's the picture painted by those familiar with Preston in 1978. That was a crucial year, for it was in the summer of 1978 that a Teamsters truck driver staged a one-man wildcat work stoppage. He refused to remove his truck from the parking lot of a Chrysler plant in Detroit because he was angry about new work rules that Preston had unilaterally imposed. "I'm going to show those S.O.B.'s in Preston who's the boss," he declared. So he sat there defiantly for several hours before returning to the Preston terminal in Detroit, feeling that he had made his point.

The driver's protest succeeded beyond his wildest dreams, though not in ways he could have predicted. His action helped provoke Preston's executives into launching a series of reforms that thoroughly altered the fifty-year-old trucking company's relations with its more than four thousand employees, most of them Teamsters union members. Today Preston's workers talk about their firm much like rabid baseball or football fans talk about their teams. Their enthusiasm about their transformed workplace has also attracted some media attention. *Business Week* ran a full-page story on Preston entitled "Letting Labor Share the Driver's Seat." *Washington Post* reporter Warren Brown concluded after interviewing numerous Preston employees that there were "no detractors, not even at the union hall." Cliff Atkinson, the Teamsters' shop steward at Preston's terminal outside Washington, D.C., told the *Post*: " 'Preston is just like a family. We can talk to the management, and they can talk to us. This is one helluva company. Heck, we don't even need a shop steward.' "

That a trucking company would have its Teamsters employees singing its praises is remarkable enough. But what makes the Preston story especially noteworthy is that it is one of the very few examples of the transformation of an admittedly bad workplace. Headquartered in the small town of Preston on Maryland's East Shore, the firm has routes that extend throughout the Northeast and along the Great Lakes down to St. Louis. Two years before the Detroit incident, Preston had merged with Chicago-based Shippers Dispatch to form the twentieth largest trucking company in terms of revenues (just over $100 million a year). The line between the management and workers was sharply drawn. Union grievances were an everyday occurrence. Suspicion and hostility characterized the relationship between the two sides.

The work slowdown in Detroit occurred at a time when the company's top management was deeply concerned about the imminent deregulation of the trucking industry. Under regulation, all truckers charged the same rates and none could enter a new territory without governmental approval. But in a deregulated industry, nothing could stop upstart competitors from horning in on an established trucker's routes and offering steeply discounted rates. Preston's leaders realized that the new competitive climate required some hard thinking about how they were going to do business.

Other trucking companies were also reassessing their options. To ward off the competition, most concluded that among other tactics, they'd cut wages and tighten up work rules. Preston decided to take a different road. The top management knew it would be shortsighted to provoke a war within. The Detroit incident had already brought home the dangers of that approach. The driver's action initially sparked Preston's management into even harsher responses that led to more slowdowns and even harsher measures by the company. The company eventually decided to punish the Detroit workers and embargoed all freight destined for that city, forcing two thirds of the workers to be effectively locked out for about three weeks. Preston won that round as the workers reluctantly agreed to come back on the company's terms. But the management realized that head-on confrontations ultimately hurt the company more than the workers. So Preston asked its employees for help in forging an unusual partnership.

This new partnership has survived in a deregulated industry that has seen more than two hundred truckers go under, including such giants as McLean Trucking, Interstate, and Spector Red Ball. It's possible, of course, that Preston would still be in business if it had adopted a different strategy. But Preston's management cites dozens of statistics showing how productivity has increased significantly in terms of shipments per employee, reduced claims, and improved maintenance. It points proudly to the U.S. Senate Productivity Award Preston won in 1986.

It isn't productivity or profitability statistics, however, that make the Preston story worth telling. There are no easy yardsticks for gauging workplace quality in the way that such statistics as earnings per share or return on equity measure financial performance. The only sure way to judge the quality of a workplace is to talk to employees. I have interviewed a variety of Preston employees in several different locations.

Like the *Washington Post* reporter cited earlier, I have found no dissenters, only boosters.

An Ongoing Revolt

Richie Storck is hardly the prototypical company cheerleader. He's the Teamsters shop steward (Local 470) at Preston's Philadelphia terminal and has been working the docks, loading trucks for Preston, for a dozen years. He told me about the working conditions at Preston before 1979:

> Everybody was under a microscope. We didn't like the company, and the company didn't like us. It was plain and simple. There was only a handful of guys who were company men. I mean, they really wanted to kill themselves for the company. The rest of us were union men.
>
> The company, more or less, had the whip on us. You got a ten-minute break, and you didn't dare go eleven minutes because you got reprimanded. You went to lunch for half an hour, and you made sure you were back in half an hour or the boss was standing there waiting for you. If you went to the bathroom, they'd say, "Where are you going? You've been in there for three minutes." It's stuff like that that used to get the men upset, and it was more or less like an ongoing revolt. Constant.
>
> It was like the bad guys and the good guys. They were the bad guys 'cause they were company. They had the right to discipline us, and we knew it. So we didn't give them a reason to. We used to hide in trucks, and when one of them started coming down the dock, we'd tell them we were working. We got the work done. Don't get me wrong. I mean, we worked, but it was just a different atmosphere [than today's].

The atmosphere in 1978 at other terminals was similar to Philadelphia's. After the incident in Detroit, Preston commissioned a management-consulting group (Behavioral Systems, Inc., of Atlanta, led by clinical psychologist Aubrey Daniels and former football star Fran Tarkenton) to conduct a survey at the Detroit and York, Pennsylvania, terminals. Detroit was picked because of the work slowdown; York because officials thought it was one of the best terminals in terms of employee morale. But the survey showed that morale was equally low at both places. For every one good comment about the company, there were forty critical ones. The consultants weren't surprised. They told Preston executives that, in their experience, morale is very poor at most companies.

Comments made by employees at the York and Detroit terminals in the 1978 survey echo Richie Storck's feelings:

• One worker said supervisors occasionally referred to workers as "scum, garbage, idiots, and so forth." Another reported, "When you have a terminal manager say, 'Down south we call them niggers and up north we call them Teamsters,' it just doesn't give a person much respect for the people they are working for."

• A Detroit employee summed up work life at Preston as: ". . . in general, chaotic. Weak management, extremely poor communication, and a high level of worker dissatisfaction all contribute to this situation. I hope that this survey opens some eyes at the corporate headquarters, but I question whether it will. The distance between management and union is of Grand Canyon proportions, and it doesn't appear that either side wants to do a great deal to close the gap."

The company did, in fact, want to close the gap. It asked its consultants to train managers and supervisors. The consultants taught a system they dubbed performance management. To an outsider, the performance-management training system may appear rather crude. It is based on decidedly unfashionable behaviorist psychological theory. (Think of Pavlov's dog or Skinner's rats.) The underlying idea is that you can alter people's behavior by rewarding actions you approve (positive reinforcement) and punishing those you disapprove (negative reinforcement). The consultants simplified the theory even more by prescribing the following: Preston's managers should find and praise four acts that an employee does correctly for every one action that they criticize.

On the face of it, this four-to-one positive reinforcement sounds blatantly manipulative. Going from being kicked in the butt all the time to being patted on the back could make anyone suspicious. Certainly it doesn't sound like the sort of thing that could fool Teamsters dock workers and truck drivers.

Yet it worked. From Storck's viewpoint, the management

stopped "hassling [the men] every day for little things." Period. The supervisors simply quit hovering over the men, waiting to pounce on errors. When a worker did something that was considered a serious discipline problem—like coming in late repeatedly—the Philadelphia terminal manager asked Storck, as the shop steward, to help resolve the issue. Almost overnight, the level of grievances filed by workers decreased to almost nothing.

This 180-degree turnabout didn't come across as manipulative. Why? Employees cite two reasons. First, manipulation generally implies secret or ulterior motives. It's extremely hard to accuse anyone of being manipulative if he puts all his cards on the table. Preston's management had *no hidden agendas.* It told everyone—from managers to dock workers and office help—exactly what it was doing and why. Everyone heard about the positive-reinforcement technique and the four-to-one ratio they were trying to achieve. And there was no mystery about why the company was using the technique. Often managements fear telling employees that their goal for a new program is to improve productivity, fearing employees will object to what is frequently seen as a code word for a speedup. Preston's managers made no bones about it. They told of the challenge facing the company from deregulation and openly proclaimed productivity as their objective.

More important, manipulation often suggests getting another person to do something differently from what he or she is already doing. In this case, employees were not being asked to change; managers and supervisors were. In the context of Preston's labor-management war, the positive-reinforcement technique had the effect of unilateral disarmament. A supervisor couldn't resort to his accustomed weaponry. The technique may have been crude, but its terms were clear. Everybody knew instantly when a supervisor violated the cease-fire.

To emphasize its commitment to the new management style, the company's top executives distributed a "mission statement" they had written. It spells out the basic principles of Preston's new operating style. This statement may have the distinction of being the only corporate philosophy statement in America to quote the German philosopher and poet Goethe: "Treat people as though they were what they ought to be and you help them become what they are capable of being." The clarity of this statement also helped to spotlight cease-fire violations.

PRESTON PEOPLE
MAKE THE
DIFFERENCE
Success Is People Working Together

Preston's most important asset is people, not tractors, trailers, terminals, or management systems. The following quotation from the German philosopher Goethe summarizes our regard for people, "Treat people as though they were what they ought to be and you help them become what they are capable of being." The means that Preston People must be regarded as partners rather than as adversaries.

The person doing the job knows more about it than anyone else. It is the responsibility of managers to ask for suggestions, to listen to possible solutions to specific problems, and to help implement productive change. Each employee has unlimited possibilities. Good managers have the ability to recognize and unleash the potential for better performance. Managers have no more important responsibility than to develop our people and continually create a better, more productive environment. At Preston improvement is always possible and is continually sought.

Every Preston employee deserves to be treated with respect. Each group of employees must understand what is important for its success and how it contributes to the progress of the Company. Supervisors are expected to hold regular meetings which will accomplish this objective. Employees are encouraged to ask any question which will give them better information about their jobs, benefits, the Company, or the performance of their groups. The better informed each employee is about his job and how it relates to other jobs, the greater will be the opportunities for making the organization more effective.

It is the responsibility of those in management to regard each employee as an effective performer until specific results indicate where there are areas for improvement. To achieve this refinement, managers first pinpoint the performance area, develop a baseline, and work with the employee to establish and reach a goal for improvement. As soon as progression is recorded, appropriate reinforcement is given.

Managers are to be fair, firm, and positive in correcting substandard performance and inappropriate behavior. Discipline such as firing or time off without pay is employed only as a last resort for flagrant violations of ethical standards or work rules which have been clearly communicated. In all areas where correction is needed, managers must first counsel the subordinate about his actions and obtain a commitment for constructive change. The manager must ask what he can do to help the employee bring about the needed improvement. . . . Warning letters are used only after the individual has been clearly informed of the problem, and then has been given sufficient time and assistance to correct it.

Although managers observe and rectify errors, it is just as important that they give credit when a job is being done properly. No healthy work environment should have more negative comments than positive ones. The obligation of managers and supervisors is to create an atmosphere wherein employees constantly gain more knowledge and are able to participate in setting challenging goals to achieve outstanding results.

Bill Terrell, Preston's head of operations, likes to tell about an incident in Chicago not long after the company adopted the new style. A manager there was annoyed that people were spending too much time socializing in the office. So one Friday afternoon, he put up above the time clock a long memo demanding that employees stop the social conversations and personal phone calls—or else. . . . One employee made a copy of the memo and sent it to the corporate headquarters, asking whether they were being managed in accordance with such mission-statement assertions as "every Preston employee deserves to be treated with respect" and "no healthy work environment should have more negative comments than positive ones." Coincidentally, over that same weekend, employees throughout the company received a quarterly report from the company that included a copy of the mission statement. The manager's wife happened to read it and asked her husband whether his putting up the memo could be squared with the company's philosophy. That did the trick. Come Monday morning, the manager himself ripped down the memo and went around the office apologizing personally to each employee. By the time Terrell called Chicago to follow up on the query from the employee, the issue had already been resolved.

Partners Rather Than Adversaries

Just as a cease-fire doesn't write a peace treaty, the positive-reinforcement technique didn't forge the terms of the new employment relationship. The company outlined its basic terms for the new relationship in its mission statement: "Preston People must be regarded as partners rather than as adversaries." The statement goes on to declare: "The person doing the job knows more about it than anyone else." In these two statements, we have the key to understanding the new Preston. It's worth looking at this idea of a partnership between management and employees in some detail.

Each party brings something of value to a partnership. At Preston, the company asserted that the employees' most valuable asset was their knowledge. It recognized that employees have minds and that the company valued their thoughts. This notion is considered rank heresy by many in the trucking industry as the highest value is often placed on brawn rather than brains. Preston's workers have little in common with the yuppies of Wall Street or Silicon Valley. There is nothing high tech about hauling freight. Yet the company was saying, in effect, that blue-collar truck drivers must be treated with the respect usually accorded only highly paid white-collar professionals.

Seen in this light, Preston's management was asserting something with profound implications by stating: "The person doing the job knows more about it than anyone else." Preston's workers immediately realized the significance. That sentence is still constantly being quoted by everyone at Preston. It is the unofficial company slogan.

The notion of partnership also implies that each partner has a distinct identity and has certain rights that other partners must recognize. By imposing the four-to-one positive-reinforcement technique, the company effectively gave employees the right to be left alone, to be insulated from the sort of abuse that characterized their previous relationship with management.

Those weren't the only rights Preston employees enjoyed. Ironically, the fact that most Preston employees belong to the Teamsters union aided the building of a genuine partnership. The union contract guarantees certain basic rights, in particular job security through the grievance process. It also assures employees a fair-market wage. Since Preston's executives made no attempt to alter the contract, the workers did not have to fear that the company was going to undermine the rights they enjoyed through union membership. Nor did the company try to undermine employee loyalty to the union, which, after all, is the employees' own organization, created to protect its members from management abuses. (In memos and meetings the company did, however, discuss frankly the economic disadvantages the unionized Preston faced in competing with new, nonunion carriers. But according to both company and union members, this economic issue was stated matter-of-factly, and was given as yet one more reason why the company had to become more productive.)

To sum up, Preston's management approached its employees with the following proposal: Let's make a deal. Instead of working at cross-purposes here, why don't we work jointly on a common project—keeping Preston Trucking afloat. You don't have to work any more hours. You don't have to change your loyalties or your attitudes. We'll assume you know best how things should be run, so we will let you run them. All we want from you is to do your work in the best way you know how.

It would be fair to say that this newly defined relationship between employees and management was based on respect— a key ingredient of trust. When you respect someone, you communicate two things: first, that you recognize limits to what you will demand or require of the other person, and second, that you acknowledge that the other person has something valuable to contribute. Preston's message to its employees conveyed both of these elements of respect. The company placed limits on its behavior toward employees (through the positive-reinforcement technique and willingness to adhere to the union contract), and it acknowledged the importance of employee knowledge. We should now look at the specific techniques Preston used to tap into that know-how.

We Ran the Show out There

In a true partnership, each partner has some say in the business. This was the clear message the company conveyed when it proposed that people in the company become "partners rather than adversaries."

For Preston even to consider involving employees in the business operations represented a sharp break with the past. Several quotes from the 1978 employee survey indicate the flavor of the old style of decision making:

- A worker at the York terminal reported: "In all my years on this job, I have never known of anyone in management even asking any one of the workers how he felt about how things are done."
- One of his co-workers added: "All decisions are made by the management, then they come to us and tell us this is the way it will be done, period. We have no say."
- In Detroit, an employee stated: "This company does not care to hear any suggestions an employee or group of employees has to say about anything, even if it would improve the operation."

What about the union? Did it object to the company's giving more of a say to employees? Many employers insist their hands are tied by the union regulations from doing much of anything, let alone from creating an entirely different basis for the relationship with its employees.

Preston's executives, however, took the position that the Teamsters contract mostly spelled out what could not be done; it did not define what was possible. The union contract doesn't prohibit management from handing over more power to the workers. On the contrary. Most companies insist on broad contract language guaranteeing management almost total control over every aspect of work—what, where, how, and when it is to be done. In labor-contract jargon, it's called management prerogatives.

So Preston, in effect, voluntarily gave up some of its prerogatives by asking employees to assume more responsibility. All managers and supervisors were required to hold regular meetings with their employees. At these sessions, employees suggested ways of improving their jobs and the company's efficiency. I visited Preston's Jersey City terminal in mid-1983, soon after employees in that terminal began holding regular meetings. One dock worker (a member of the International Longshoremen's Association) said he was initially skeptical of the company's intentions. His attitude changed when the company implemented one of his suggestions—installing a brighter lighting system on the loading docks. Other Preston workers I talked with at other locations related similar stories. It wasn't the meetings that made the difference. It was that the company acted on the suggestions, many of them seemingly minor matters like new snack and coffee machines.

These seemingly minor issues often served as major symbols to employees. At the York terminal, employees had long been upset about the state of their lunchroom. In fact, the most memorable comment in the 1978 survey related to the York lunchroom:

> You've got to wonder at the future possibilities of a multi-million-dollar company that cannot handle the improvement of a twenty-by-twenty-five-foot lunchroom. Ah! the infamous lunchroom. It has become the personified example of all the problems at York. Our request for an improved lunchroom was nowhere near unreasonable. And patiently, for sixteen months, we've waited. And not so patiently, we've sat amid searing summer heat, hordes of flies, and armies of mice, even a few rats, while Preston obtained a fleet of trailers and tractors—all new, all paid for.

When long-standing sore points like the York lunchroom and the lighting on the Jersey City docks were finally addressed, suspicions about the company began to break down. Workers began to respect the management more. After all, most workers always assumed they knew more about how to do their own jobs than their supervisors did. They thought the management at Preston (and almost any other workplace) was living in a dream world to think otherwise. They had little respect for managers who acted as if they knew the work better than the employees. Once management stopped insisting on something that wasn't true, change became possible.

Richie Storck explained the process:

We started having meetings, company meetings, with supervisors and the men, and they started getting more input. They started asking, "What can we do to change things?" And then the men started seeing maybe they really do care about our concerns and our ideas. I mean, we got some good, smart guys out there. There's not any cowards on that dock. They know their business. They know what they're doing. And that's important.

They started listening to us, our suggestions as before they didn't. Then they started more or less leaving us alone, and we more or less ran the show out there. If we had a problem, we took it to the supervisor. Everybody gave a little bit. We talked about things. Like faith. Just leave the guys alone, they'll do the job. Now there's quite a few Saturday and Sunday nights the supervisor will be late or something, we have men come in and open the doors up and start working with nobody supervising.

The company went beyond merely listening to and implementing employee suggestions. An important corollary to the idea of partnership is sharing information. The company set forth the policy in the mission statement: "Employees are encouraged to ask any questions which will give them better information about their jobs, their benefits, their Company, or the performance of their groups. The better informed each employee is about his job and how it relates to other jobs, the greater will be the opportunities for making the organization more effective."

In other words, the company told employees that they could have access to any information that was also available to the management. Literally. Both employees and supervisors give numerous examples of memos and reports that are now freely shared with all employees. There are no secrets permitted. This broke down the notion that management possessed more data than did employees. It further reduced the power gulf between the two sides.

Laughingstock of the Industry

Anyone familiar with American management techniques of the past decade will immediately recognize the basic technique Preston adopted. It employed a variation of quality circles—a technique of Japanese management that became a fad at many American businesses in the early 1980s. This is a technique of participatory management that numerous business-school theorists have advocated over the past quarter century. An MIT industrial psychologist named Douglas McGregor framed the concept for participatory management with his distinction between Theory X and Theory Y managers. Theory X managers believe employees are fundamentally lazy and must be prodded to work harder. By contrast, Theory Y managers believe that employees want to be productive, so they need only a good "atmosphere" or "managerial climate" to flourish. (This philosophy can be traced to the human-relations movement. Elton Mayo, for instance, stressed the need to create the right "environment" to achieve "spontaneous cooperation.") Preston's outside consultants were disciples of McGregor's and as can be seen from Preston's mission statement, the company explicitly set out to create a good "atmosphere" and a "healthy work environment."

Still, it would be an error to give credit for what happened at Preston to a strict following of the McGregor/Theory Y principles. In one important respect, Preston varied from the Theory Y philosophy as spelled out in McGregor's classic book, The Human Side of Enterprise. McGregor saw participation as "a special case of delegation" and, hence, a technique that maintains the basic status quo in workplace power relationships. Part of the reason for this is McGregor's rather benign view of conflict between workers and management. For instance, he explained worker complaints about not getting a "fair break" in purely psychological terms—their "safety needs are thwarted." But Preston's executives had simply sat across the table from Teamsters negotiators for too many years to believe that labor conflicts are merely psychological problems.

Preston's executives knew from the outset that the name of the game is power. They knew there was no way employees could achieve more control over their work without real tradeoffs taking place. In other words, it could not be merely a form of delegation, because the supervisors actually had to give up some authority for the process to work.

Everyone at Preston agrees that managers did in fact lose authority because of the changes. Managers had to learn to live, in the words of one Preston executive, "with their egos at their ankles." Bosses couldn't be absolute bosses anymore. The result: About 25 percent of Preston's managers, from first-line supervisors to regional managers, left the company *because of* the change in management philosophy. Many of those who left had been with the company for ten, fifteen, twenty years or more. Few were actually fired for refusing to go along with the new style. Most quit simply because they didn't agree with or couldn't adjust to the new Preston policies. One regional manager told a corporate vice-president that he was resigning so that he would no longer have to be associated with "the laughingstock of the industry." The departure of a quarter of Preston's managers was no small matter. Since Preston did not make any organizational changes when it changed managerial styles, all departing managers had to be replaced.

The management exodus underscored that what happened at Preston was genuinely different from what happened to most experiments in participatory management. Even where the efforts were less ambitious than at Preston, managerial opposition usually stopped the programs cold. *Fortune* ran a major article in 1986 describing that most participatory-management programs installed in the early 1980s had already been scratched because the top executives had succumbed to opposition from middle managers. Participatory techniques were too threatening to American managers. There's no theory of management, no concept of the manager, that proposes reducing the manager's power over the workplace. After all, management theorists from the time of Frederick Taylor have shared the aim of increasing, not decreasing, managerial control over the workplace. Even the proponents of Theory Y have a blind spot when it comes to power. Calls for "empowerment" of workers by the Theory Y-style managers often have a hollow ring because they don't address the trade-off essential to any real empowerment. More power to the workers means less power to the managers. That's just how power works.

As we've seen, Preston's management faced this issue head on. I asked Preston's top officials about it. Will Potter, Preston's president, insisted that the top officials tried to keep the changes from "threatening" managers. The company didn't intend to push anyone out of Preston. It said it made every effort to retrain managers and sell them on the new program. But *credibility* with the entire work force was an even higher priority. And to be credible, you have to be consistent, Potter said. You can't retreat just because there's some opposition. You can't afford to look like you're following the latest in managerial fads:

> If we were trying something a little bit different every other year, this would create a problem. It would get to be manipulative. We said in terms of performance management, "This is it and it's here forever, and we're going to continue to refine it. We can't tell you how, but we can give you examples through time where people have done things that we never even dreamed about."

Potter often refers to his own management motto: "Do what you say you are going to do when you said you were going to do it." He has no patience for people who don't follow through on their promises. It undermines trust. He estimates that it took two to three years to build up the management's "integrity and credibility" within the organization. Credibility is a perishable commodity that must be kept fresh. Nothing destroys it more quickly than broken promises.

Bruce Kennedy, Preston's head of marketing, offered another perspective on credibility:

> People can see right through you. When you say you respect the ideas and the intellect of every person in the organization but you don't act in a way that's consistent with that, they see right through it. Then you're labeled as hypocrites. And then all respect, all trust, comes tumbling down.

To be consistent with the new relationship with employees, the company began calling employees associates and supervisors coordinators. Other companies (J. C. Penney, Wal-Mart Stores, for instance) refer to employees as associates. It implies the sort of partnership that Preston was trying to build.

The term *coordinator* is Preston's own attempt to cope with the altered status of supervisors. It's a term that reflects their new role within the company. This name change is not mere window dressing. The role of managers *is* different at Preston; in a few short years, the tradition of American management going back to Frederick Taylor had been thrown out. The separate managerial class, with its unchallenged authority over the workplace, has no role at the new Preston. It has not been replaced by a cadre of human-relations specialists à la Elton Mayo or by professionals à la Peter Drucker or by cheerleaders and coaches à la Tom Peters. Managers act as *coordinators*— the folks who organize things so that work done by one part of the organization can be used effectively by another part. Or they connect the work done by the organization to the outside world. Their role is *not* to supervise the work of others in the usual sense of the term. As Preston employees like to reiterate: "The person doing the job knows more about it than anybody else."

We Took Chances with People

As Preston's employees gained more confidence that the company's management was sincerely interested in their efforts, they gave more of themselves to their work. They did "work smarter"—to use the catchphrase of the day. Their increased cooperation in turn encouraged Preston's managers to take more risks, too. This was especially apparent among Preston's so-called city drivers, the ones who pick up freight from various customers and bring it back to the local terminal, where it is sorted and put on long-distance trucks. As these drivers became more comfortable with the new Preston, they often volunteered to solicit more business from their regular customers. Soon, they were being called driver-salespersons, making Preston's drivers the only ones in the industry who actually helped make sales. At other trucking companies, salespeople make all the sales calls, while drivers simply pick up and deliver the freight. It's the old brain-versus-brawn distinction. The two different functions are carried out by two different types of employees, one white-collar, the other blue-collar. Trusting Teamsters drivers to *talk* directly with customers was the sort of change that made Preston the industry's laughingstock in the eyes of some detractors.

But it's hard to quarrel with results.

Larry Regosch has dozens of stories about the new system's paying off. As Philadelphia terminal manager (and Richie Storck's boss), Regosch says he used to ride workers as much as any other manager in the company—a fact Storck and others will testify to. But he has become an ardent supporter of the new style. He says that the changes meant "we took chances with people."

Regosch's favorite example is what happened at American Honda, which is the distributor for the Japanese automaker and the Philadelphia terminal's largest account. John Wilson, the Teamsters driver on the route, learned from the American Honda traffic manager that there had been an increase in damaged-freight claims, among other problems. So Wilson went to Regosch and said: "I feel if I'm given the proper equipment and the proper time to handle Honda, I could reduce the damages at Honda." At the time, Wilson loaded all the Honda freight (mostly car parts) into one trailer and drove it to the terminal, where it was off-loaded and reloaded on trucks bound for different locations. Wilson suggested that Preston park *four* different trailers there every day. Each trailer would only be loaded with freight slated for a specific destination. For instance, one trailer would only be filled with Honda freight headed for Washington, D.C. At the end of the day, that trailer would be driven to the Philadelphia terminal, where other freight also bound for Washington would be loaded. Because of the reduced handling, Wilson argued, there would be less of a chance of damage.

The terminal manager agreed with Wilson's plan and agreed to put four trailers at the distributor's warehouse (about $100 per trailer per day). Honda was so pleased with the results that it began giving more of its business to Preston. In the first year, Preston's Honda account doubled in revenues, and it increased by another 50 percent the following year (1986). By early 1988, Preston was using a dozen trailers daily—all because it was willing to take a risk on one of its drivers' suggestions.

Terminal manager Regosch fully appreciated the element of risk inherent in the situation:

Oh, there's just no question that was a very high risk situation. But I knew the potential at Honda, and I knew that the person I was speaking to about it—John Wilson—had thought it all out. I figured, Why not? It's never been done before. If it fails, it fails. We made a mistake, we'll try something different. But it happened to work out fabulously.

In this business environment, especially in the trucking industry, with massive discounts and bidding wars between
trucking companies, you have to be aggressive. And you have
to take a shot once in a while. If you don't, you're going to be
dead in the water. Our drivers are like that, too. They look for
the extra bit of freight every day. They bring this in, try this,
try that. It happens all the time. Every day with a multitude of
drivers. "Give me a shot, I can do that for you," they say to the
customers. "Our company can perform that service." And that
kind of stuff makes us different from someone else on the street.

We could, of course, take a very cynical look at this entire
story and say: Sure, this manager is happy because his workers
are now doing a lot more work for the same amount of money.
These drivers have been tricked into working as salesmen, but
they are not getting any sales commissions or any other benefits
for their extra labor. I asked Richie Storck, the Teamsters steward, whether Preston's employees weren't simply getting more
work for the same money. He answered indignantly:

Would you rather drive home and feel whipped, and feel that
you'd been through hell that day? Or would you rather get the
personal satisfaction when you went home that you did something to help the company and your fellow men by getting more
freight? That's why other outfits went out of business, because
they just did their eight hours' work and went home. They had
no concern for the company. Or the company showed the men
that they had no concern for the men or the company itself.

Employees have not received only psychological rewards
from their additional efforts. In 1984, Preston introduced a
Scanlon bonus plan, through which employees share directly
in the financial savings resulting from their higher productivity. It was the first and, as of this writing, only trucker to have
such a program.
    It would be unfair to end our consideration of Preston giving
the impression that all problems have been resolved. As Storck
explained:

It's one big happy family. But I know the [terminal manager]
is a company man, and he knows I am a union man. We may
have different views about different situations, like a man and

a wife. But if another major truck company in the city says, "Let's go after Preston's freight," then all of a sudden, we're one. Then it's not a union and a company anymore, it's Preston, and we'll go get 'em.

Storck insists, in other words, that he hasn't been tricked at all. If you had to sum up his current attitude, he'd say that instead of being a hired hand—an employee—he's now a *partner* in the business. Rather than the management's having sole responsibility for whether the firm keeps in operation, Storck feels he shares that responsibility with everyone else in the firm, including the management. He sees himself on a more equal plane with them.

Even though the company has made no organizational changes, all the employees I interviewed—dock workers, drivers, clerical workers, and mechanics—reported that they felt that hierarchy had been eliminated because of the changes. At the corporate headquarters, for instance, I interviewed a group of clerical workers. Joyce Cohee was one of them. She has been handling claims for a dozen years. Like Richie Storck, she describes a transformation:

> When I first started work here, I felt every day when I came to this office that somebody, especially my supervisor, was watching me. You know, every move I made, I just felt uncomfortable. I just felt that the guy was out there to get me, to find me doing something wrong. And with the change of management concept, I feel more relaxed about what I do. I feel that they're trusting me in what I do. They're giving me the opportunity to perform my duties in the way that I see best.

Another clerical worker, Sandy Redd, in the accounts-receivable department, adds:

> I noticed a distinct attitude change when the management concept changed because instead of thinking, Well, we'll accept this the way it is, we decided to start thinking, How can we make it happen this way? or, What can we do to improve things? And I think the attitude also made each person feel like they're an associate and not an employee.
>
> The more you start thinking in terms of I'm an associate and we work together, instead of, I'm coming in today, I'm gonna

report to my supervisor as to what I should do or how I should go about this, you start eliminating the feeling that you're just one here and one there. Instead you become a group and a team, and you start thinking that way.

Testimonials like these are common around Preston today. Among employees there is a newfound sense of pride in themselves and their company. If you refer to them as employees, however, you may find yourself corrected. They are *associates* now, you are told. Aside from the increased pride in themselves and their company, it seems that Preston associates feel that a great side benefit of the changes is the relaxed atmosphere within the company. In other words, not only is the relationship with the company better and the relationship with the job improved, so is the relationship of employees with each other. Mike Callahan is a mechanic at the Preston, Maryland, terminal. He explained:

> It's gone from all these different levels to everybody's on the same level really. Whereas before you don't have coffee with the vice-president or you don't have a discussion with the president. There's just not that animosity and the tensions there used to be. I'm not interested in doing Will Potter's [the president's] job, and he's only interested in me doing a good job. But he is *interested*, and it makes a difference.
>
> We still have our problems, but we just seem to be able to work them out a lot simpler, because we work them out among ourselves. It makes it a lot easier.

This has meant, among other things, that there's a lot more socializing among the workers. It's more fun to work at Preston. Another mechanic, Jerry Meredith, described the new situation:

> We start work at seven o'clock, and twenty minutes of seven, the parking lot's half full. We don't have nobody running to punch the time clock—everybody has been here for ten minutes anyway. So if people didn't like it here, they wouldn't be coming in. People don't grab every minute they can from the company. You don't have people sitting around the clock. When we come in early, we sit there and drink our coffee and chat.

A third mechanic, Howard Bradshaw, is used to people's reacting skeptically to such tales of happy workers. He tells a story of one group of customers who made a tour of the mechanics' shop and heard stories of how the mechanics were now doing jobs in two hours that used to require eight hours, because of the productivity improvements the mechanics have implemented. One of the visitors returned shortly after the rest of the group had left and took Bradshaw aside. As Bradshaw tells the story:

> This guy snuck back here and he said: "Are you for real?" He didn't believe it. I said, "What do you think?" He said, "I had to ask you." He just didn't believe what he was hearing. He thought I was bull-shitting. He thought I was telling a bunch of lies, and that the company was making me do it. It was neat. I said, "Yeah, it's all true, and I believe in all of it."

When Bradshaw told me that story, I asked, "Do you think you will believe in all of it ten years from now?"

Bradshaw shrugged his shoulders: "Come back in ten years and ask me."

Bill Terrell, a Preston executive, knew exactly what Bradshaw meant. He said: "People don't give you their trust and respect. They only *loan* it to you."

11
THE ROLE MODEL
THAT CRASHED
People Express

In 1880, exactly a hundred years before People Express was incorporated, the Pullman railway sleeping-car company started construction of its model industrial community eight miles south of Chicago. To attract the best workmen and help them to become "elevated and refined," George Pullman built an aesthetically pleasing village with an artificial lake, broad avenues, and a large indoor shopping arcade. Pullman fully expected his great experiment would usher in "a new era . . . in the history of labor." Pullman's dream of a new era had turned into a nightmare fourteen years later, when President Grover Cleveland ordered the Seventh Cavalry into the community to quell the worst labor disturbance of the century.

People Express offers few direct parallels to the Pullman story. Pullman still exists as an entity (though it now makes truck trailers and aerospace parts), while People Express's brown aircraft have all been repainted with Continental Airline's red-and-white colors. But People Express, too, was a social experiment on a grand scale—probably the most elaborate (and certainly the most highly publicized) attempt at corporate democracy in the modern era. As a social experiment, People Express certainly did not prove to be the ideal workplace its founders had hoped for.

People Express was launched with the noblest of intentions.

Donald Calvin Burr, the airline's president, once said: "The single predominant reason that I cared about starting a new company was to try and develop a better way for people to work together." He named the company *People* Express to underscore the firm's commitment to a people-oriented management philosophy.

The company's people philosophy was translated into wide-ranging policies aimed at transforming employees into "owner-managers." There were no supervisors, secretaries, or vice-presidents at People Express. All employees were given the title of manager, and performed a variety of jobs. Most were customer service managers, who rotated monthly, weekly, or even daily among jobs—in the air as flight attendants, at the airports as ticket agents, or behind the scenes in the accounting or scheduling departments. They were guaranteed lifetime job security. They shared in the profits—one third of the corporate profits were distributed to employees. And they all owned a minimum of a hundred shares of the airline's stock. The airline trumpeted this fact in one of its newspaper ads: "When you fly People Express, an owner is never more than a few steps away."

A few months after its planes were flying routes along the eastern seaboard, Burr and several cofounders sat down to codify the airline's goals. They settled on six "precepts," including one asserting that People Express should be a "role model for other airlines and other businesses." It was. Many outsiders eagerly embraced People Express. Dozens of newspaper and magazine reporters wrote articles lauding People Express and its humane management philosophy. It was included in *The 100 Best Companies to Work for in America*, based on interviews conducted in 1983. Harvard Business School published a case study of the airline for its students. A professor there, named D. Quinn Mills, asserted that People Express was "the most comprehensive and self-conscious effort to fit a business to the capabilities and attitudes of today's work force." Another Harvard professor, D. Daryl Wyckoff, declared, "Anyone who isn't studying People Express and the way they're managing people is out of their minds." And the two most popular management consultants of the day—John Naisbitt and Tom Peters—extolled People Express and its founder Don Burr as living embodiments of their managerial principles. They cited People Express repeatedly in their best-selling books—*Re-inventing the Corporation* and *A Passion for Excellence*—and they spread the People Express gospel in dozens of speeches on the business lecture circuit.

Management gurus weren't the only ones attracted by the airline's people-oriented style. Indeed, People Express used its unconventional management philosophy as its primary recruiting tool. One of its recruiting ads heralded: "People Express is growing fast because we put people first!" Another proclaimed: "Teamwork takes on a whole new meaning at People Express!" It continued:

> People Express has a whole new approach to running an airline! As a Customer Service Manager, you'll be a vital part of our management team, working in all areas. . . . Instead of doing just one limited job, you'll be involved in both line and staff activities—so you can learn the airline business fully. Faced with our variety of challenges, you'll develop and use all your decision-making skills. That's how bright people grow at People Express . . . by finding simple creative solutions to complex problems . . . solutions that contribute to our productivity and growth . . . and yours.

The recruiting pitch worked. When People Express interviewers showed up in a town, thousands of applicants turned out. According to *Inc.* magazine: "As hokey as the term may sound, the so-called people structure has the drawing power of last call at a Saturday night beer blast." So many responded that the airline hired only one out of every hundred applicants.

Once on board, People Express employees entered an intensive five-week, six-day-a-week (without pay) training program. The highlight came when company president Don Burr addressed them. Those who saw him in action portrayed Burr as an "evangelist" who preached his "new management" gospel with "messianic zeal." *New York Times Magazine* writer Sara Rimer attended a 1984 training session. She wrote:

> Burr never misses an indoctrination session. He cracks jokes. He preaches, sometimes taking *Star Wars*, his favorite film, as his text for a sermon on the forces of good and evil in the business world. And he inevitably ends with his own vision of People Express: The Good Company.

"You're not a commodity," he told the recruits. . . . "You're not a beaten-down worker. You're a manager. You're an owner."

After two hours under his spell, the recruits rewarded Burr with a "resounding ovation." One of the employees "practically floated out of the room." He told the reporter: "I think the man's a wizard. This is the opportunity I've been waiting for all my life. This is my road to self-actualization."

That comment typified the employees' reaction to their first taste of life inside People Express. It's no wonder that the former head of competitor New York Air said, "Don Burr is a motivational genius." Ten- and twelve-hour days were the norm at People Express. This translated into high productivity. People Express operated with about fifty employees per airplane, about half the industry average. Not only did People Express expect its employees to work hard, it also expected its "manager-owners" to work cheap. In 1986, for instance, the firm paid its workers an average of $28,200, compared with the industry average of $43,200. (They were paid more on average, however, than the employees of Continental Airlines.)

There's no doubt that the highly productive and relatively cheap labor force helped fuel People Express's phenomenal growth. People Express was the Cinderella story of the decade. By some measures, it was the fastest-growing company in American business history, shooting from zero to more than $1 billion in revenue in less than five years. It became the biggest carrier serving the New York metropolitan area from its headquarters at Newark Airport. With its purchase of the ailing Frontier Airlines in late 1985, People Express became the nation's fifth largest airline. But its expansion was costly. Too costly. Buying the nearly bankrupt Frontier Airlines drained People Express. Burr agreed to sell the entire airline to Texas Air, which merged it into that company's Continental Airlines subsidiary on February 1, 1987.

Because People Express's people-oriented management style was so highly publicized, many people were quick to conclude that the airline's demise proves that corporate democracy doesn't work. The New York Times, for instance, ran a front-page article headlined: "Behind People Express's Fall: An Off-beat Managerial Style." The Wall Street Journal, chimed in: "Airline's Ills Point Out Weaknesses of Unorthodox Management Style." But such conclusions may have been unfair. There were no similar articles, for instance, about the flaws in conventional and orthodox management styles when other airlines floundered or went under. As demonstrated by several dramatic bankruptcies (Air Florida, Braniff, Continental) and the disappearance of a number of familiar carriers because of mergers into the surviving so-called megacarriers (Republic into Northwest, PSA into USAir, Western into Delta, Ozark into TWA). Strong arguments could be made that if anything, People Express's labor policies helped prolong, rather than interfered with, the company's survival. At any rate, People Express failed as a business proposition. Why it failed is a topic that will undoubtedly be discussed for years to come in many business schools.

Our concern, however, is with People Express as a place to work. To gain more insight into the dynamics of work life at People Express, I talked at length with numerous People Express employees during two trips to the airline's headquarters in Newark. My last visit came during the final week of the airline's existence as an independent entity. For the most part, the employees still believed in the ideals that had attracted them to the airline, but almost all were bitter about what had happened at People Express. They talked of feeling "ripped off," "betrayed," "lied to," and "manipulated." They stressed that these feelings surfaced on a large scale *before* the airline flew into the financial turbulence that caused it to be sold to Texas Air. The financial problems only exacerbated the already serious morale problems that existed at People Express. In short, the reality of People Express as a workplace did not correspond to the rhetoric about corporate democracy. Employees cited serious problems with both key "people policies" and the philosophy behind those policies.

The Start-up Syndrome

Part of what happened at People Express has occurred at countless other companies. There's an infectious excitement about being involved in launching a company. Everyone believes and understands the organization's goals and purposes. Everyone feels needed and useful, as there's so much to be done. The rigid, bureaucratic, and routine ways of doing things haven't come into being as yet. People Express's cross-utilization and job-rotation policies were ideally suited to the start-up phase. They allowed the company the kind of flexibility it needed to grow rapidly.

The early years were exciting times for People Express employees. They felt like winners, and they could see tangible results from their hard work. But working for a start-up can have a darker side as well. The astonishing rate of growth meant many employees worked long, uncompensated hours, since the airline was almost always understaffed. This wreaked havoc on personal lives. It was stressful; it precipitated numerous divorces. As managing officer Lori Dubose told researchers for a Harvard Business School case study in 1982: "And start-up team members—oh my God, they've got ulcers, high blood pressure, allergies, a divorce . . . it's one thing after another. . . . We've all been physically run down."

How an employer deals with the human strains of its start-up phase indicates a great deal about the kind of relationship it intends to have with employees over the long run as well. Top managers often get so caught up in the whirl of growing the business that they become blinded to the strains placed on the individuals around them. Some employers don't even see it as a problem. They may, in fact, perpetuate a start-up environment indefinitely because of the benefits of running a company with employees who are so swept up in the excitement of the enterprise that they work long—often uncompensated—hours. Sooner or later, many employees, including managers, lose their personal bearings and quit to rebuild their lives. But some bosses could care less, because they believe departing employees can always be replaced with others who are attracted by the glamour and energy of the intense working atmosphere.

The question becomes: Is the company operating in a start-up mode for legitimate business reasons? Or does the start-up style mask an exploitative relationship? Is the company taking unfair advantage of its employees' love of excitement and novelty? If so, trust between the company and employees becomes impossible because employees are treated as replaceable cannon fodder, not as individual human beings with something unique to contribute.

In the perpetual start-up environment, employees are often deceived because they are given so much responsibility. Over

time, it becomes clear that lots of responsibility is merely part
of the job description. The responsibility is good, but the employer doesn't reward employees for their above-and-beyond-
the-call-of-duty efforts. The company takes their hard work for
granted.

People Express showed signs of being addicted to this start-
up syndrome. Its cross-utilization and job-rotation policies
certainly helped maintain a kind of electric tension. These
policies fostered a constant crisis atmosphere because the frequent changes of assignments made developing routines impossible. It is certainly revealing that Don Burr himself had
little sympathy for the human problems created by the airline's
rapid growth. He told the Harvard researchers:

> Now there are a lot of people who argue that you ought to
> slow down and take stock and that everything would be a whole
> lot nicer and easier and all that; I don't believe that. People get
> more fatigued and stressed when they don't have a lot to do. I
> really believe that, and I think I have tested it. I think it's obvious
> as hell and I feel pretty strongly about it.

Burr also argued that the short-run stresses were unfortu-
nate, but there were overwhelming benefits that would accrue
to everyone from the rapid-expansion plan. But few longer-
term employees I interviewed bought that argument. Instead,
they felt Burr got hooked on bigness for its own sake and lost
sight of the airline's original goals. Burr himself gave credence
to that view when, in late 1985, he justified to a business
reporter the airline's constant expansion:

> Leadership is not pandering to what people say they need.
> It's defining what the hell people need. It's not saying, "Oh,
> yeah, you want another candy bar? Here, rot your teeth." That's
> not what builds empires. . . . All I want to do is win.

Burr's justifications sound similar to the language of other
CEOs, men who make no pretense of trying to create a good
working environment. In retrospect, there appears to have been
a clear conflict between Burr's winning-is-everything attitude
and his espousal of humane management. At many companies,
the top management doesn't suggest that it has any goal for

the organization besides fattening the bottom line and creating a bigger enterprise. But People Express appeared to be different, and many (if not most) employees signed up for the airline because of the eloquence about its enlightened management style. They placed their trust in the organization. When they saw that things were *not* different, they felt betrayed.

A customer service manager named Vicki summed up the feelings of many employees. Attracted by the concept of self-management, Vicki was an early recruit, joining the airline before its planes were flying. She says:

> The basic problem was that people felt they were continuing to put out and put out, but not getting anything in return. We began to see that it would always be like that. I worked 16 and 17 hours a day. I put in $65,000 a year worth of work, but was paid about $25,000 a year. I never would do that again for anybody.

Every Employee a Manager: Prescription for Autocratic Rule?

One of the biggest complaints I heard from employees was the lack of "managerial direction" as the company grew. Yes, that's right. The highly motivated "self-managers" of People Express wanted *more direction* and coordination. They said they were often confused about what to do next. They said the top officers of the company didn't communicate clearly about where the company was going, and they frequently felt at a loss.

How can we account for this apparent anomaly of self-managers demanding more direction? Let's look closely at the concept of every employee a manager from a political viewpoint. If everybody is a manager, it follows that nobody is a manager. It also leaves a huge power vacuum between the people at the very top of the organization and everybody else. In most large companies, a power vacuum is inconceivable precisely because people in the middle layers of the organization carve out bureaucratic niches.

At People Express, bureaucratic structure was anathema. It represented everything that was moribund about corporate America. People Express sought to be different. Instead of a bureaucracy, it would, in Burr's words, "create an environment which would enable and empower employees to release their creative energies." Employees participated directly in decision making. Without supervisors, employees worked in small teams, which decided how to do things. This was an aspect of People Express that all employees I talked with found stimulating and fulfilling. They felt they had an impact. It was a heady experience, setting up a major airline.

But as the firm expanded and the work force grew, the gulf between the top and everybody else grew wider. There were no mechanisms to bridge that gulf. The company had relied on a variety of vehicles that gave employees a sense that everyone was a "manager" in the sense of having a say in the running of the company. There was an extensive internal communications network. There were monthly employee question-and-answer meetings with the top management. And there was a fifteen-minute daily news video shown on color monitors throughout the company's facilities. And the top executives, including Burr, were great practitioners of the management-by-wandering-around style touted by management guru Tom Peters.

When things were going well, the elaborate communications system worked beautifully. The system was well suited to disperse good news. But there were no viable mechanisms for handling employee complaints or concerns when the news turned sour, and employees began having major questions about the wisdom of executive decision making. In a word, the entire system assumed a kind of harmony between the employee-managers and the top executives; it made no provisions for serious conflicts.

One example. There was no real grievance system at People Express. The airline relied on an open-door policy: If you had a problem, you could voice it directly to Burr or one of the group of managing directors. A customer-service manager named Jack said that at first, Burr insisted his door was always open and he would listen to any employee complaint. But according to Jack: "Later, he would still let you come in to see him, but he wouldn't listen. He had the attitude that he had had his picture in *Time* and *Business Week* and *Fortune* magazines, and that he was the one who had made People Express, so he didn't have to listen to us anymore."

What's Wrong with Being a Secretary?

In a column he prepared for *The Wall Street Journal* in 1985, Donald Burr wrote:

> Every worker at People Express is a manager. . . . No one has a secretary at People Express. We run a company that will do about $600 million in volume without having one secretary. I answer my own phone and I hand write my own letters. Needless to say, I don't write much.

At first blush, Burr sounds like a working-class hero. Not only did People Express have no secretaries, but because of the cross-utilization/job-rotation policy, no employees could find themselves in a boring, repetitive job.

Let's step back and ask: What is the matter with being a secretary? Thousands of secretaries love their jobs. They take pride in doing it well. They feel they are making a meaningful contribution to the organizations they work for. Even if they despise their *bosses*, they may nevertheless feel that their *job* is interesting and challenging. Not all secretaries feel this way, of course. But it is not the *job* of being a secretary that's fundamentally wrong. It's frequently the servile *relationship* with their bosses that many secretaries find objectionable. Even highly paid engineers and scientists can have degrading relationships with their superiors. So it's not always the nature of a job's tasks that makes people hate their work. Other factors often account for unhealthy boss-worker relationships, including an organization's failure to respect individuals as individuals. By publicizing its lack of secretaries, People Express was trying to say that it had no menial jobs. In proclaiming that every employee is a manager, the company was saying: You're not just a flight attendant or a ticket agent, you're a *manager*.

Just as we asked earlier, What's wrong with being a secretary, we can ask, What's so great about everybody being a manager? Sure it's important to feel you have some control over your own work, that you don't have to be bossed around by some nincompoop. But nonmanagerial tasks are important, too. The trouble with People Express's setup was its underlying bias: that only managers do significant work in this world. There was unspoken contempt for those who do the humdrum tasks. As the employees quickly learned, running an airline is comprised of lots and lots of prosaic tasks. Most People Express employees did jobs that were almost identical to those performed by their counterparts (often unionized) at other airlines.

It's also ironic that Don Burr told new recruits: "You're not a commodity." There was something very commoditylike about the airline's personnel system. Because everyone was trained to do a variety of tasks and was regularly rotated, employees themselves were treated like interchangeable parts. To use a distinction from an earlier chapter, it would appear that there was more of a division of *labor* than a specialization of *work* operative at People Express. Employees were not encouraged to specialize. Instead, the overall tasks were divvied up according to how much manpower was around. That process makes sense from time to time. Delta Air Lines, for instance, has resorted to a cross-utilization policy to avoid layoffs in difficult periods. But if such a policy is standard operating procedure, as it was at People Express, an employee's individuality and sense of accomplishment can be lost.

At first, calling everybody a manager and moving employees around at an almost frenetic pace probably obscured the mundane aspects of ticketing passengers and serving them coffee. The constant movement seemed like fun to many employees. When the novelty wore off, however, employees were still ticketing passengers and serving them coffee. Only it wasn't quite as challenging as it had been at first.

Nevertheless, employees insist that People Express was basically a "fun" place to work, even in its last weeks of operation. Many of them claimed that what made working there fun was *not* the job-rotation system itself, except at the beginning of their employment. It was their relationships with other employees. The job-rotation setup allowed people to "keep up with" other employees, as several of them put it. And the cross-utilization policy contributed to a lack of social and political hierarchy at People Express. That also helped create a relaxed social environment. People Express employees reported a genuine camaraderie within the organization. Employees enjoyed the "people" of People Express. In other words, the job-rotation system may have failed in its ostensible purpose of improving employees' relationship with their jobs, but it helped create better relationships among the employees themselves.

In terms of two of the three basic workplace relationships, then, People Express gets high marks for creating a sense of community among employees. It gets only mixed reviews for the employees' relationship to their jobs. The crucial element of pride was often lacking because employees were always changing assignments. Employees were so much part of the team effort that their sense of pride depended on how the team was doing. When the People Express team was doing well, they felt good about their jobs. When the firm began to stumble, there was little or nothing for them to be proud of individually. In other words, because many employees had their sense of accomplishment wrapped up in the fortunes of the enterprise, they took the company's failures quite personally. This added to the bitterness.

It's certainly too soon to write the last word on the People Express experience. As we've seen, in certain respects the company did create a good workplace. Workers were given considerably more responsibility than is typically the case. There was great camaraderie among the employees themselves. While the firm was flying high, they were also extremely well rewarded. At one point in the fall of 1983, it was estimated that as a result of the large number of shares most People Express employees owned that the average employee's holdings were worth about $40,000. In that regard, the company certainly did create policies that gave employees a genuine stake in the success of the company. But that sudden wealth evaporated when the company's fortunes—and People Express's stock—took a nosedive, causing many of the workers to lose their life's savings. Longtime employees tell horror stories of co-workers who lost their homes and cars. I talked with one woman who had lost well over ten thousand dollars in savings she had invested in People Express stock. She was bitter about the lack of conservative financial advice from the company and the airline's policy of requiring employees to own stock as a condition of employment.

Although many of People Express's problems can be traced to its policies, in the final analysis the basic problems with the airline as a workplace were probably not with the policies themselves. Instead, People Express failed as a viable role model as a place to work because of a more fundamental way in which trust was undermined.

A former People Express employee named Jeff Cohen was interviewed by the *Bergen Record*'s Sid Karpoff several months after the demise of the carrier. Cohen stated the issue sharply:

> I came to People Express because of what they were trying to do: to create a unique environment to work in and for people to fly in. It was a grand experiment that could have worked. But Don Burr let it get away from him. I don't know a single person who worked for People that doesn't feel bitter about what happened and what it could have done to reshape the way corporations treat their people. But now, instead of others pointing to corporate democracy and saying, "See how good it worked," they'll point to People Express and say, "You can't let people have freedom to get their jobs done."

As Cohen points out, the problem was that sad part of the People Express story was ultimately the betrayal of trust. In the conventional labor exchange, the employer agrees to pay employees a specific sum of money for carrying out certain tasks defined by the management. That's the extent of the relationship. Much more was going on at People Express. The airline made a series of promises. It promised employees stimulating work. It promised them they would be part of the "management team." As "manager-owners" rather than "beaten-down workers," top management was promising them that they would have more responsibility for their jobs (and, to some extent, the direction of the company) than in most workplaces. But as we've seen, the reality of working at People Express often didn't match these promises.

The case of People Express illustrates that it's more important what is delivered than what is promised. Or more accurately, it's more important that what is promised is what is delivered.

Another way of putting the same point may sound a bit old-fashioned. A good workplace depends on people's honoring their commitments. At People Express, many employees discovered that broken promises lead to broken dreams.

PUTTING
IT
ALL
TOGETHER

Drawing from the observations and insights from earlier chapters, we can now put forth a fuller framework for analyzing workplaces, that is, explaining why some are so good—and most, so bad.

12
BEYOND A
WORKPLACE
OF "ROBOTS"
A "People" Company

At good workplaces, it's common to hear employees talk about working in "a people-oriented company," or to hear them say, "They treat you like a human being around here." Or, "You feel like you can be yourself." Employees of good workplaces assume that it's a normal part of their working environment to feel like a human being.

What makes such statements significant is that they are usually made by employees who previously worked elsewhere. Dan Malone used to work for a test controls company before joining Federal Express. He now answers customer phone calls in the Memphis office. He reports: "It's a kind of family atmosphere. Everybody is out to help you out. This is a people company." Malone did not find his previous employer to be at all people oriented. You did your job and that was that.

Several years ago, Chicago folklorist Studs Terkel wrote *Working*, the definitive book on work life in contemporary America. According to his chronicle, at least, few workers claim to be working for a "people company." Terkel interviewed 133 people about their jobs and their feelings about work. The book reads like a veritable laundry list of insults, of affronts to self-respect, of adults being treated like children. In his introduction, Terkel observed that work has become synonymous with "daily humiliations." Indignities occur across the board:

> The blue-collar blues is no more bitterly sung than the white-collar moan. "I'm a machine," says the spot-welder. "I'm caged," says the bank teller, and echoes the hotel clerk. "I'm a mule," says the steelworker. "A monkey can do what I do," says the receptionist. "I'm less than a farm implement," says the migrant worker. "I'm an object," says the high-fashion model. Blue-collar and white call upon the identical phrase: "I'm a robot."

The endless round of put-downs takes its toll. Many people feel their humanity is stolen from them at work. That's why they compare themselves to inanimate objects or animals.

If we had to sum up in a word what makes a good workplace good, it's that the people working there feel treated like human beings. They do not experience the constant dehumanization catalogued by Terkel's people. They feel that the workplace brings out what's uniquely human.

Talk about a people company and feeling like a human being may sound too subjective and abstract or too touchy-feely to have much meaning. Yet it obviously does have meaning for those working in good workplaces. So if we are going to understand what makes a great workplace different from others, we need to grapple with what is meant by the concept of human being in the context of workplace relationships. One approach is to distinguish between the concepts of human being and robot. Let's start by listing some of the differences between the two concepts—most of which seem obvious. But they're apparently not obvious enough to be reflected in workplace practices.

• *A human being is unique, not duplicable.* No two human beings are alike. Each person has his or her own quirks of personality. We rebel when our uniqueness goes unappreciated. We each know we're different from anyone else. And at work we are usually intensely aware of ways in which we make distinctive contributions (or could make them if permitted). So when an employee talks about being treated like a machine or a robot, he or she means, in part, that the employer doesn't recognize what makes each individual special.

In her book *Pink Collar Workers*, Louise Kapp Howe gave an example of this point. Howe interviewed several clerical workers at a large insurance company located in downtown Chicago. At one point, the company launched a job-enrichment program. The company considered this an enlightened move, as it was designed to give somewhat more variety and responsibility to the clerical work. But a worker named Diane saw it differently:

> "They seem to think we all want the same thing. I don't think that's true. I think some women, some *people*, want more responsibility and some don't. Some like to work slow and careful and some quick and forget it. Some want to be with other people. Then there are those like me who prefer to work alone. But they act like we're all alike."

Diane is saying that her employer does not recognize that people have individual skills, abilities, and limitations. Nor does her employer recognize that people have their individual likes and dislikes, which affects how effectively they work. Without this recognition, Diane says, the company is not seeing her as a full human being. By contrast, recognizing people's individuality, that they are *not* all alike, is a key feature of good workplaces.

At the same time, good workplaces recognize that a company with five hundred employees does not have just one relationship with employees. It has five hundred different relationships with employees. People notice when they are not treated individually. Sure, company-wide pay and benefits policies contribute significantly to the overall tenor of a workplace. If people feel they are underpaid, they will probably feel exploited no matter what an employer does. But in addition to overall policies, people note the little things—the pat on the back for doing a good job, the unsolicited (if genuine) inquiries about one's family, the willingness of top company officials to talk informally with employees.

Such acts indicate that the company cares, respects, and values *people as people. The 100 Best Companies to Work for in America* cites scores of these institutionalized little things: from the free taxi ride home that Time Inc. offers staffers who work overtime to the personal birthday cards Mary Kay sends employees to Federal Express's naming each of its new airplanes after the child of an employee (picked by lottery) to the twenty-fifth-anniversary parties at Hallmark, where an employee can invite any of his or her friends throughout the company and which are usually attended by the company chairman.

- *A human being is self-determining, not programmable.* A human being can initiate and control his or her own actions. We feed ourselves, clothe ourselves, move ourselves from place to place, and so on. We determine what we are going to do, when we're going to do it, and how it is to be done. That doesn't mean that we ever exist in a state of pure freedom. There are frequently social constraints on our actions. And there are lots of limitations in any workplace. When you work for others, you aren't entirely free to do what you want to do from day to day—or in some cases, from minute to minute. Like any society, each organization imposes implicit and explicit restrictions on its members. The objectives and priorities of the organization must be accommodated. But workplaces vary greatly in the extent to which individuals feel they are in control of their own actions. In the workplace, being in control depends on *participation*, having an active say in how you do your job. People who feel like a robot are suggesting they feel no latitude for their own initiative. They are merely following orders, with no ability to do tasks as they wish to do them. They are controlled, programmed by others.

The controlled workplace environment takes its toll on human beings. In *The Work/Stress Connection*, Robert L. Veninga and James P. Spradley cite unnecessary organizational rules as a major reason for job burnout. They write:

> With the growth of large industrial organizations, rules to control the mass of workers have become commonplace. . . . Often aimed at the rank-and-file worker, stringent rules are made on the assumption that you will work more efficiently with close supervision and narrow boundaries. . . . Although the pinch of rules doesn't squeeze all workers in the same way, many feel restricted that their jobs seem to be a dead end.

When people are stifled, their health often suffers. The National Institute of Occupational Safety and Health recently cited lack of control over one's work as a major factor in work-related stress, which contributes to hypertension, heart disease, ulcers, and depression. One work-related-stress researcher puts a price tag to American industry of $150 billion in annual losses because of stress-connected absenteeism, reduced productivity, and medical fees.

Not all people react to being frustrated by turning inward, which can cause personal health problems. Some turn outward in revolt against those who are causing the frustration. Aside from the obvious examples of worker sabotage (a common occurrence among frustrated assembly-line workers), many people engage in personal slowdowns, expressing their revolt silently.

No one tracks the positive impact of a positive work environment—where people have more of a sense of control over their destiny. It's difficult to measure the value of a fulfilled life.

• *A human being is capable of intelligence and has an emotional life.* Mike Lefevre works in a steel mill near Chicago. He told Studs Terkel: "The first thing that happens at work: When the arms start moving, the brain stops." Many employees believe there is no point to thinking on the job. They are told repeatedly that they are "not paid to think." Nobody is interested in their opinions. Nobody wants to know whether they have any ideas about how to improve the work process, as they are assumed not to have any. But it goes deeper than that. Nobody cares about their feelings. People are often thought of as mere appendages to the machines they work with. The emotions that drive them, their dreams, their ambitions, their concerns about their families are considered, at best, irrelevant to the job.

Barbara Garson describes an incident involving an insurance company clerk named Ellen in *All the Livelong Day: The Meaning and Demeaning of Routine Work.* Ellen noticed a discrepancy on one of the forms she was typing. Because numbers had been placed on the wrong lines of a store owner's policy, his store was insured for $165,000 against vandalism but only $5,000 against fire. For the sake of the store owner,

Ellen wanted to tell her supervisor of the error. But she immediately thought better of it:

> "Wait a minute! I'm not supposed to read these forms. I'm just supposed to check one column against another.... If they're gonna give me a robot's job to do, I'm gonna do it like a robot."

Ellen's reaction was a common one. If treated like a non-thinking creature, many workers act that way—to the detriment of not only the company, but also of themselves. There is another familiar reaction, however. When author Garson checked later with Ellen, she discovered that the young clerk had told her supervisor about the error after all. As Garson noted: "For most people it is hard and uncomfortable to do a bad job. . . . Work is a human need following right after the need for food and the need for love."

Garson's point is well taken. People are often treated as if they are mindless, but their sense of dignity often refuses to let them play the roles they are given. Even though the workplace often dehumanizes people in this way, they find countless means to hold on to their sense of self-worth. Sometimes they do it by inventing games with themselves to make the work itself more interesting. Or they daydream on the job. Or they socialize with others. Or they find ways of subverting the boss. One way or another, people do use their mind and show their feelings. In bad workplaces, people's expressions of themselves can frequently be destructive. In better workplaces, employees can channel their intelligence and emotions constructively.

• *A human being grows and learns; a robot is limited by its programs.* From birth on, a human being grows. We never stop learning. We acquire more knowledge and skills. We become capable of doing increasingly complex things. As we've seen, scientific management, as exemplified by the assembly line, makes no provisions for this aspect of human beings. Workers are to fit into preordained slots. There is no provision for them to gain more responsibility as they become increasingly competent at their jobs. Responsibility is in the hands of management alone.

In good workplaces, human growth is part of the system. Jobs are expanded as people gain more skill. People are given more responsibility as they grow. A promotion-from-within policy communicates that personal growth is rewarded. There's also a recognition that jobs must often be fitted to people rather than the other way around. Employees at good workplaces often remark that there are no rigid job descriptions in their company because people grow in unexpected ways. Growth is encouraged, too, by the emphasis on training at good workplaces, often including subsidized college-level education.

Trust as Alchemist

The following chart sums up this distinction between people and robots:

ROBOT	HUMAN BEING
1. duplicable and disposable	1. unique and irreplaceable
2. programmable	2. self-determining
3. devoid of thoughts or feelings	3. rational and emotional
4. inherently limited	4. capable of growth

The notable thing about the list of attributes under "Human Being" is that all of them become assets when trust enters the picture and liabilities when there is distrust. Take the rational and emotional nature of humans, for example. When trusted, a human being can use intelligence to deal with unforeseen problems. The emotions come into play when we "warm to a task," and the job gets done faster and better. If, on the other hand, we are distrusted and expected to perform a task a certain way no matter what, intelligence become a nuisance, a distracting voice that says, "Try a different approach." The emotions rebel, draining our energy away.

The best workplaces not only treat people as their most important assets, but they also learn how to call forth the best attributes from what a human being is—a creature that flourishes with trust. Conversely, to withhold trust is to dehumanize and to bring out the worst in people.

Social scientists have preferred to blame other factors for the demoralized, dehumanized workplace chronicled by Terkel and many others. Some have pointed the finger at the Industrial Revolution and the consequent subordination of workers to machines. Automation certainly ought to be considered a major contributing factor, as is obvious in the work of auto workers and steelworkers like Mike Lefevre. Machines also dominate the working lives of countless white- and pink-collar workers. For instance, Studs Terkel interviewed Sharon Atkins, a receptionist "at a large business establishment in the Midwest." Atkins echoed the complaints that have been voiced by thousands of workers since the inception of the machine age:

> "The machine dictates. This crummy little machine with buttons on it—you've got to be there to answer it. You can walk away from it and pretend you don't hear it, but it pulls you. You know you're not doing anything, not doing a hell of a lot for anyone. Your job doesn't mean anything. Because you're just a little machine. A monkey could do what I do. It's really unfair to ask someone to do that. . . . You're there just to handle the equipment. You're treated like a piece of equipment, like the telephone."

The profit motive is also often blamed for workplace discontent. In Marxist terms, the capitalist system reduces workers to the status of commodities. To obtain ever higher profits, the capitalists inevitably resort to exploiting the workers. This analysis, too, has its merits. There are lots of notable examples of greedy exploitative employers.

Still others have suggested that large-scale bureaucratic organizations are inherently dehumanizing. In his classic book *Small Is Beautiful*, E. F. Schumacher writes:

> Nobody really likes large-scale organization; nobody likes to take orders from a superior who takes orders from a superior who takes orders . . . Even if the rules devised by bureaucracy are outstandingly humane, nobody likes to be ruled by rules, that is to say, by people whose answer to every complaint is: "I did not make the rules: I am merely applying them."

Each of the three factors listed above—the machine age, the profit motive, and large-scale bureaucracies—takes its toll. But how is it that good workplaces manage to exist despite the conditions described above? They exist in industries where employees work with machines. Steelworkers at Worthington and Nucor, factory hands at Fisher-Price Toys, insurance clerks at Northwestern Mutual Life prove that you can work with machines all day without feeling like one yourself. Good workplaces exist in companies that are highly profitable. In fact, as will be discussed later, good employers often are more profitable than their competitors. And good workplaces exist in large-scale organizations.

All my experience visiting and researching workplaces has led me to believe that where mutual trust exists, it functions at a deeper level to offset the realities that tend to dehumanize. In other words, the presence or absence of trust is the most powerful influence in any workplace.

13
TRUST
AT WORK

The Difference Between
Commodity and Gift Interactions

During the Iran-contra hearings in the summer of 1987, Secretary of State George Shultz told of an incident early in his Washington career when his mentor told him that to get along in the capital Shultz should always remember that "trust is the coin of the realm."

The same might be said of workplaces. Trust is the currency of good workplace relationships. Without trust, the workplace can easily become dehumanized. Employees feel detached from their work; they feel like robots. But with trust, workplace relationships can flourish. People can feel more pride in what they do and achieve deeper enjoyment from relationships with others with whom they work.

Despite trust's importance to workplace relationships, it has rarely been addressed as such by those writing about the workplace. So the following discussion about trust puts us into largely uncharted territory. As an initial effort to unravel this most elusive ingredient of good workplace relationships, this chapter can be no more than a sketch of a fuller theory about trust in the workplace. But it's a start.

A Story About Trust

Quad/Graphics prints dozens of major national magazines ranging from *Time* and *Newsweek* to *Black Enterprise*, *Playboy*, and the *Atlantic Monthly*. Founded in 1971, Quad has grown rapidly, becoming the nation's largest national weekly magazine printer with 1987 sales in excess of $400 million. Its presses run around the clock, seven days a week, rolling off more than three million magazines a day at the rate of twenty million pages an hour. Each of Quad's twenty-nine state-of-the-art web presses is worth nearly $6 million; its three gravure presses, $10 million. Because of the speed of the presses and the value of the equipment, a relatively minor mistake can cost thousands of dollars; major ones can cost tens of thousands.

Once a year, Quad's four hundred managers and supervisors leave the printing plants entirely in the hands of the three thousand workers. The reason: Quad's annual "spring fling." When the company was smaller, the spring fling was a one-day event during which the managers held a retreat at the lakefront summer house of company founder Larry Quadracci. You might think the spring fling would have been discarded as the company grew larger and mistakes could cost more money. Starting in 1986, however, the company expanded the spring fling into a two-day, three-evening affair, including seminars at a local college. During the entire period of time, none of the managers is to set foot inside the printing plants unless an employee makes a request for emergency help. No manager has ever been called in.

Quad's spring fling matches our commonsense notion about what trust is all about. We would say that, at least on those two days a year, Quad trusts its employees. Because it's such a graphic example, let's look more closely at what's going on here.

Trust implies risk. When the managers let the workers run plants, they relinquish operational control over the business. This makes the company vulnerable. The workers can perform their jobs as usual but they can also goof off or conceivably even sabotage some of the plant's machinery. Even if the workers don't create problems, something unforeseen could happen about which the workers on duty might make bad decisions, costing the company money. There is no way around it—the company is taking a risk. As Quadracci says, "We trust them, but we also hope the mistakes will be small ones."

The risks involved in trust aren't undertaken blindly. If Quad didn't have good reason to believe the workers could handle the printing presses on their own, the managers would be fools to walk away. Trust is, in other words, a calculated risk made with one's eyes open to the possibilities of failure, but it is extended with the expectation of success.

Finally, an act of trust, like Quad's spring fling, promotes a kind of social bonding with which most of us are familiar. By bestowing trust, the company is in effect saying that the employees are a vital part of the business. It creates a new kind of relationship with the employees, blurring a rigid distinction between management and employee. An act of trust suggests that both are part of the same team. The spring fling has the effect of making both sides reevaluate their own roles and their relationships with each other. The managers see that their role should not merely be one of hovering over the workers, and the workers come to appreciate more of the managers' day-to-day responsibilities that free the workers of many concerns, allowing them to concentrate on doing their own work well. If things go as expected, both sides feel strengthened and grow from the experience. Growth is possible because both sides care about the relationship itself. Because each side respects what the other brings to the relationship, both feel it important to strengthen the bond between them.

From this example, we can see that what may appear to be a straightforward act of trust is exceedingly complex. It involves risk and vulnerability. It involves judgments about other people's attitudes and abilities. It involves questions of power and control. Trust is not extended lightly. It is, however, part of the fabric of some good workplaces as can be inferred from the Quad/Graphics company credo.

Trust in Trust at Quad/Graphics

- The Trust of Teamwork. Employees trust that together they will do better than as individuals apart.
- The Trust of Responsibility. Employers trust that each will carry his/her fair share of the load.

- The Trust of Productivity. Customers trust that work will be produced to the most competitive levels of pricing, quality and innovation.
- The Trust of Management. Shareholders, customers and employees trust that the company will make decisive judgments for the long-term rather than the short-term goals or today's profit.
- The Trust of Think-Small. We all trust in each other: we regard each other as persons of equal rank; we respect the dignity of the individual by recognizing not only the individual accomplishments, but the feelings and needs of the individual and family as well; and we all share the same goals and purposes in life.

Building the Trust Reservoir

Trust doesn't just happen. It's the product of what has happened within the workplace over time. In this regard, trust in workplace relationships is no different from trust in personal relationships. Certain acts seem to add to the quantity of trust we feel toward another person, while other acts reduce it. We're all familiar with this process. If somebody fails to return a book we've loaned them, our level of trust in that person may be affected. Similarly, if we tell someone a secret and that person respects our confidence, our level of trust in that person may increase.

One way of describing this phenomenon is to talk in terms of a *trust reservoir*.

Consider the following illustration. Before the radical transformation at Preston Trucking described earlier, the company commissioned an outside consulting firm to conduct a survey. At the York, Pennsylvania, terminal an employee offered this assessment of the typical career pattern of a Preston employee:

First, the new employee starts out eager to please and a hard worker. Second, after his probationary period, he continues to be an industrious worker. Third, after a time the lack of any praise, or even opinion of his work, and the negative attitudes of his fellow veteran employees who've already gone through the same thing takes its toll, and he begins to slack off. He becomes lackadaisical about his performance. He forms the opinion that if the company doesn't give a damn, why should he. Fourth, by this time he has reached the crossroads. He can (a) revamp his performance and try to influence the company by his positive attitude, or (b) just put in his time and no more than that. Unfortunately, (b) is too often the common choice because (a) never seems to do any good.

The feelings expressed by the Preston employee are familiar indeed. We could interpret his description in the following way: The worker joins the company with his trust reservoir at a high level. He wants to do a good job. He's even willing to extend himself beyond the narrow definitions of a job description. He assumes that the employer can be trusted to recognize and reward him for his commitment and loyalty. Little by little, as his expectations are not met, the employee perceives that the employer doesn't care about him. The worker's trust reservoir gets depleted. Finally, he stops extending himself. Without trust, the worker feels that the only kind of relationship which makes sense is the one offered by the company—a straightforward commercial transaction where he puts in his hours and takes home a paycheck. Subjectively, he feels dehumanized, like a robot.

After such an experience, many employees simply assume the worst and expect no more than a robotized existence on the job. The most common reaction to the erosion of one's trust reservoir is cynical emotional withdrawal at work. But sometimes workers react by striking back, trying to regain the human dignity that is stripped by the reality of a trustless workplace. Union-organizing drives, for instance, can typically be traced to the erosion of trust. In every organizing drive I've observed as a labor reporter, workers express a sense of betrayal. Unionizing drives are usually precipitated by a noteworthy event—an unjust firing or an arbitrary change in the work rules or benefits. That event, or series of events, typically convinces employees that they need to force the relationship with the employer into a more formal mode—specifically in the form of a union contract. No longer can the employer's word be trusted. Workers invariably assert that they can no longer rely on the employer to look after their best interests. That's why they turn to the union for protection.

In his most recent book, *Tales of a New America*, Robert B.

Reich describes what happens when trust breaks down in society:

> This systemic erosion of trust precipitates all manner of pre-
> cautions. Commercial dealings are hedged about by ever more
> elaborate contracts. There is a proliferation of work rules, codes,
> and standards to be followed. Requirements and expectations
> are well documented in advance; enforcement procedures are
> minutely delineated.

Reich's observation applies directly to what commonly happens in the workplace. Besides pushing the relationships toward a more formal mode, the erosion of trust can be seen as
the root of various other pathologies—such as higher levels of
personal stress and lower productivity.

Let's consider the opposite process, when trust reservoirs
are augmented. That's what happened at Preston Trucking in
the years after the interview cited earlier. It's also what happens in great workplaces. In fact, the constant replenishing of
trust reservoirs is the single most distinguishing characteristic
of great workplaces. Employees recognize that the company
cares about them and respects them. This recognition makes
them feel freer to commit themselves to the relationship and
to their work for the company. At the same time, the company
sees that the risks it has taken (its willingness to reward and
recognize work, the willingness to give more control to the
employees) have met the company's expectations. Meeting
their expectations makes the company willing to extend itself
even more to employees. These kinds of interactions build the
trust reservoirs that can help the relationship survive the difficult times that any company (or relationship) goes through
because of outside pressures. This dynamic provides a good
foundation for future interactions. It's what makes a good
workplace good.

Gifts and Commodities

How do great workplaces build up trust reservoirs? To answer
that question we need to look more closely at the nature of
interactions that build trust. Because of certain kinds of in-

teractions, employees of better workplaces often talk about
feeling that they have "more than a job" and about feeling part
of a "family" or "partnership." At the same time, other interactions in good workplaces are not totally unlike what happens
in other companies. Employees put in hours on the job and
take home paychecks to provide for themselves and their families. Looking at a good workplace from the viewpoint of employees, it's as if employees regularly participate in two
distinct types of exchanges or interactions—one familiar to
any workplace and another that is peculiarly related to good
workplaces. Put another way, it's as if employees are operating
on two different levels simultaneously.

Not long ago I came across a book that helped me appreciate
what makes good workplaces tick. In *The Gift*, poet and es-
sayist Lewis Hyde provides an explanation for the place of
creativity in our market-oriented society. Hyde puts forth the
idea that a work of art is a gift rather than a commodity. Works
of art, therefore, exist in two parallel economies—the market
economy and the gift economy. The market economy is gov-
erned by the law of supply and demand. A painting, for example, may be sold for a thousand dollars at an auction. But
the painting also has a separate life as a gift. Aside from the
subjective aspect of the artist's gift (or talent) needed to create
the work, those who view the work consider it a gift:

> That art that matters to us—which moves the heart, or revives
> the soul, or delights the senses, or offers courage for the living,
> however we choose to describe the experience—that work is
> received by us as a gift is received. Even if we have paid a fee
> at the door of a museum or concert hall, when we are touched
> by a work of art something comes to us which has nothing to
> do with the price. . . . The work appeals, as Joseph Conrad says,
> to a part of our being which is itself a gift and not an acquisition.

Anthropologists have written extensively about the customs
and mores of the gift economy, which predates money or even
barter. In the typical gift exchange, acceptance of a gift obliges
the recipient to certain implied duties. Often the recipient is
obliged to give a gift in return; sometimes the obligation may
only be that of being friendly or expressing appreciation or

goodwill to the gift giver. In all cases, there is a distinct social bond created whenever gifts are exchanged. As Hyde puts it: "It is the cardinal difference between gift and commodity exchange that a gift establishes a feeling-bond between two people, while the sale of a commodity leaves no necessary connection." Both sides recognize that whenever a gift is given, the giver is giving part of himself or herself, which helps to explain the basis for the "feeling-bond" between parties of a gift exchange.

While reading Hyde, I was struck by the similarities between what happens in great workplaces and his description of the operation of a gift economy. Interactions between company and employees are acted out according to implicit rules that both sides understand as being somewhat like the unstated rules of gift exchanges. When the Preston driver described in Chapter 10 offered to take over the American Honda account, he did so as if he were offering the company a gift—his creative work. It was not a tit-for-tat offer where the worker was saying he would be willing to do more work if he received more money. The company recognized the nature of his suggestion and responded appropriately. His manager not only gave the driver the appropriate equipment and time to do the task, but he expressed appreciation in a variety of ways for the gift that had been offered.

The analogy of the gift economy strikes a resonant chord for another important reason: *Human work is not just a commodity.* What struck the Preston workers most strongly about the company's transformation was that the management no longer treated them as if they only offered a commodity—time on the job. That is, before the changes, the company related to the workers purely in terms of a simple time-for-money exchange. Much of that exchange was spelled out in detail in the Teamsters' contract between the two sides. Work, on the other hand, cannot be so carefully circumscribed. Work encompasses individual initiative and creativity. When people work, as opposed to merely laboring for money, they are offering part of what they consider their individual essence, part of what distinguishes them as human beings. Employers who recognize this dimension of work effectively communicate that they recognize that their workers possess those human, nonrobotlike

qualities, which we spelled out in the previous chapter—
unique, self-determining, rational and emotional, and capable
of growth.

Note, however, that it is precisely the giftlike nature of work
which allows an insensitive employer to completely ignore
the human element of his relationship with the workers: A gift
can be refused. There is an element of free will attached to the
offering or acceptance of gifts. If a company refuses to accept
the work freely offered by its employees, it is entirely free to
do so. Indeed, generations of management ideology has encouraged employers to blind themselves to anything but the
commodity aspect of work. The Preston worker at the York
terminal quoted earlier in the chapter described what it is like
for an employee to have his work gift ignored by the employer.
What makes good workplaces special is that the company recognizes the possibilities of giftlike exchanges with employees
and actively cultivates those interactions.

This distinction between commoditylike and giftlike work
helps us to understand the two levels of interaction at great
workplaces. The exchange of gift work is *not* a substitute for
the straightforward agreement between a company and an employee to do a certain job for a specified amount of pay, that
is, a commodity exchange. Rather, gift work coexists with that
level. In other words, commoditylike and giftlike exchanges
of work are not mutually exclusive ideas. They represent two
different aspects of work life. They are distinct modes of exchange within the workplace.

We could briefly sketch some of the major differences between these two types of workplace interaction:

In commodity interactions, both sides give up something to
receive something else roughly equivalent in value. The
worker gives up forty hours of work and receives a weekly
paycheck in return. By contrast, giftlike exchanges are more
complicated because they rely on the extension of trust. The
essence of the trust is that one side gives up something without
having a guarantee about what, if anything, it will receive in
return. So, for instance, in Quad/Graphics' spring fling, the
company has its expectations of trustworthiness, but there's
an element of risk involved that doesn't exist in simple one-
for-one exchanges.

Another significant difference: If something goes wrong in

a commoditylike exchange, adjustments can be made based on the terms of the original exchange. If an employee is an hour late, his or her paycheck can be docked by an hour. Not so in a work exchange where trust is involved. In the Quad/ Graphics example, let's say a press crew decided not to produce as usual and intentionally failed to print thousands of copies of a big order (something the management could never prove) because they wanted to go fishing instead. There's no adequate remedy for the wrong. If someone violates trust, the other party may consider itself betrayed—a highly charged term. A feeling of betrayal invariably affects the relationship with the person who took advantage of one's vulnerability.

Part of the reason for the feeling of betrayal is that trust occurs within the context of open-ended relationships. This presents another sharp distinction with one-shot, commodity exchanges. Both parties in the commodity exchange always have other options. The printer can always hire others to hire other workers, and the workers can quit and look for work elsewhere. Giftlike interactions suggest, on the other hand, an ongoing relationship. From our example about the spring fling, the pressmen cannot assume that there would be a limit to how long the management's feelings might be affected. The management may well be upset with the delinquent press workers if it discovers years later that the workers had betrayed their confidence.

There is one other significant difference between gift and commodity exchanges. In a commodity transaction, the terms for the exchange are generally available to all. The $10 hourly wage will be available to anyone willing to do the job. This is part of the employment relationship at Quad/Graphics or any other workplace, good or bad. An exchange involving trust is different. The terms can vary completely depending on who is involved and what is at stake. The management doesn't just turn over the printing plants to the first person who comes along. Quad spent years training the workers before they placed trust in their technical competence. A trust interaction, then, is highly individualized, highly personalized.

The highly personalized nature of trust is perhaps more clearly understood if we step back to compare the dynamics of a commodity exchange versus the dynamics of a gift exchange. In the commodity exchange the rules of the game are clear: both sides give up as little as possible while trying to extract the maximum value from the exchange. Classic economic theory is based on the assumption that everyone plays this game of enlightened self-interest. Adam Smith, among others, claimed that the greatest good for all comes from everyone's following his or her self-interest.

Giftlike interactions dictate a different set of rules. They are not competitive games, with each side trying to maximize itself at the other's expense. Rather than seeking individual gain, giftlike interactions require both sides to give up things that are in their power to withhold. Each side is willing to give up something because it trusts that the other side will recognize its sacrifice as a gift toward building something in common, a better relationship. As Hyde explains, giftlike interactions assume that "it is not when part of the self is inhibited and restrained, but when a part of the self is given away that community appears." Because the ensuing community, or better relationship, is founded on trust, a giftlike relationship exists only so long as both sides are willing to trust each other and continue to give. That's why trust is the basic currency of giftlike interactions, just as money is the fundamental medium of exchange in commoditylike interactions. Just as commodity exchanges require money, giftlike interactions demand trust. By the same token, the more trust that exists (the larger the trust reservoirs), the more the parties are able to participate in giftlike interactions and build a stronger relationship.

The dynamics described above have special relevance to the workplace. As the relationship between the parties grows, the parties can do things together that are not possible otherwise. In other words, trust heightens the ability of people to cooperate with each other. Achieving the cooperation of the workers has, of course, been an objective of management for generations, since the days of Frederick Taylor, as we saw in earlier chapters. But management theory has, almost entirely, sought to achieve that cooperation through a commodity-type interaction with employees. Or to put it more precisely, many management theorists, especially those espousing various motivation techniques, try to get the employees to give up part of themselves for the common good without sacrificing any management power. The fact that only one side is playing according to the rules of the gift-type exchange is why motivational techniques are often viewed with such distrust by employees. Both sides have to willingly and freely participate in gift-type interactions for genuine cooperation to exist. It's the willingness of managements of good workplaces to engage in gift-type interactions that distinguishes them.

The accompanying chart sums up the differences between the two types of interactions:

CHARACTERISTICS OF:

COMMODITY INTERACTIONS	GIFT/TRUST INTERACTIONS
One-for-one exchange	Varying responses possible
Low risk	High risk
Easy to rectify bad exchanges	Betrayals hard to repair
Relationship must be renewed after each exchange	Open-ended relationship
Terms available to all	Terms highly personalized
Each side maximizes its advantage at expense of other side	Both sides give up something for common goal
Goal is individual advantage	Goal is mutual growth
Currency is money	Currency is trust

Making Work into a Commodity

Because of its obvious advantages in achieving cooperation, giftlike exchanges ought to be extremely common in the workplace. Yet in many workplaces, giftlike transactions are virtually nonexistent. How can this anomaly be explained? There is a good historical explanation. According to anthropological studies of the evolution of the market, the gift economy represented the first form of exchange among peoples. Over time, barter was introduced, followed by the money economy that dominates today. To make this transition, the items of exchange had to be objectified. When one tribe offered its fish to another in a gift economy, everyone understood that the fish carried with it something of the giver. That's why accepting the gift implied entering into a relationship with the giver. By the time the full-blown market economy came into

being, however, buying fish no longer carried any obligations
to the seller. That's because the fish had become a commodity,
an object of exchange, with a monetary value determined by
the law of supply and demand. The market economy requires
commodities—impersonal objects—to function.

Work cannot be so easily objectified. In a 1926 book sur-
veying the evolution of the market economy entitled *Primitive
Trade*, economist Elizabeth Ellis Holt discussed the difference
between the exchange of goods and the exchange of services
(people's work):

> ... an object or article of exchange may be regarded as a thing
> merely, but a service can never be entirely disassociated in
> thought from the individual who performs it. His presence is
> a continual reminder of the personal element in service.

We could somewhat unfairly suggest that some managements
act as if the presence of their employees doesn't seem to remind
them of the "personal element." Some employers seem to have
had no difficulty making a complete transition to a market
economy even when people are involved. Or, in our terms,
they operate as if the completely objectified, time-for-money
commodity exchange is the only reality of the workplace, completely ignoring the elements of the giftlike work exchange.

Certain companies are not the only ones who act as if the
relationship with employees can be treated like other forms
of commodity exchange. Economists and management theorists have generally ignored giftlike work (as opposed to time-
for-money labor) as a valid subject of study. This helps explain
the lack of concepts to appraise companies as workplaces
rather than as businesses. Economists have developed elaborate models to describe how the labor exchange operates, using
such concepts as the law of supply and demand to explain
pay scales. Similarly, management theorists have done the
same when looking at the workplace. With productivity as
their standard of value, they have claimed that if management
puts in a new form of compensation and benefit package or
adopts the latest motivational technique, the employees will
produce more at a faster rate than before. Even the most enlightened management theorists, as we saw in earlier chapters,
typically place their motivational techniques (often using

words like "trust" and "pride") squarely within the context of financial success. The financial bottom line remains the only bottom line. The interactions between the company and the employees are evaluated solely in terms of a cost-benefit analysis. Hence the workplace is ultimately seen through the accountant's prism, reducing the employee's contribution to an interchangeable commodity, totally ignoring or distorting an important aspect of workplace relationships.

There is, of course, some merit in evaluating workplaces according to various financial and productivity yardsticks. Commodity exchanges represent *one* reality of the workplace. People do spend time on the job in exchange for money. But the commodity-type labor exchange is not the *only* reality. As we've seen throughout this book, great workplaces have distinctive patterns of interaction. The maintenance and growth of trust between the employer and employees is a central concept. So is the need for pride in one's job and the sense of enjoyment of the relationships with others one works with. The lexicon of the time-for-money commodity exchange has no entries for the elements of trust, pride, or fun. Those qualities cannot be produced through a simple tit-for-tat, commodity-type exchange. Such qualities can only be nurtured through giftlike interactions that bring out that which is most distinctively human in both sides of the employment relationship.

14
WHAT MAKES
SOME
WORKPLACES
SO GOOD

"People are our most important
asset." Organizations throughout the land welcome newly
hired employees with variations of this slogan. Orientation
sessions and employee handbooks convey the same message:
"This company values you as a person." "You are important
to this company." "You can rely on us to look after your best
interests because we care about you." Unfortunately, such sen-
timents often bear little resemblance to the reality of the workplace. Employees at many companies correctly conclude that
such platitudes have been lifted from a business-school text-
book on human relations.

To complicate matters, genuinely good employers greet their
new employees with similar declarations. Advanced Micro
Devices has long used the slogan "People first, products and
profits will follow." IBM's employee handbook proclaims that
"respect for the individual" is the first tenet of its business.
And Publix Super Markets has plastered its stores with banners
saying "Publix People Make the Difference."

The problem is that almost all organizations would like to
convince employees (and potential employees) that they are
good bosses, that they care about their people. Many companies sincerely intend to create a good place to work. As time
passes, the pressures of the marketplace tend to open a gap
between a company's good intentions and the reality of work

life. So you can't evaluate workplaces merely by listening to company slogans.

The best way to judge a place to work is to visit the company and talk with employees. That's the only sure way to find out what it's really like to work there, and it's the method my coauthors and I adopted to research *The 100 Best Companies to Work for in America*. The best way is not, however, always the easiest way or the most practical.

Another approach is to see what can be learned from a company's personnel policies and practices. It isn't the presence or absence of specific policies, however, that determines whether a company is a good place to work. It's what those policies say about the nature of the workplace relationships. In examining policies and practices, we can see that they have a double life in that they operate on two distinct levels. On the base-line level, which we are calling the commodity level, policies represent a straightforward time-for-money agreement between the employer and employees. But any policy simultaneously makes a statement on the trust level that conveys information about the company's underlying attitudes. Our focus is on the trust level. Some policies broadcast a message that undermines trust, while others build up trust by acknowledging the giftlike aspect of human work. Great places to work are characterized by the latter—with policies and practices that consistently increase the amount of trust in workplace relationships.

Let's look at a variety of workplace policies to see how evaluating workplaces by this method works:

Terms of Employment

There are two elements of the basic workplace exchange—time and money. The basic terms of employment, then, are policies concerned with that exchange. In particular, they include a company's compensation policies and policies it may or may not have regarding job security.

Time is what employees have to give. By taking a job, they make a major sacrifice. They give the company the bulk of their waking hours and much of their productive energy. All leisure activities must be shoehorned into the rest of the day or into their days off from work. Employees also give a great deal of themselves to the job, whether or not they fully intend to. It's no wonder that the job is the primary way in which people are identified socially; that is, as carpenters, bankers, or secretaries. There is no getting around the fact that a job, even a lousy one, represents a significant personal commitment in terms of time, energy, and sense of self.

On the most elementary level, good workplaces make sure to hold up the company's end of the time-for-money exchange by establishing wage-and-benefits compensation that is considered fair and equitable. Most good workplaces have a reputation for paying well. Some, like Trammell Crow and Goldman Sachs, pay their people exceptionally well. But building trust isn't determined by the size of paychecks alone, though paying well can go a long way to making people feel that their personal sacrifices are appreciated. What's important is that the company is fair and is making an honest attempt to pay as much as the company can afford. That's why it's difficult for employees to feel that theirs is a good place to work unless their firm pays at least as well as comparable firms in the same industry or part of the country. Unusual benefits or opportunities have little effect in the long run if the company appears to be taking financial advantage of employees. Unfairness in the basic time-for-money exchange poisons the trust reservoir.

Good workplaces also see that the employees' commitment of time requires more than decent wages and benefits. Many good workplaces also make a commitment of their own—job security. Nearly a third of the *100 Best* companies, for instance, have no-layoff policies or state explicitly that they will attempt to maintain full employment unless, as Federal Express's Fred Smith puts it, the company is "at death's door." Smith is not referring to major changes in corporate strategy, either. In 1986, the company eliminated Zap Mail without zapping any of the hundreds of employees who worked directly or indirectly on its money-losing electronic mail service. All were reassigned elsewhere in the company. Other firms with no-layoff policies include Delta Air Lines, Digital Equipment, Hallmark Cards, Hewlett-Packard, IBM, and Johnson Wax. A no-layoff policy makes a powerful statement on the trust level. It says that the company considers that it has a *relationship* with employees,

CHECKLIST FOR A GREAT PLACE TO WORK

Basic Terms of Employment

1. Fair pay and benefits:
   a. compare well with similar employers
   b. square with company's ability to pay
2. Commitment to job security
3. Commitment to safe and attractive working environment

The Job

1. Maximizes individual responsibility for how job is done
2. Flexibility about working hours
3. Opportunities for growth:
   a. promotes from within
   b. provides training
   c. recognizes mistakes as part of learning

Workplace Rules

1. Reduces social and economic distinctions between management and other employees
2. Right to due process
3. Right to information
4. Right to free speech
5. Right to confront those in authority
6. Right *not* to be part of the family/team

Stake in Success

1. Shares rewards from productivity improvements
2. Shares profits
3. Shares ownership
4. Shares recognition

NOTE: A great workplace cannot be equated with the presence or absence of a particular set of policies or practices. *What's* important is the quality of the relationship that gets developed between the company and its employees. With that in mind, we can use this checklist as a way of taking the pulse of a company's workplace relationships. Great places to work tend to have most or all of the attributes listed above.

not merely an agreement to pay employees for the time they spend on the job. It says that the relationship is a serious one— like a marriage rather than a one-night stand.

Companies that are willing to make a long-term commitment to employees stand in stark contrast to most companies of the contemporary corporate world. At the first sign of trouble, many companies pare their payrolls, making clear that any relationship with employees is one of convenience at best. Hundreds of thousands, even millions, of workers get laid off whenever there is the slightest downturn in the economy. But it doesn't even require an economic recession or depression to precipitate layoffs. In the past few years, more than a half million American workers have been thrown out of their jobs as a result of what is known as corporate restructurings— mostly changes brought on by takeovers or mergers engineered by financial speculators. These speculators may have purchased a perfectly healthy company but they quickly gut it of many of its most valued employees. Such tactics are justified because they provide short-term profits. Employees as such show up only as liabilities, not assets, on financial balance sheets.

Takeover artists and corporate executives are perfectly within their legal rights to throw long-term employees out of their jobs. In fact, American law states clearly that employees have no reason to expect any kind of long-term relationship with any company. At the turn of this century, American courts enunciated a doctrine called "employment at will." It assumes that the employee and the employer are essentially equals in a free labor market. Just as workers are free to sell their labor for whatever price they can get, a company has the right to prescribe the conditions of the employment. If workers don't like the conditions, they are free to go elsewhere. By the same token, if the company doesn't like the way a worker is performing, it can fire the worker and find someone else from the labor market who will perform as desired. According to this doctrine, the only obligations either party has to the other are whatever agreements they make with each other. In a legal sense, then, the employee-employer relationship is defined only by their contract with each other. But the great bulk of American workers are not unionized and do not have individual employment contracts. Even in unionized companies, the company has few, if any, restrictions on its right to lay off employees. With few exceptions, union contracts only generally spell out how layoffs are to be accomplished; that is, who gets laid off first. So the at-will doctrine means a firm's management is under no obligation to maintain employment. In this context, it's all the more notable that some companies go out of the way to make a commitment toward job security.

There's another good reason a no-layoff policy helps build trust. It implies that the company is willing to impose a burden on itself for the sake of its relationship with employees. That is, there's some risk involved which, as we saw in the previous chapter, denotes a principal ingredient of trust. At Hallmark Cards, J. D. Goodwin, a plant manager in Kansas City, explains, "Our attitude is that when we have a downturn, it's the managers who have a problem. It shouldn't be an employee problem." This is not merely rhetoric, either. During the recession of 1981–82, Hallmark loaned about six hundred production employees to other departments to do a variety of jobs (such as repainting) and even had a crew of workers do volunteer work, for which they were paid by Hallmark, in the community. The company spent a total of $10 million to maintain jobs for its surplus workers until business picked up again. At Olga, company founder Jan Erteszek explains that such a no-layoff policy "creates a very pressing and demanding discipline. It means the company has to plan for employment just like we plan for profit." When the Los Angeles-based women's lingerie maker's plans don't work out, the company seeks creative solutions to maintain job security. During the 1982 recession, Olga avoided layoffs by enrolling in an obscure California state program called Workshare, enabling employees to work four-day weeks with the state absorbing part of their pay for the fifth day.

Finally, a no-layoff policy communicates that everyone in the company is considered important, not just those at the top. H. B. Fuller, a Minnesota-based glue maker, has a job-security policy that makes this point dramatically. Everyone who has been working at the company for at least two years will be affected equally by any reductions at a particular plant. During the 1982 recession, for instance, everyone at a vacuum-cleaning division was cut back to a four-day work week, including the vice-president of the division.

In some highly seasonal or cyclical industries, a no-layoff policy is simply not practical. The toy industry, for instance, manufactures most of its products for the Christmas season. So Fisher-Price Toys regularly lays off several hundred workers (as much as a quarter of the work force in some plants) at its upstate New York plants after the Christmas rush. But the company does everything within its power to let employees know what to expect as far in advance as possible, and it lays off people according to a well-established seniority system. So the employees are provided with a message that the company has a long-term commitment to them, despite the possibility of occasional layoffs.

The Job

Work involves more than spending a prescribed number of hours at a company. It implies doing certain tasks, doing a job. There are three kinds of job-related policies we shall look at: *how* and *when* jobs are to be done and *who* is to do them.

How jobs are to be done: When we work on a job, we generally want to accomplish something in the process and to feel proud of our work. This is true even in the most deadening jobs. Henri de Man interviewed dozens of German industrial workers during the mid-1920s. In his classic book *Joy in Work*, de Man concluded that despite the mind-numbing nature of their jobs, "every worker aims at joy in work, just as every human being aims at happiness." He cites a woman who wrapped an average of thirteen thousand filament lamps in paper every day. Yet even she could find meaning in her work by frequently changing the way in which she wrapped them. He found the impulse toward doing a good job strong, although he argued that most workplaces seem determined to put hindrances in the way.

People generally put more effort into their jobs than the minimum that is absolutely required. Good workplaces recognize the desire to do a good job that is, in effect, a gift to the company, as it is over and above the absolute minimum required. They acknowledge this gift by accepting it. That is, good workplaces provide ways for people to assume an increasing share of *responsibility* for their own work.

In our chapter on Northwestern Mutual Life and Preston Trucking, we saw how two companies engaged in this process of increasing employee responsibility for how to do their jobs. We noted how at Preston, for instance, the company adopted as its unofficial slogan "The person doing the job knows more about it than anybody else." This phrase communicates that the company believes the employees have an important contribution to offer, one which the company is willing to accept. Both companies employed participative-management techniques as ways to accept increased employee responsibility— a job-enrichment-style program at Northwestern, quality circles at Preston. But it would be a mistake to think that these techniques alone made the difference. Participative-management techniques by themselves may only affect the commodity level of the workplace relationships. Other factors determine whether increased participation in decision making translates into building trust in the workplace.

For one thing, participative-management techniques can be seen as thinly disguised efforts to undermine employees' job security. It's hard to imagine an employee finding credibility in a program that she believes may eventually eliminate her job. That's why, for instance, Northwestern's management gave written guarantees that no one's job would be at stake when the company began redesigning jobs. At the same time, participative programs may fail as a means of improving trust if they are perceived as either a means of forestalling unionization or undermining an already existing union. At both Northwestern and Preston Trucking, the managements went out of their way to involve the unions in the process. By doing so, they made it easier for employees to believe the company when it said its objective was productivity. Trust is impossible when there's an obvious conflict between what the company says it is doing and what it actually does.

Participative-management programs are also especially susceptible to broadcasting conflicting messages precisely because they are, in general, creations of management consultants steeped in psychological theories. As we saw in the chapters on Elton Mayo and Tom Peters, such psychologically based techniques proceed from the assumption workers would work harder if only they were happier. Since much recent work in industrial psychology has suggested that job dissatisfaction comes from feeling a lack of control over one's work, management theorists have advocated participative management programs like job-enrichment or quality of work-life programs currently popular in the American steel and auto industries. These techniques often do make workers feel better because they provide a forum for workers to express themselves. There's nothing wrong, of course, with employees being happy in the workplace. But as we saw in the case of the Chicago insurer, it is extremely difficult to convince people that there is not an ulterior motive to making them happy through more enriched jobs or having regular work discussion groups. That suspicion can destroy the very morale the programs are supposed to improve.

What distinguishes good workplaces is the openness and honesty about the real motivations of such productivity techniques as quality circles (used at Preston Trucking) or job enrichment (used at Northwestern Mutual Life). Employees understand that the actual objectives correspond to the stated ones. On that basis, trust is possible. Similarly, good workplaces don't shy away from the political implications of greater employee responsibility either. A decision now left to the employee may be one that would, previously, have been made by someone higher up. At Preston Trucking, we saw that many of the supervisors and managers couldn't abide by the added responsibility employees were taking, so they left the company. So-called participative programs that merely make employees feel good but don't actually change the power relationships in the workplace probably have not actually increased the amount of the employees' responsibility.

One final point. There is no way to increase employee responsibility for their jobs without some increase in risk. That's why at Marion Labs, the company stresses that the management must be willing to accept honest mistakes. If employees are not given the ability to fail, to make mistakes, they probably don't have any genuine responsibility. Because increased responsibility involves risk, it taps directly into the dynamics of trust (as described in the previous chapter). Trust implies some risk. James Treybig, chairman and founder of Tandem Computers, explains that his company offers considerable responsibility to employees because it believes employees are capable of creativity:

Creativity is a process. It's not just an accident. It's bringing different ideas together and different kinds of people and working at it and letting it kind of grow. Most people want to destroy the thing before it gets started. But it's like a little tree. Creativity takes accepting different kinds of people and accepting failure. People have to know that if they are creative, they won't be abused, and if it fails, that would be OK.

When work is to be done: A good example of a policy that acknowledges the desire to do a good job is flextime. Flextime gives employees choices about their working schedule. So, for instance, employees who work eight-hour shifts can arrive between seven and nine o'clock in the morning and leave between three and five o'clock in the afternoon. Viewed as part of the time-for-money exchange, flextime doesn't change the employees' agreement to put in their eight hours a day. But on the trust level, flextime makes an important statement: It says we, the company, trust you, the employees, to determine when to do the job. It demonstrates respect toward the employee's own desire to do a good job, while at the same time finding the best hours to work their shift from the viewpoint of their personal lives.

When Northwestern Mutual Life instituted flextime in the early 1970s, it was one of the first major companies to do so. Many of the female clerical workers with children comment that this policy acknowledges a genuine problem many of them face. Some Northwestern workers contrasted their flextime provisions with a policy which was in effect until mid-May 1988 at Miller Brewing's corporate headquarters located across town. At Miller, employees were required to be in the office by eight o'clock. At that time, the doors to the office were locked and entrance could be gained only by inserting an employee identification card in a slot, which identified the latecomer. Every time an employee was late, he or she received what was known as a nastygram, a letter of reprimand. After the third nastygram, an employee could be terminated. That kind of inflexibility and insensitivity certainly undermined trust in the workplace as it did not demonstrate fundamental respect. It was worse, according to former Miller employees, than the old-fashioned time clock.

Who does the job: One of the main ways of allowing employees to assume more responsibility is to provide them with the opportunities that arise from the firm's growth. Business enterprises are growing organisms. As they grow, they expand and take on more employees. They produce more goods or add new services. Good workplaces assume that a firm's growth is due largely to the efforts of the people working there. So they have policies and practices that offer those people the opportunity to grow with the enterprise.

For this reason, promotion from within is gospel at virtually all good workplaces. Unlike the practice at many firms across the country, where the best jobs are open to outsiders, most good workplaces make a strong point of trying to hire from within first. Many have job-posting systems, where openings are announced (through internal company newspapers or bulletin boards) within the company before any outsiders are even considered. When Delta Air Lines needed two staff writers for the company newspaper, the editor assumed that no one within the firm would have the proper qualifications, forcing him to hire an outsider. He was surprised, therefore, when nearly a hundred Delta workers applied, eighteen with journalism degrees, and ten with prior broadcast or newspaper experience. The winning candidates had been with the company between three and seven years. Because the company assumed that its own employees were its main resource, it was able to uncover a lot of hidden talent. At the same time, such a policy lets employees feel that they are considered capable of growth and that they are recognized as more than a ticket agent, a stewardess, or whatever job slot they happen to occupy.

Making sure employees share in the company's growth through job promotions is only part of the picture. Good workplaces often have strong in-house training programs which communicate, among other things, that the company considers the employees' growth is the basis for the company's growth. One of the best in-house training programs in the country is at J. P. Morgan Bank in New York City. It is aimed at new management recruits and lasts a full six months during which time the trainees are exposed to all facets of the company. Leonard Langer, a vice-president with responsibility for the training program, explains one of the major purposes of the program:

We want to make sure that the people don't feel that they are working for the bank but that they are really part of the bank. . . . We have very much of a partnership attitude.

The tremendous investment the bank makes in the education of the trainees demonstrates that the bank genuinely does consider them as part of the bank, as partners, not merely as people who've been hired to do a job.

Workplace Rules

Every workplace has a variety of policies and practices that determine how individual employees are to be treated both by those in authority and by fellow employees. Some of these policies are codified as rules in employee handbooks. Others are unwritten practices that have a profound impact on relationships within the workplace.

In accepting a job, an employee puts himself at the mercy of the company in a variety of ways. He can be ordered to do unpleasant tasks. He can be promoted or demoted without explanation. He can be intimidated. He can be fired or laid off without warning. Much of an employee's vulnerability can be traced to the employment-at-will doctrine mentioned earlier. Rights Americans enjoy as citizens simply do not exist as employees. For instance, the Bill of Rights to the U.S. Constitution protects free speech, prohibits unreasonable search and seizure, and provides for due process and trial by one's peers. Yet with very few exceptions, companies throughout the country routinely violate these same rights on a daily basis. Employees can be penalized for speaking their minds. Management can search employees' desks without anyone blinking an eye. Employees can be required to submit to urine tests for drugs, and employees are routinely fired without warning, let alone having recourse within the organization. A federal study entitled *Work in America* put it this way:

The United States must resolve a contradiction in our nation—between democracy in society and authoritarianism in the workplace.

Unions can and do reduce an employee's vulnerability. Union contracts make individual employees less likely to be singled out for abuse, but unions can do little to prevent employers from behaving badly toward all employees as a group. By the same token, laws have been passed to protect employees from certain abuses. There are laws regarding minimum wages, overtime pay, antidiscrimination. There are far more stringent health and safety codes in effect today than a half century ago, but for most day-to-day problems, the law offers little comfort. In practice, an employee who considers that she was fired unfairly has only the right to sue (typically for breach of contract). In practice this means little, and relatively few workers bother to challenge dismissals because the process is so time consuming and costly.

Good workplaces recognize the vulnerability of employees and go to great lengths to provide safeguards to assure fairness. Without fairness, the employee's gift of work can get destroyed. It is because good workplaces respect the employees' desire to work that they insist there be an environment where the work can be appreciated.

Assuring fairness requires addressing two major problems: the huge imbalance of power of the organization over the individual employee and the proclivity for management to be treated as first-class citizens and other employees as second-class citizens at best. Good workplaces typically have a variety of practices that reduce class distinctions. Few of the companies we visited while researching The 100 Best Companies to Work for in America had executive dining rooms. If they did, the executive dining rooms usually had a clearly understood function of being a place to dine certain customers. Often they could be made available to any employee or employee group with a good reason for using it. They were not understood as off-limits to the second-class citizens of the workplace.

Good workplaces also try to eliminate other kinds of obvious executive perks that tend to accentuate the existence of a privileged class. Some firms, like Marion Labs, extend this to benefits. For instance, all Marion employees get stock options, a benefit usually reserved only for top executives in most corporations. The most graphic example of the lack of managerial perks we encountered was at Advanced Micro Devices, which does not have executive parking lots. That means that when its flamboyant founder Jerry Sanders arrives to work late, he has to park his Rolls-Royce in the outer parking lot and walk just like any other latecomer.

Countering the imbalance of power between the organization and the individual requires *extending rights* to employees. Marion Labs, for instance, hands all new employees (called associates) a list of their rights. It reads:

Each associate has the *right* to:
• Be treated as an individual.
• Be paid for performance.
• Know what is expected on the job and where he or she stands in relation to that expectation.
• Get problems resolved and be heard.
• Share in the growth of the company through personal and career growth.

Very few good workplaces actually follow Marion's example and publish an employee bill of rights. But most have clearly articulated policies on several key issues. When a company guarantees rights, it places limitations on its own power. That is why policies which extend employees rights go a long way toward building trust in the workplace. Rights show good faith on the part of the organization by directly addressing the very real problem of employee vulnerability. Here are several examples of the kinds of rights that characterize many good workplaces.

Right to due process. The most basic right is that of appealing decisions that the employee considers unfair. Federal Express's Guaranteed Fair Treatment procedure, discussed in an earlier chapter, shows how such a policy helps to build trust among employees. Not only is the GFT an elaborate grievance procedure, but the final decision might be handed down after a trial by one's peers. The GFT also underscores the fact that all employees are equal citizens in the workplace community because it is also used by management employees when they feel they have been unfairly treated, such as being passed over for a promotion.

Right to full and accurate information: Federal Express employees also have the right to information. A company policy enables any employee to see any piece of information with only three exceptions: other employees' personnel records, plans that could be used by competitors, and sensitive financial data that the Securities and Exchange Commission does not permit to be distributed prematurely. So, for instance, if a courier wants to know how his wage compares with that of drivers for competitors, he would be able to ask for and be shown wage surveys and comparable wage scales at United Parcel Service and Emery. A policy of no secrets does much to build trust throughout the workplace community if for no other reason than it can help stop rumors that erode people's confidence in each other. By giving everyone access to the same information, people can form their own opinions about issues of common concern.

The right to obtain information is only part of the picture, however. Most good workplaces have elaborate communications systems that provide ongoing information about all aspects of the company. Widely dispersed information isn't restricted to the highly sanitized version of reality often seen in glossy company magazines. Federal Express's Fred Smith insists that approach is hopelessly out of step with the times:

> You are dealing with a very sophisticated work force today. They may not all be highly educated formally, but they can tell you about the federal deficit, about the Japanese, about the MX missile. Even if they get all their news from TV, they see all kinds of issues discussed there—corruption, abortion. And the nightly news is showing people getting blown up. So, to have a corporate publication that mambie-pambies around and talks about nothing but five-year pins is not going to have any credibility at all with employees. You ought to talk about it when we get crummy letters from customers or that there are terrible wrecks involving our vans or that somebody gets caught by the FBI. You ought to put the news in there.

Some good workplaces take this advice to heart and make it a point to demystify the usually sacred issue of compensation. In the annual Pitney Bowes jobholders' report, for instance, there are detailed charts that show how much money various levels of employees receive, from the lowest-paid clerical workers to the chief executive officer. Security Pacific

Bank, headquartered in Los Angeles, has a similar practice. It hands each new employee a card that lists the salary ranges and performance rating ranges for each of the thirty pay grades within the company. Making this kind of information widely available helps put every employee on the same footing in the workplace community. Some make more money than others, but at least those who make less have the same right to information as those who make more.

Right to free speech: The freedom of speech enjoyed by the Tektronix employee newspaper, discussed in an earlier chapter, is a good example of this right in action. Tek employees not only have the right to have their own opinions on work issues, but they also have the right to broadcast those opinions widely without fear of retribution. The company newspaper isn't the only vehicle for expressing opinions. Tek's area representative activity enables employees to ask questions and obtain answers about anything of concern from anyone in the company, including the president.

Tandem Computers takes a high-tech approach to free speech with regular companywide gatherings using an in-house TV satellite network that links Tandem offices and plants throughout the country. Employees not only get the opportunity to hear the latest information directly from the top officers of the company, but they can also ask questions during these sessions. The company never edits what is said in these TV meetings.

Tandem employees also have immediate and constant access to each other through the computer terminals sitting on their desks. Any employee can send a message to any other employee through this network, which is called electronic mail. This means that if the management makes a decision, it can get immediate feedback. When the chief financial officer instituted a new procedure for employees recording their travel expenses, he soon received more than four hundred electronic mail letters—all negative. The policy was quickly changed. As company president James Treybig points out, "The point was that it was a bad policy, and people expressed that to him. It's an example of the value of direct communication. He probably talked to the people who worked for him before he started the policy but they didn't say anything to him."

Right to confront those in authority: Through an open-door policy, another common feature of good workplaces, an employee who is dissatisfied with her treatment by her supervisor is entitled to appeal to others higher up in the hierarchy without fear of retribution. In many companies, the employee can appeal directly to the company president. On the commodity level, this can be seen as simply another rule in the company handbook, comparable to a policy stating whom you are supposed to call if you are sick. But an open-door policy is more than just another what-to-do-if rule. By extending a right to employees, the open-door policy tells them that the company cares whether they are being treated fairly, even if they are lower down in the hierarchy. It says that no one, not even managers, can mistreat those who are offering part of themselves to the mutual enterprise.

The Pitney Bowes annual jobholders' meeting, where any employee can ask any question publicly of the top officers, is another example of the right to confront those in authority. This right communicates that everyone in the workplace, especially management, can be held accountable to his fellow employees for his actions. It offers an antidote to the tendency to create two, distinctly unequal classes of employees—one with all the power and privileges and one without.

Right not to be part of the family/team: Employees at most good workplaces say they feel their company has an atmosphere like that of a family or a team. However, this same family feeling can translate into social pressure to conform. It can be one of the worst ways in which an organization can tyrannize the vulnerable individual. Good workplaces often have a tolerant attitude toward the loners and eccentrics. As one Tektronix employee explained: "I feel I can be me here." In this sense, good workplaces are very much like real families in that people don't have to do anything or prove anything to be part of it.

A tolerant attitude toward individual differences also means that good workplaces accept those who want to have no more than a commodity-type exchange with the company. Donald Hall is chairman of Hallmark Cards, one of the most familylike of any company in America, yet he states emphatically that "there has to be a place for those who only want to put in their eight hours a day and go home. There has to be a place for those who don't want to be part of the family." This is an extremely important feature of good workplaces that is often missed when people focus on the terrific familylike or teamlike spirit of companies such as Hallmark Cards or Delta Air Lines.

It's worth noting that the kinds of policies we have discussed in this chapter are ways in which companies respond to the employees' gift of work. The company accepts that gift and responds by offering various ways employees can more fully give their gift of work. For instance, good workplaces may offer increased responsibility for those who wish to give more of themselves to the enterprise, but employees can always refuse more responsibility. Similarly, rights only exist when they are exercised. Federal Express employees may have the right to virtually any information but they don't have to exercise that right. Policies that offer employees rights or responsibilities offer a basic kind of respect toward the individual to decide his own level of involvement.

Like other rights, the right not to be part of the family or team represents a risk. Some employees will want to place strict limits on the organization's control over their lives, while others may want to give the major part of their existence to the organization. A company's management may prefer a workplace of workaholics but, as we saw from the example of People Express, such an environment exacts a tremendous toll on the human beings who work there. A good place to work is, above all, a place where people thrive. People cannot thrive unless they have some say in how much they wish to contribute. For a company to genuinely acknowledge the giftlike nature of human work, it must provide a role for those who don't wish to engage in more than a time-for-money exchange with the company. Work is not a gift if it must be given only on terms dictated by the recipient.

A Stake In Success

Good workplaces recognize that compensation alone does not adequately recognize the contribution people make to an enterprise. These firms acknowledge that the role of employees is central to a firm's success or failure. So they make sure that employees have a genuine stake in enterprise so that they can share the rewards of their joint endeavors. This is accom-

plished largely, but not entirely, through sharing profits and/
or ownership.

Sharing rewards: More than half of the firms listed in *The
100 Best Companies to Work for in America* have explicit
profit-sharing plans. On the commodity level, profit sharing
could be considered as only a means of compensation that is
reflected in employees' paychecks. In other words, *profit sharing* represents part of a basic commodity exchange of time for
money. On the trust level, however, profit sharing has an entirely separate meaning. By paying part of its profits directly
to employees, a company is saying that employees are valuable
enough to the enterprise to share rewards of the firm's success.
David Packard, cofounder of Hewlett-Packard, explains that
his company initiated one of the first industrial profit-sharing
plans nearly fifty years ago for the simple reason that "employees should participate in the success they helped make
possible." For that reason, profits should be shared not only
with those who put up the capital—the shareholders—but also
with those who put their lives into their enterprise—what's
sometimes called sweat equity. Employees, like shareholders,
deserve to reap the rewards of success.

Several good workplaces, including Dana, Donnelly Mirrors,
Herman Miller, and Preston Trucking, have elaborate systems
called Scanlon plans through which employees are awarded
a share of the financial gains resulting from their improved
work. These plans generally reward work groups for their improvements. A more conventional approach is suggestion
awards through which a company splits savings with the individuals who offered the suggestion. Perhaps the most elaborate suggestion-award system is at Maytag, where nearly 95
percent of those eligible participate by offering suggestions.
Like the Scanlon plans, these systems acknowledge personal
initiative with tangible rewards.

Like participative-management techniques, profit-sharing or
other incentive techniques are not panaceas. Companies institute profit-sharing plans for a wide variety of reasons, so
they are subject to a wide variety of interpretations by employees. Many firms, for instance, see profit sharing as merely
another device to bolster productivity. If increased productivity is the sole reason for profit sharing, the policy suggests

little more than a direct commodity exchange: Work harder and you will get more money.

At many good workplaces, the company makes clear that increasing productivity is only part of the reason for profit sharing. It's instructive to look back at one of the first known profit-sharing plans. Edme-Jean Leclaire owned a painting company in Paris when he first began sharing profits with employees in 1842. By 1882 the firm's one thousand workers were receiving annual profit-sharing bonuses equal to 22 percent of their wages. Leclaire argued that because of profit sharing:

> [The workers] are no longer mere journeymen who act like machines and quit their work before the clock has sounded its last stroke. All have become partners working on their own account: in virtue of this, nothing in the workshop ought to be indifferent to them—all attend to the preservation of the tools and materials as if they are the special keepers of them.

It is this sense of feeling a part of the company that sharing of the rewards of the company's success brings out. Tektronix offers one of the more generous profit-sharing plans in the country. It gives employees 35 percent of all corporate profits. Tek, however, pays slightly lower base wages than some of its competitors, which means that in bad years, Tek employees may earn less than those at firms like Hewlett-Packard or Intel. But when times are good, Tek employees earn more. The crucial role profit sharing plays in employees' livelihoods is only part of the picture. Profit sharing is an absolutely fundamental policy in terms of the company's relationship with employees. As Earl Wantland, Tek's president, explains:

> Profit sharing [means] that the employee should be considered more than an eight-hour-a-day person. An employee should have other real, tangible relationships with the industrial enterprise. So we have structured our profit sharing so that the employees as a group benefit to the equivalent extent as the shareholders as a group, in terms of our margin and our performance. That way employees have a real stake. We structure our salaries so that profit sharing is an integral part of the pay

at Tektronix. So employees have the opportunity to earn more
if we collectively are more productive.

Sharing ownership is similar to profit sharing in that it is
another means of giving those who helped create a firm's success a share of the spoils. A high percentage of good workplaces
offer some form of employee ownership. They range from 100
percent employee-owned companies like Publix Super Markets and Quad/Graphics to firms that have a sizable percentage
of employee ownership, like Lowe's Companies and Hallmark
Cards, where between a quarter and a third of the company is
owned by employees, to companies where only a small percentage of the firm is employee owned, like Preston Trucking
and Dana. In some firms, employee ownership is considered
as merely another benefit, particularly if it is linked to pension
plans. But most good workplaces stress another dimension to
ownership. Employee ownership implies that employees are
not just working for someone else, for an absentee shareholder;
they are working for themselves.

Sharing recognition: Profit sharing and sharing ownership
aren't the only ways of sharing rewards within the workplace.
One of the most critical forms of reward is recognition.
Whether someone is adequately recognized can play a critical
role in the building—or destroying—of trust in the workplace.
When employees first start working for a company, they are
generally willing to extend themselves, to show how much of
a contribution they can make. This could be interpreted as a
willingness to make a gift of part of themselves to build a strong
relationship with the company. Unless this trust is recipro-
cated by recognition of the extra effort they put forth, employees often feel hurt, even betrayed, and retreat into themselves.

Not only newcomers can feel betrayed in this way. Because
work is so central to what makes us feel human, it's difficult
for us to consider what we do as simply part of a straightforward commodity exchange of money for time. Most of us put
more of ourselves into our work than even we realize. So without recognition of that fact, typically by our immediate supervisors or co-workers, we begin to give less and less of our
creative efforts to our job.

Most good workplaces seem to have dozens of formal and

you done

GOOD,

_____
(name)

WHEN YOU

_____
(sign)

informal ways of recognizing people's work efforts. One Delta employee said that what he likes most about the company is that you are always acknowledged for doing good work. He says people have a feeling that they are working in a "climate of approval."

The most unusual form of recognition I've ever come across is at Tektronix. Joe Floren likes to tell the story of the You Done Good Award. A former communications manager, Floren recalls having coffee a number of years ago with his boss, a vice-president. The boss said he'd been thinking about a problem stemming from the company's rapid growth. He thought the company was getting so big that it needed a formal recognition program. So he had read some personnel handbooks on the subject and began telling Floren of several variations of the traditional golden watch given for time served.

The entire proposition sounded ludicrous to Floren. Taken aback, the boss challenged Floren to come up with something better. Floren suggested drawing a certificate called the You Done Good Award and letting any employee send it to any other employee.

To Floren's surprise, the vice-president agreed, so Floren got some printed and started distributing them. They caught on and it has become part of life at Tek. To Floren: "Even though people say nice things to you, it means something more when people take the time to write their name on a piece of paper and say it. Employees usually post them next to their desks, but management folks generally keep them in their drawers where they look at them now and then."

15
SPOTTING
BAD
WORKPLACES
From Exploitation to
Paternalism

After having looked at a variety
of policies and programs that exist in great workplaces, we
need to again stress a point we made at the outset of the book:
A great workplace is greater than the sum of its parts. Having
most or even all of the kinds of policies listed in the previous
chapter do not create a great workplace. More important is
how various policies or practices fit together to form a pattern
that encourages employees to trust those they work for, have
pride in what they do, and enjoy their relationships with other
employees, including managers.

Unfortunately, few workplaces fit that kind of description.
Most workplaces that employees are likely to encounter have
patterns of policies and practices that undermine trust. There
are, of course, a wide variety of bad workplaces. What follows
are descriptions of the four most familiar patterns of bad
workplaces.

Exploitative

Enforced bondage is not the only form of exploitation. Observers of the early stages of the Industrial Revolution saw
little difference between factory life and servitude. In his description of English textile mills, Friedrich Engels compared

the plight of the factory worker of 1845 with that of the "Saxon serf under the lash of the Norman barons of 1145." He cites various rules imposed by the factory owners, such as at the Kennedy mill in Manchester, where workers were fined for lateness, leaving their work stations without permission from the overseer, failing to supply their own tools, or for being "detected speaking to another, singing, or whistling." Adding insult to injustice, the employers collected the fines "with the most heartless severity, and for the purpose of piling up extra profits." There was no point in objecting to the system, however, because:

> Here ends all freedom in law and in fact . . . [Inside the factory] the employer is absolute lawgiver; he makes regulations at will, changes and adds to his codex at pleasure, and even, if he inserts the craziest stuff, the courts say to the working man: "You were your own master, no one forced you to agree to such a contract if you did not wish to; but now, when you have freely entered into it, you must be bound by it."

A half century later, Upton Sinclair describes similar conditions in *The Jungle*, his novel set in the Chicago slaughterhouses in the early 1900s. Talking of one employer, he writes:

> Here was Durham's, for instance, owned by a man who was trying to make as much money out of it as he could, and did not care in the least how he did it; and underneath him, ranged in ranks and grades like an army, were managers and superintendents and foremen, each one driving the man next below him and trying to squeeze out of him as much work as possible. And all the men of the same rank were pitted against each other; the accounts of each were kept separately, and every man lived in terror of losing his job, if another made a better record than he. So from top to bottom the place was simply a seething cauldron of jealousies and hatreds, there was no loyalty or decency anywhere about it, there was no place in it where a man counted for anything against a dollar.

Sinclair's meat packinghouse, like the English mills and various forms of slavery, typifies the exploitative workplace. It can be defined as one in which the employer systematically takes unfair advantage of the employees. Using terms from the previous chapter, employees of such firms have few or no rights, are given tasks without responsibility, and don't share in the rewards of the enterprise. More specifically, exploitative workplaces share the following characteristics:

1. *No rights; arbitrary rules:* There is no justice—or hope for justice—in an exploitative workplace. Injustice most distinguishes it from other types of workplaces. In societies that permit servitude, the law of the land gives the bondsman no (or almost no) rights before the law. Marriages of American slaves, for instance, had no legal standing. Even in cases where employees have full citizenship rights, their *rights as employees* before the courts may be a mockery, as the quotation above from Engels demonstrates. When there is no appeal over the heads of the employer, the employer often believes he can act with impunity and rule by whim. This can lead to despotism or tyranny—to the workplace as jungle.

In the United States today, employees have considerably more legal protections than at the turn of the century, though they have far fewer than the employees of the major industrialized nations of Europe and Japan. And the employment-at-will doctrine, described in the previous chapter, permits exploitative workplaces to be created because the American legal framework is weighted so heavily in favor of the employer. This is especially true in industries where there is an oversupply of labor, which gives unscrupulous employers little incentive to offer more than the legally mandated minimum requirements of pay and safety. When employees are not entitled to full citizenship rights, such as illegal immigrants, some employers don't even show concern for meeting the legal minimums.

Unionizing drives most commonly are precipitated by the lack of justice in a workplace. Union organizers invariably raise the rallying cry of exploitation. They typically point to capricious firings, unfair wage cuts, blatant acts of favoritism, or reckless endangerment of people's health or safety. In the face of injustice and chaos, a union contract provides some measure of fairness and stability—a welcome counterbalance to the arbitrary power wielded by exploitative employers.

2. *Abusive supervision:* In an account of a wildcat strike

several years ago in the gypsum industry, author Alvin W. Gouldner quotes how one worker perceived his supervisor:

"The only word I know for him, like the men call him, is just a plain prick. He is a guy that wants the men to work on their job and stick a broom up their ass and sweep the floor at the same time. He's looking out for himself. He's the kind of a guy who'd stick a knife in you when he could. Wants to make a name for himself. He wants to make things look good, get production up. He doesn't give a damn for any of the men. The men resent the whole setup. They don't like anything about it."

Left unchecked, this kind of supervisory behavior destroys a workplace. Workers justifiably begin to see themselves in a master-slave relationship. An employer who lets overseers abuse workers apparently cares little for their well-being.

Good workplaces have a strong system to curtail arrogant managers. As Federal Express's Fred Smith explains, the company's Guaranteed Fair Treatment policy is more than a grievance procedure. It also serves as a mechanism for spotting offensive supervisors. David Packard, co-founder of Hewlett-Packard, adds:

There seems to be a kind of a human tendency that when a fellow becomes a boss, he wants to throw his weight around. Now a first-line supervisor is the boss of the largest number of people in the company. If he doesn't behave properly, he can screw up the whole damn thing; and if he does behave properly, he can transmit the right philosophy to all the rest of the people.

3. *Disregard for employee well-being:* Upton Sinclair's novel details horrifying disregard for employee health and safety. According to Sinclair, each job in the slaughterhouse had its particular danger. The butchers, beef boners, and trimmers regularly cut their thumbs and fingers with their knives; those in the pickle rooms had their hands eaten by touching the acids; the men in the refrigerator rooms were afflicted with rheumatism; those at the stamping machines often had part of a hand chopped off. Worst of all, Sinclair writes, were the fertilizer men and those who worked in the cooking rooms:

These people could not be shown to the visitor for the odor of a fertilizer man would scare any ordinary visitor at a hundred yards, and as for the other men, who worked in tank rooms full of steam, and in some of which there were open vats near the level of the floor, their peculiar trouble was that they fell into the vats; and when they were fished out, there was never enough of them left to be worth exhibiting—sometimes they would be overlooked for days, till all but the bones of them had gone out to the world as Durham's Pure Leaf Lard!

Today, we have some more stringent laws on the books to penalize the Durhams of this world. In one recent case, a company owner and manager were convicted of murder for exposing employees to toxic chemicals. But the statistics about workplace accidents and illnesses are still shocking. More than ten thousand work-related cases of cancer are diagnosed each year. As in *The Jungle,* many of these accidents occurred because of exploitative employers who did not believe that, in Sinclair's words, "a man counted for anything against a dollar." According to the federal Occupational Safety and Health Administration, fully 25 percent of those cases stem from instances where the employers willfully violate OSHA standards on exposure to toxic substances.

4. *Divide-and-conquer policy toward employees:* One of the worst aspects of exploitative workplaces is how workers are pitted against one another. This practice robs employees of the possibility of enjoying one of the fundamental workplace relationships—working together with other employees. We saw that among the rules of the Manchester mill described by Engels, employees were punished for talking to other employees during working hours. It's doubtful that this policy was installed to increase work efficiency. It makes sense, however, as a policy aimed at keeping employees from banding together to form unions. In a master-slave relationship, the master feels strongest when he can deal with slaves individually, not collectively. So it works to his political benefit to pit the slaves against one another.

Mechanical

The assembly line is the most well-known symbol of industrial civilization. It represents the triumph of the machine over people, the system over the individual. It is also the paradigm of the mechanical workplace.

Charles R. Walker and Robert H. Guest spent two years talking with workers on an automobile assembly line, conducting a total of 180 in-depth interviews. Published in 1952, *The Man on the Assembly Line* remains the classic study of the subject. The workers paint a depressing picture:

> "The assembly line is no place to work, I can tell you. There is nothing more discouraging than having a barrel beside you with 10,000 bolts in it and using them all up. Then you get a barrel with another 10,000 bolts, and you know every one of those 10,000 bolts has to be picked up and put in exactly the same place as the last 10,000 bolts."

> "The worst is the pressure. It's like on a dog-sled. As soon as the whistle blows, they yell 'Mush,' and away you go producing cars. The company should at least give us a five-minute break. Or the pace could be slower. The *only* good thing the company has is a hospital, and that is really good."

> "You cannot get quality and quantity. That's my big worry about the place. I don't like it. I always like to be proud of my work. But I can't be on this job very much. Everybody is working under too much pressure for speed and 'get it out.' "

These quotes illustrate the problems most often cited about assembly-line work: it's boring, repetitious, mindless, pressured. Walker and Guest point out, however, that the most psychologically disturbing result of assembly-line work is "the sense of becoming de-personalized, of becoming anonymous as against remaining one's self." Workers described themselves as feeling like "robots," "just so much horsepower," "a cog in the wheel," "one of the machines," "interchangeable." That these workers should feel depersonalized is no accident. Frederick Taylor, the intellectual father of the assembly line, saw scientific management as taking the human element out of the work process. There is an impersonal, objective authority— science—that determines the "one best way" to do a job. There is no room for personal discretion, no room for individuality, no room for the qualities that make people people and not robots.

As can be inferred from an automobile assembly line, the mechanical workplace has three main characteristics: the pace of the work is dictated by the demands of a machine (or machinelike system); jobs are highly defined and specialized; and an impersonal authority is the final arbiter of workplace standards.

The mechanical workplace can be seen outside of factory assembly lines. Many big financial institutions have organized clerical work as if the work were part of an assembly line. And the mechanical workplace can be seen in bureaucratically organized institutions as well. In *Contested Terrain: The Transformation of the Workplace in the Twentieth Century*, economist Richard Edwards describes how managements of modern corporations exercise power over employees. Instead of relying on authoritarian supervisors, modern corporations develop systems. Edwards explains:

> Bureaucratic control is embedded in the social and organizational structure of the firm and is built into job categories, work rules, promotion procedures, discipline, wage scales, definitions of responsibilities, and the like. Bureaucratic control establishes the impersonal force of "company rules" or "company policy" as the basis for control.

From the employee viewpoint, there is little difference between working on an assembly line or for an organization that operates through what Edwards calls bureaucratic control. The individual is subordinated to the system to such an extent that he or she feels like a mere appendage to the process—a part of a machine. The feelings of depersonalization, of being no more than a robot, are the outcome in either instance.

On the plus side, the same factors that make the mechanical workplace so boring—its rigid adherence to rules—also contrast with the arbitrary lawlessness of the exploitative workplace. Again, this can be seen in the writings of Frederick Taylor. He asserted repeatedly that workers should welcome scientific management because it frees them from petty and often bitter arguments about whether their work is acceptable.

Everybody knows whether an employee is doing the job right because there is a right way to do it. Employees may not have a role in creating the rules, but at least there are rules that are consistently applied. This respect for law and order helps place restraints on abusive supervisors.

Unions in mechanical workplaces help assure that management honors the rules. A union contract, after all, is nothing if not a rule book prescribing how management and labor are to interact. It's an interesting footnote to the history of scientific management that although Taylor himself was a staunch foe of unions, many industrial engineers who followed him worked cooperatively with unions in the 1920s and 1930s. The alliance between labor and management in many big industrial enterprises has certainly eliminated many egregious exploitative practices. But it has led to mechanical workplaces where everything is "done by the book."

Entrepreneurial

Nothing is done by the book in entrepreneurial workplaces, which most often exist in newer companies, ones led by a strong, even charismatic leader. The leader often preaches a gospel of flexibility, of change, of creativity, of challenge. These companies display a special social dimension as well. The entrepreneurial workplace often appears to be one big happy family in the sense that employees feel that everybody is "in it together." Unlike in the mechanical workplace, people are not compartmentalized into job slots, so everybody pitches in together to do the work.

Appealing? You bet it is. Especially to people with ideals. Especially to young people, as entrepreneurial firms seem to be staffed largely by those new to the job market. Especially to people who've never worked in such an environment before. There's much to be said for entrepreneurial workplaces. Employees often get a tremendous amount of genuine responsibility. They are not merely assigned tasks as in the mechanical workplace, but they may fully participate in a major project, as at People Express, the prototypical entrepreneurial workplace, where brand new employees found themselves making significant decisions that had direct effects on how the airline was to be run.

Just as the entrepreneurial workplace does not put individuals into predetermined job slots, it tends to avoid hierarchical relationships. If anything, there may be a distinctly nonauthoritarian tinge to an entrepreneurial workplace. Everybody appears to be part of the same team, not just the same family.

The entrepreneurial workplace may even appear utopian. In *Brave New Workplace*, journalist Robert Howard uses that phrase to describe a very sophisticated version of the entrepreneurial workplace, exemplified by firms in California's high-tech Silicon Valley:

> . . . the corporation [is] conceived, not as an impersonal bureaucracy, but as a caring community; the workplace as a realm of self-fulfillment; business enterprise as the fundamental source of identity in modern society. . . . They promise a world where traditional dissatisfactions dissolve in an atmosphere of unity and good feeling, where conflict and division are abolished, and where the ambivalences of modern industrial life disappear behind the glittering façade of a utopian business culture.

Behind the "glittering façade" of the entrepreneurial workplace is another reality. Although employees are given considerable responsibility for their work, they rarely have any rights. For as in exploitative workplaces, justice in the entrepreneurial workplace is based on whim rather than any clearly established rules. Why? The gospel of flexibility. In an entrepreneurial workplace, the management prefers to reserve its options. And establishing rights, such as due process, ties management's hands.

There's another, more insidious, reason why managements of entrepreneurial workplaces avoid tying their own hands. They benefit from the employees' long hours of work. After a period of time employees can burn out, and those who aren't willing to maintain the grueling pace can find themselves subjected to ostracism from the happy family.

A good place to work makes specific provisions for people *not* to participate in the great big happy family. It provides room for those who only want to put in their eight hours of work and go home. More important, it makes it possible for people to have other commitments besides work in their lives, such as family, friends, and personal hobbies. From an employee perspective, this is a fundamental issue of fairness. It's simply not fair for an entrepreneurial-style workplace to demand that work be the only thing in people's lives. It gives people no room to grow or become more fully human.

Paternalistic

The most difficult type of workplace to distinguish from a great workplace is the paternalistic one. An incident that occurred during my research on this book illustrates the problem. While interviewing the two top officials of Publix Super Markets, I asked whether they thought paternalism was a bad thing. Both men responded at once. The chairman and founder, George Jenkins, answered that he thought it was a good thing, while the president, Mark Hollis, said he thought it was bad. Each man, it appears, had a slightly different understanding of the term. Jenkins understood paternalism to mean that the company cared about the employees as a father cares about his children. Hollis thought the concept had overtones of a dictatorship, where a fatherlike figure imposes his will on the childlike employees.

Paternalism has both of those meanings, and many more as well. It is a highly charged term when applied to the workplace. In union struggles, the term is used as an epithet. So it's important from the outset to be clear about what's meant by a paternalistic workplace.

During the nineteenth century, there were several well-known examples of paternalistic employers. During the early part of the century, the textile mill in Lowell, Massachusetts, was set up to be a model for industry in a healthy rural setting. The workers were young women from the surrounding area, who would come and work at the mill for a few years. The employer took the position that it had the responsibility to care for the women *in loco parentis* (in place of the parents) while they were at the mill. And the management imposed very strict rules on the women about what they could do in their time off from work as well as on the job.

It's partly because of the history of Lowell, Pullman, and similar industrial experiments that paternalism has such a bad name today, especially among trade unionists. There are two main elements of the paternalistic workplace, both of which distort workplace relationships:

1. *Control through gifts*: Gift giving is the most obvious characteristic of paternalistic employers. They shower benefits on their employees, many more than employees may expect. In this regard, gift giving may appear similar to what occurs as a matter of course in good places to work. For good employers may also offer employees more than they could expect from other jobs. But paternalistic gift giving has at its root an entirely different motivation. The paternalistic gift giver seeks control. A famous magazine magnate known in his day as a paternalistic employer, was once quoted as saying: "Spoil them! Like spoiled children they'll grouse about you all the time and jump the moment you call."

This technique often works. Because of the paternalistic employer's overwhelming generosity, employees incur a debt they cannot ever repay. No matter what they do for the company, it is never enough. As the magazine publisher recognized, he cannot buy the employees' love by this tactic. Employees will grouse because they resent the unfairness of their predicament. Usually employees in such workplaces just let themselves be controlled because the paternalistic employer does, after all, meet their security needs. Often, however, the resentment turns into rage, as we described earlier in the case of Pullman. Workers often lash out at the paternalistic employer with even more anger than they do against the purely exploitative employers because the stifling paternalistic environment is such an affront to people's dignity.

In contrast to paternalistic gift giving, the dynamics of a good workplace starts with the employee's gift of work. In various ways a good employer acknowledges and recognizes that gift. A good employer may respond with giftlike gestures of going beyond the norm and doing more than what most other employers do. But the context is always that of responding to what is being offered. As Marion Labs' Ewing Kauffman emphasizes, he doesn't give gifts to employees, they "earn" what they receive. Whatever benefits the company has to offer employees are not the result of the employer's largesse. They exist because of the work employees contribute to the enterprise. Where the paternalistic employer tries to get employees to be grateful to him for his act of providing benefits, the good workplace focuses on the work that made the benefits possible to exist in the first place.

2. *Shielding from reality*: Douglas Strain, founder of Electro Scientific Instruments, says that paternalistic employers tend "to shield or protect people from the vicissitudes of the world." He thinks management has no business trying to play this role, as it also reflects an attempt to control employees rather than empower them.

Richard Sennett calls paternalism "false love." In his book *Authority*, Sennett says that the paternalistic employer tries to appear to his employees as a loving father. But, he writes, "the essential quality of nurturance is denied." That is the key difference between a good workplace and a merely paternalistic one. In a good workplace, the respect and care shown toward employees have the effect of helping them grow for their own benefit as well as for the benefit of the company. In the paternalistic workplace, the paternalistic care stultifies personal growth. The irony is that in the long run, it also stifles the company.

Like all typologies, this schema for describing types of workplaces should not be seen as a description of specific workplaces. Most workplaces have a combination of these patterns. The same is true of companies that we've been describing as good workplaces throughout this book. None of them is great in the sense of perfect in every respect at all times to all people within the organization. Bad policies are implemented, individual supervisors abuse their employees, people are not given jobs that challenge and fulfill them. Looking at it from a larger perspective, companies like IBM and Publix Super Markets have paternalistic aspects to them. Companies like Quad/Graphics and Federal Express have touches of the entrepreneurial workplace. Companies like Pitney Bowes and Preston Trucking have elements of the mechanical pattern. The following chart offers a guide to help you classify a workplace.

TYPES OF WORKPLACES

Relationship:	GREAT Partners	PATERNALISTIC Parent/Child	ENTREPRENEURIAL Leader/Follower	MECHANICAL Machine/Part	EXPLOITATIVE Master/Slave
Rights	+	−	−	+	−
Responsibilities	+	−	+	−	−
Rewards	+	+	+	−	−
Consistency	+	+	−	+	−
Patience	+	+	−	−	−
Openness	+	−	+	−	−
Accessibility	+	+	+	−	−
Commitments	+	−	−	+	−
Fairness	+	−	−	+	−

WORKPLACE AND SOCIETY

Workplaces not only reflect their society, but they define the kind of society in which people live. By examining the relationship between a good workplace and a profit-making enterprise, the role of management, the impact of the workplace on society, we can understand the need for a new workplace ethic, implicit in the concept of a great workplace.

16
THE RISE AND
CORRUPTION OF
THE MANAGERIAL CLASS

A Case for Employee Ownership

The scene was a small plaza beneath the Crown-Zellerbach building in downtown San Francisco. A half dozen or so employees were sitting at card tables eating sandwiches. All were about to be laid off—casualties of corporate raider Sir James Goldsmith's recent hostile takeover of the paper company. Besides throwing a going-away "banquet" for themselves, the employees were also registering a symbolic protest.

A few weeks earlier, the top sixteen Crown executives had thrown their own farewell party at the posh Blue Fox restaurant. To commemorate the occasion, the executives were given a large cartoon version of Leonardo da Vinci's "The Last Supper." The panel depicted chief executive officer William Creson as Jesus Christ, with his fifteen "apostles" along the table beside him. Including limousine service, the estimated tab for the evening was more than ten thousand dollars, paid for entirely out of the company treasury.

To the employees, the contrast between their brown-sack lunch and the executives' "Last Supper" suggested an apt analogy. For they and hundreds of other longtime Crown-Zellerbach employees would soon to be out on the streets looking for a job. The sixteen top executives, however, were leaving the company with severance payments ("golden parachutes") totaling $9.2 million. CEO Creson alone was walking away with a cool $2.3 million.

The respective farewell parties took place in the spring of 1986 as corporate America was being "restructured" by take-overs, mergers, leveraged buyouts, the selling off of assets, and the assumption of huge debts. It was the biggest upheaval in American business since early in the century, when J. P. Morgan and others fashioned huge industrial combines. As a direct result of corporate restructuring, more than a half million people were thrown out of their jobs between 1984 and 1986 alone. Many of the casualties had spent ten, twenty, or even thirty years with a company. Like the Crown-Zellerbach employees, most had only a slight chance of finding comparable work.

What about those left behind? In one of his weekly newspaper columns, CBS's Andy Rooney talked about the effects the restructuring process has had on his business—TV news:

> Many of my friends who have enjoyed their loyalty to the news divisions at NBC, CBS or ABC for 20 years or more, are bitter and disillusioned. All three [networks] are undergoing great changes, accompanied by layoffs . . . These new takeover business leaders are going to eliminate unnecessary jobs and increase the profit. They have little interest in the quality of their product and not much faith that quality makes any difference. They're going to eliminate the fat, even though they wouldn't know fat from muscle on a sirloin steak. It matters not to the businessmen that they often are firing loyal employees who made the business worth acquiring in the first place.

The human toll of these changes has been enormous. But it would be an error to think that this was simply another chapter in a long history of workers as victims. Properly understood, the current wave of hostile takeovers and the restructuring of hundreds of American corporations should be seen as a political struggle, not merely as an economic phenomenon. At root, it's a fight over who is to own and control the American corporation. When the smoke clears, the shape of the corporation may be changed irrevocably. The outcome may spell the end of the era of the professional manager. At the very least, the battles raging across the land will have profound implications for the workplace well into the next century.

From the perspective of the late twentieth century, managerial control of the corporation has appeared to be the natural order of things. But it hasn't always been that way. In Adam Smith's day (or even in Karl Marx's, a century later), most employees worked in small enterprises where the owner was the boss. As industrial firms grew in size and complexity, one man couldn't control everything. The owner had to hire managers to run day-to-day operations of the business.

By the early part of this century, then, it was common for the owner (sometimes one man or his family, often a partnership) to run the financial end of the business while managers and foremen ruled the workplace. Frederick Taylor offered an ideology for the managers. Scientific management was a gospel of productivity intended for the shop floor, not the executive suite. Similarly, Elton Mayo and the other human-relations management theorists found a receptive audience among the same strata of management—those who dealt with employees every day.

However, neither scientific management nor the human-relations school had much to say about the big picture, the running of the entire organization. That was to happen later as a result of the economic transformation that occurred after Taylor's death in 1915. To grow larger, many industrial enterprises needed infusions of capital. So they turned to the stock markets, where thousands of investors eagerly snapped up new offerings. These investors thereby became the nominal owners of many large enterprises. By 1930, U.S. Steel, the successor company to Andrew Carnegie's steel empire, had over sixty thousand stockholders, with the largest single shareholder owning less than 1 percent of the total stock. That same year, General Electric had nearly two hundred thousand shareholders; its largest investor held only 1.5 percent.

The structure of corporate ownership in America was laid bare in 1932 by Adolf Berle and Gardiner Means in their trailblazing book The Modern Corporation and Private Property. Based on their study of the two hundred largest industrial companies, Berle and Means concluded that ownership and control of the modern corporation had become separated. Nearly two thirds of the largest corporations were actually owned by thousands of individual stockholders. As absentee owners, the shareholders more properly should be described as "investors" rather than owners. Shareholders typically paid little or no attention to the day-to-day workings of these enterprises. Since most held a portfolio of stocks in a variety of companies, the owner-investors noticed only the quarterly earnings and dividend reports, if they noticed anything at all about individual companies. And in general, few investors had any commitment to a particular firm. They were quick to sell their stock whenever they saw a better investment opportunity. According to Berle and Means, the stockholders were only "passive property owners" who had "ceased to have power over or to accept responsibility for" the corporation. Power had quietly passed into the hands of the professional managers.

In a matter of decades, then, managers were no longer merely hired hands who worked alongside the employees they oversaw. A separate class of executives had emerged, and they exercised undisputed control over corporations. James Burnham, in his 1941 book *The Managerial Revolution*, talked of the takeover by the "managerial class." Burnham argued that this revolution was comparable to the one Karl Marx had described a hundred years earlier. Where Marx depicted the capitalist revolution against feudalism, Burnham described a managerial revolution against the capitalists: "In ever widening sectors of world economy . . . the managerial prerogatives of the capitalists are being progressively whittled down. The completion of this process means the elimination of the capitalists from control over the economy; that is, their disappearance as a ruling class."

Why should anyone have been upset about the emergence of the managerial class? After all, professional managers offered administrative expertise. They presumably were as qualified, or even more qualified, to manage complex enterprises than anyone else, including the original entrepreneurs. Early observers like Berle and Means acknowledged that point. They were bothered about another issue: By what right did managers hold the reins of power?

The question of management's legitimacy has special relevance to the workplace. For a company to operate smoothly, there cannot be any serious question about the authority of those in charge to give direction to others. The legitimacy of top management cannot rest merely on the fact that it is at the top of a hierarchical pyramid. Sociologist Reinhard Bendix explains this point in his classic book *Work and Authority in Industry*:

> Whenever enterprises are set up, a few command and many obey. The few, however, have seldom been satisfied to command without a higher justification even when they abjured all interest in ideas, and the many have seldom been docile enough not to provoke such justifications.

How did the new managerial rulers justify their authority? They had a ready response: Management exists to serve the shareholders, who in turn are interested in the bottom line—the profitability and growth of the enterprise. This became the shibboleth of the managerial class.

The management-as-trustees-for-the-shareholders served as an appropriate justification of managerial authority for a number of reasons. For one thing, professional managers had historically been acting at the behest of the entrepreneurial owners. When the entrepreneurs were no longer on the scene, the management appeared only to be continuing to act in the same role, although with greatly expanded power. At the same time, the claim was technically correct. Corporate law does give management the legal right—indeed, the fiduciary responsibility—to represent the firm's owners, the shareholders. Finally, this slogan has a great moral appeal simply because management is seen as acting on behalf of someone else. Rather than pursuing their own selfish interests, the professional managers are the servants of thousands of anonymous people who may have invested their life's savings in the corporation.

From the outset, however, the management-as-trustees-for-the-shareholders justification has been flawed as an accurate depiction of reality. As Berle and Means pointed out, the shareholders exercised no effective control over the managerial elite. Shareholders could only assert their ownership prerogatives through the board of directors. But these boards were often no more than rubber stamps for the top managers. That left the managerial elite alone to do what it wanted.

Listen to Harold Geneen, who ran ITT for nearly two decades. In his 1984 autobiography, the quintessential professional manager wrote the following:

Polite lip service is always given to the concept of the primacy
of the stockholders in the corporate setup, but there is an internal arrogance on the part of professional managers and longtime (professional) board members that leaves uninformed
stockholders out in the cold. How independent are those outside directors? . . . If there ever is a direct conflict and confrontation between a board member and the chief executive,
who stays and who goes? It is well known and accepted that
only those men and women who can "get along" are nominated
and elected to the board.

After a lifetime at the very pinnacle of the corporate world,
Geneen concluded: "There are few, if any, real checks or bal-
ances upon the power of the chief executive within our large
corporations."

Berle and Means foresaw this eventuality. Writing a half
century earlier, they warned that the lack of a countervailing
power could pose serious problems. Either management could
act: 1. "for the sole benefit of the security owners"; 2. "in their
own interests" and "divert a portion of the asset fund of income stream to their own uses"; or 3. for the benefit of "all
society," by setting "forth a program comprising fair wages,
security to employees, reasonable service to their public, a
stabilization of business, all of which would divert a portion
of the profits" from the stockholders.

Berle and Means left no doubt that they preferred the third
option. Indeed, they argued that it may be "essential if the
corporate system is to survive—that the 'control' of the great
corporations should develop into a purely neutral technocracy,
balancing a variety of claims by various groups in the community and assigning to each a portion of the income stream
on the basis of public policy rather than private cupidity." But
the authors were skeptical of that outcome without some
changes in corporate law. History, after all, has been replete
with examples confirming Lord Acton's often-quoted statement "Power tends to corrupt; absolute power corrupts
absolutely."

Just because the managerial elite could act irresponsibly
does not mean it did. So it's worth considering what has actually taken place during the past half century. For years, even
decades, the fact that the professional managers running public

companies didn't own them made little difference. For the most part, one could argue the managers have done a good job as trustees for the shareholders. And for many companies, one could also argue that management acted on behalf of "all society," as Berle and Means had urged, by paying fair wages and benefits to employees and making positive contributions to their communities.

Corporate managers kept a low profile and generally didn't take personal advantage of their position. It was the era of "the organization man," a phrase made popular by William H. Whyte's 1956 book by the same name. Peter Drucker and others began developing an ideology for the professional manager. No longer did management theory concern itself only with specialized functions, such as improving productivity on the shop floor à la Taylor and Mayo. The professional manager oversaw the whole show, and management theorists to the present day, including Tom Peters, write from that perspective.

Management became a highly respected profession. In 1942 Peter Drucker surveyed the landscape and wrote, "There has never been a more efficient, a more honest, a more capable and conscientious group of rulers than the professional management of the great American corporations today."

Perhaps we would expect such a statement from a conservative business-school professor and management consultant. But a quarter of a century later, the liberal economist John Kenneth Galbraith echoed Drucker's observation. In his best-selling book *The New Industrial State*, Galbraith described a "technostructure," which extends beyond the management to include "all who bring specialized knowledge, talent or experience to group decision-making . . . the brain of the enterprise." In other words, he felt that the top management executives had for the most part submerged their own interests into that of their organizations. They had become the "purely neutral technocracy" Berle and Means had advocated. Galbraith further noted that "management does not go out ruthlessly to reward itself—a sound management is expected to exercise restraint." He cited several studies which revealed that the salaries of top corporate managers weren't especially high, and their stock holdings were generally small or nonexistent. He also pointed out that this restraint was all the more remarkable considering the top managers' "advance

knowledge of products and processes, price changes, impend-
ing government contracts and, in the jargon of our time, technical breakthroughs. Advantage could be taken of this
information. . . . But these are not the sort of thing that a good
company man does; a remarkably effective code bans such
behavior."

Today no one—conservative or liberal—could make such a
statement with a straight face. Events of the last decade have
seriously harmed, if not permanently crippled, the managerial
class's self-described claim for legitimacy. Berle and Means's
fears about the dangers of unchecked managerial power have
come to pass with a vengeance. We're talking here about corruption. And, for the most part, entirely legal corruption.

Take the issue of executive pay. The "restraint" Galbraith
reported only twenty years ago is becoming extremely difficult
to locate, especially when considering the largest companies,
where the *average* chief executive officer, at a salary of about
$1 million a year, gets paid more than *fifty* times what is paid
the average worker. By contrast, the top European and Japanese
executives only get paid about one fourth as much, or about
ten times as much as their typical workers. This disparity
cannot be explained by citing the terrific performance of American companies as opposed to their Japanese and European
counterparts in the last few years. On the contrary, the opposite
seems to be true, as has become painfully obvious from the
enormous trade deficits caused largely by the erosion of America's market share from steel and cars to textiles and computer
chips.

That something is truly amiss here can be seen most graph-
ically by looking at the size of some of the individual paychecks. In its annual survey of the highest paid corporate
executives, *Business Week* reported that 220 American corporate executives in 1986 had incomes in excess of $1 million,
up from just four executives only six years earlier. In fact, the
magazine noted that the CEOs' paychecks jumped an average
of 26 percent in just one year. And the amount some of these
men took home was astronomical. The top twenty-five executives received more than $3 million apiece; four got over $10
million for one year's work. The biggest winner of all was
Chrysler's Lee Iacocca, who drew over $20.5 million.

Owen Bieber, the head of the United Auto Workers (nearly

forty thousand of whose members have been laid off by Chrysler during Iacocca's tenure), was predictably outraged: "No one individual can possibly be worth that much money to a corporation. Compensation like this sends the wrong message of greed and complacency in an industry that can't afford that kind of thinking." As far as serving the stockholders was concerned, *Business Week* pointed out, Iacocca's $20 million a year earned him the dubious distinction of being on the magazine's list of the ten chief executives who gave shareholders the least return for their pay for the second year in a row. (He was paid $11.5 million the previous year.) For his part, Iacocca bristled at the criticism. When a reporter asked, "Mr. Iacocca, don't you think your compensation is out of line?" he retorted, "I'm not a socialist. I believe in the American system."

Do these multimillion-dollar paychecks really represent the "American system"? It may be more accurate to say that they represent an entirely new development. Previously, the creation of wealth in capitalism has been linked to risk. There are countless examples of the traditional entrepreneurial story. A man thinks of a great idea for a business. He pools together his life's savings and launches a company. The entrepreneur may need some investors for more capital. They also put up some, or all, of their money. If the business succeeds, the entrepreneur and the investors are rewarded. That reward can be beyond anyone's wildest dreams if the idea takes off like McDonald's or Apple Computer. But if the company fails, the entrepreneur and the investors can lose their shirts.

Let's look at how the millionaire executives are amassing their riches. They start at the bottom of the corporate pyramid. (Actually, armed with an MBA, they more typically may start at the bottom of the managerial ranks.) After years of service to the company (or to several companies), they find themselves in the executive suite. Now they are sitting at the helm of power that controls great wealth. Their rubber-stamp board of directors approves their hefty executive compensation packages and, voilà, they're rich.

Granted, a lot of personal sacrifice is required to get to the top of the corporate heap—long hours, numerous trips away from the family, and so on. The personal sacrifice of the executives could be considered to be on a par with the legendary personal sacrifices of the prototypical entrepreneurs fighting to keep their businesses afloat. But where's the risk? More particularly, how can the corporate executive lose his shirt as can the entrepreneur or the investor? For it's not for personal sacrifice that capitalism justifies the enormous wealth an entrepreneur can amass. It's the fact that the entrepreneur puts his capital at risk that the capitalist system rewards. The truth is the corporate executive never has to put one penny of his own at risk. He just has to make it to the top.

Consider stock options, the main device that has enriched Lee Iacocca and most of the other highly paid executives. In simplest terms, a stock option is the right to buy shares of stock at a later date. The price is determined at the time the option is granted. For example, assume a company's stock is selling for $10 a share today. The executive may be granted the right to buy 1,000 shares of the stock over the next three years at a guaranteed price of $10. Assume that in three years the stock moves to $25 a share. The executive can then exercise his options, that is, buy 1,000 shares for $10 apiece (or $10,000), then turn around and sell the shares at the current market price of $25 each (or $25,000) and pocket the difference (or $15,000).

One could argue that there's some risk involved here because the company's stock may be worth only $5 in three years, making the options worthless. But that's not risk, only uncertainty. There's no down side, just possible disappointment. The executive can't lose any money on the stock options— only the chance to clean up. He's certainly not about to lose his shirt, because he's guaranteed a handsome salary regardless. (If he does lose his job, there are the huge executive severance payments, like the $11 million Thomas Wyman got after being ousted from his post as CBS chairman in 1986.) In short, there's no discernible risk involved in the executives' get-rich-quick tactics. It's the culmination of the managerial revolution.

It's notable that Marion Labs and Apple Computer, for instance, have offered stock options to *all* employees, not just the top brass. And for the most part, the top executives of companies cited as good workplaces in *The 100 Best Companies to Work for in America*, for instance, have paychecks at the lower end of the executive-compensation spectrum. There are exceptions, like IBM, which had executives on *Busi-*

ness Week's top twenty-five lists in 1984 and 1985. The pressures toward self-enrichment are strong among top executives if for no other reason than the follow-the-leader syndrome among American managers. In particular, there has become what Robert B. Reich calls the "cult of the CEO," where the business community and the public at large have placed the top executive on a pedestal, as if that person were a breed apart from the rest of a corporate enterprise.

Executive compensation is only the tip of the iceberg of managerial corruption. Other examples are the "golden parachutes," like those that cushioned the fall of the Crown-Zellerbach executives. The worst is the management leveraged buyout (LBO), which promises to dwarf all previous executive enrichment techniques. Donald Kelly may be the first professional manager to have climbed into the realm of the superrich. *Forbes* estimates his worth at $200 million, placing him among the four hundred richest Americans. Kelly got there through a management LBO of Beatrice. We'll return to the management LBO shortly.

It should be underscored that managerial enrichment is a relatively recent phenomenon, even if it has its roots in the unchecked power of corporate executives. It has significant implications for the workplace. In the first place, we should recall a theme we've reiterated several times in this book: Managers are employees, too. The top brass may have a different function within the organization than an assembly-line worker or a cashier at a check-out stand. It's only fair that the managers' greater responsibility should be reflected in their compensation. But what has been happening in the past few years no longer has any relation to a just reward for a greater contribution to the organization. It's a reward based on power— the ability of those sitting on top to grab as much as they can from the till while they're in a position to do it. In that sense, Lee Iacocca's comment about the American system rings a cynical chord. There is indeed a strain of every-man-for-himself philosophy within the American system. But it is a philosophy that can undermine corporate endeavor.

The every-man-for-himself ethic is supposed to be applied outside the corporation, in the competitive world, where it is truly dog eat dog. Applying a cutthroat ethic internally can only lead to disaster. Self-enrichment of top executives will undoubtedly create increasing problems within the corporation, especially in the ranks of middle managers. If the payoffs for reaching the top spot are not merely power and glory but also fabulous wealth, the internal power struggles are going to take on an increasingly nasty quality. The highest premium within a corporation must be placed on cooperation among the various parts of the organization. As we've seen, cooperation is enhanced by trust. Managerial enrichment destroys both the trust of fiduciary responsibility (putting the organization first) and the trust of fair play. It shows that the management has failed live up to its self-described role as trustee for the shareholders. Those who wholeheartedly subscribe to the every-man-for-himself ethic are hardly to be trusted to be anybody's trustees.

Worse, managerial enrichment communicates the message that there are two classes of employees within the corporation. This philosophy has long been true in practice. But previously it has been applied only to power relationships. As we saw earlier, management theorists since the days of Frederick Taylor have sought to justify the two-classes-of-employees concept. But these theorists have only done so in terms of power, like Taylor's division between brains and brawn. It's difficult, however, to limit a philosophy that justifies two classes of employees to only one sphere. It was perhaps inevitable that the managerial elite would ultimately take the two-classes-of-employees idea to its logical conclusion and use it to justify two *economic* classes of employees. Top management previously could look forward to leading an economically comfortable existence, but it was still within what sociologists would call the upper middle class in terms of wealth. Not so anymore. The astronomical pay schemes are creating family fortunes that may last for generations.

Finally, managerial enrichment ignores those who are the actual "shareholders" in contemporary America. In the past few decades, the actual ownership of large corporations has become increasingly concentrated. So-called institutional investors, such as insurance companies, mutual funds, and pension funds, have become the largest players in the stock market. Ironically, the biggest players of all are the employee pension funds, which now own more than a quarter of all publicly traded stock. Peter Drucker was the first to note this extraordinary development, and he was disturbed by it, as can be discerned from the title of his 1975 book, *Unseen Revolution: How Pension Fund Socialism Came to America*. So even if management is going to live up to its own justification as trustee for shareholders, it needs to realize that it is already a trustee for employees.

The era of the management elite has reached a crucial crossroads, and employees could wind up one of the unintended beneficiaries. It appears that the managerial elite has sown the seeds of its own demise. Managerial corruption has not gone unnoticed by the so-called investment community.

Corporate raiders like Carl Icahn and T. Boone Pickens, who first appeared on the scene in the early 1980s, were not part of the gentlemen's club. They were outsiders. They hadn't climbed to the top of the corporate ladder. Instead of legions of employees spread all over the globe, they often employed tiny staffs of sharp financial analysts. They portrayed themselves as investors and claimed that they, not the corporate managers, represented the true interests of shareholders. They also appropriated the tactic of the hostile takeover, that is, acquiring a company against its wishes (at least against the wishes of its top management). The raiders certainly have not been friends of employees, either. Their tactics have ruthlessly forced thousands of layoffs and plant closures. But what has special relevance to our story is how they typically accomplished the financing of hostile takeovers. They borrowed huge sums of money from big investors and issued junk bonds. In issuing the bonds, they used the assets of the target company itself as collateral. This maneuver became known in financial circles as a leveraged buyout (LBO).

Not to be outdone, a number of corporate managements have resorted to a variation of the same financing technique to ward off the raiders. The management makes an alliance with a group of investors, who put up the money to buy all of the company's stock. For its participation, the management receives a sizable number of shares of stock in the new company. To effect the deal, management puts itself in the ethically tenuous (though apparently legal) position of being both buyer (as a representative of the stockholders) and seller (as part of the purchasing group) in the same transaction. As part of the deal, the new owners get huge loans to buy their shares of stock. As do the corporate raiders, the new owners use the assets of the company itself as collateral. This management leveraged buyout has been employed by the corporate managers of a number of companies, including Safeway, Beatrice, and Macy's. Management LBOs have made Beatrice's Donald Kelly and other professional managers fabulously wealthy.

What's ironic about the leveraged-buyout technique is that it works precisely the same way as an employee stock ownership plan (ESOP) buyout. As conceived by Louis Kelso in the 1950s, the ESOP provides a way employees can buy their own company in much the same way that the corporate raider or the management of a Safeway or a Beatrice or a Macy's did. Buying 100 percent of their own company through an ESOP is precisely what the employees of Weirton Steel have done. In more than eight thousand different companies, ESOPs own varying pieces of ownership of their own companies.

What makes an employee LBO superior to a management LBO is not the financing, however. Its main strength lies in its much stronger claim to what Reinhard Bendix called a "higher justification." A management LBO is ultimately justified on the grounds that there are two classes of employees. An ESOP buyout says that managers are employees, too. The management of an employee-owned company cannot justify its actions to employees by saying that it is responsible to someone outside of the firm and hence ought to have special privileges—including getting enormously wealthy by, as Berle and Means put it, diverting "a portion of the asset fund of income stream to their own uses." There are no outsiders involved in an employee-owned firm. The management is legally responsible only to the people who are working there.

Employee ownership is not a panacea for all people problems within companies. Three recent highly publicized cases (Hyatt Clark, Rath Packing, and South Bend Lathe) saw the employee-owners engage in work slowdowns or strikes against the managements of their own companies. And employee ownership does not by itself create a great workplace. As we've seen, a great workplace ultimately depends on the quality of the relationships that are developed and maintained among everyone within a company, managers and other employees alike. That is not settled once and for all by any personnel policy or management technique or system of ownership.

Employee ownership does, however, offer one solution to what has become an increasingly serious problem of the separation of ownership from control. Alternative solutions, such as hostile takeovers and management buyouts, to that problem are currently tearing apart the corporate American workplace, as testified by the half million employees thrown out of their jobs in the past few years because of the hostile takeovers and restructurings. Other solutions are doing even more damage to the inner fabric of the workplace as the two-classes-of-employees justification for the enrichment of the managerial elite continues to create a fabulously wealthy elite at the top of the corporate pyramid.

Above all, employee ownership exemplifies one of the most important lessons of good workplaces—the implicit (and usually explicit) acknowledgment that management is accountable to the people working there. Any management rationale for its legitimacy that doesn't list accountability to employees as its first tenet is always going to have a hollow ring.

Full employee ownership is, of course, not applicable to every company. The varying capital needs of enterprises make unrealistic a blanket prescription of immediate 100 percent employee ownership of every firm in the land. And employee ownership has no obvious applicability to educational institutions, governmental departments, and nonprofit agencies as workplaces. But the principle of management accountability to employees is relevant to every workplace. Management's legitimacy cannot be based only on serving those outside the organization. Management must also be seen as the servant of the people who are putting most of their waking hours into the organization. This perspective requires a different kind of workplace ethic, one that sees serving employees as integral to the very purpose of the institution.

17
DO NICE
COMPANIES
FINISH LAST?

What about the bottom line? That's the inevitable question that anyone advocating a better working environment must face. People in business want to know the effect of a good environment on the firm's profitability. They ask: Great workplaces may be terrific for the people working there, but don't the owners get shortchanged?

Underlying this question is a skepticism about anything that might detract from the unbridled quest for profit, and it is in contrast to this skepticism that good workplaces should be seen. In a great workplace, importance is attached to means as well as to ends. The ends may be the same in both outlooks— to run a financially viable operation. But in a great workplace, it also matters *how* that end is achieved. The welfare of employees is not compromised to achieve ever higher profitability. In this respect, a great workplace collides with the dominant business ethos. Our culture assumes that business and morality don't mix. In the rough-and-tumble business world, it's thought that those who relentlessly pursue their own self-interest are winners; those who don't are losers. As baseball manager Leo Durocher put it, "Nice guys finish last."

But how valid is the presumption that good employers jeopardize the financial viability of their enterprises? Is it true that success shines only on the greedy?

Nice Guys Versus Tough Guys

There are plenty of well-known examples of avaracious individuals who've succeeded in business. J. Paul Getty was purportedly the richest man on earth at the time of his death in 1976. Numerous anecdotes reveal the oil billionaire's ungenerous spirit. He installed pay phones for guests at his fabulous English seaside estate. He thought nothing of pitting his sons against each other in vicious games, ultimately driving one of them to narcotics addiction and another to suicide. When the wife of one of his sons once complained, "Your lawyers are killing my husband," Getty reputedly told the lawyers: "Keep killing my son."

American business history is replete with characters like J. Paul Getty, John D. Rockefeller (who forced his own brother into bankruptcy), and Jay Gould (the railroad entrepreneur who was referred to by his contemporaries as "the most hated man in America," "a despicable worm," and "the worst man on earth since the beginning of the Christian era"). There are many contemporary examples as well. Take, for instance, the *Forbes* 400, the annual listing of the four hundred richest Americans. Near the top of the list is Harry Helmsley, whose real estate holdings include the Empire State Building and a hotel chain run by his wife Leona. Among the most famous of those on the *Forbes* list, the Helmsleys were the subject of a May 1988 *People* magazine cover story after their indictment for income tax evasion. The magazine's cover ran the headline "Greedy, Greedy, Greedy: 'Queen of the Palace' Leona Helmsley & billionaire hubby Harry face jail. His charge: tax fraud. Hers: extortion. But that's nothing compared with their despotic, skinflint ways with employees and family. Here's how some of the rich get richer." (The Helmsleys pleaded not guilty and their case was scheduled for later this year.)

The Helmsleys may not, however, be prototypical of the superrich. When researching America's best workplaces, I was struck with how frequently companies considered good employers were founded by people who had become extremely wealthy. Out of curiosity, I placed a *Forbes* 400 list alongside a list of the firms picked for *The 100 Best Companies to Work for in America*. Among the *Forbes* 400 are sixty-five individuals or families whose fortunes come from having founded or run one of twenty-one companies listed among the *100 Best*. The companies are: Anheuser-Busch, Trammell Crow, Dayton Hudson, Digital Equipment, Walt Disney, Du Pont, Federal Express, Hallmark Cards, H. J. Heinz, Hewlett-Packard, Intel, Johnson & Johnson, Johnson Wax, Knight-Ridder, Levi Strauss, Marion Laboratories, 3M, Nordstrom, Tektronix, Wal-Mart Stores, and Weyerhaeuser.

To personalize this point, seven men interviewed for *The 100 Best Companies to Work for in America* or this book show up on the 1987 *Forbes* 400 list. They are:

- Sam Walton, reputedly the richest man in America, head of Wal-Mart Stores (net worth: $8.5 billion)
- David Packard, ranked as the fourth richest American, founder of Hewlett-Packard (net worth: $2.8 billion)
- Ewing Kauffman, founder of Marion Labs drug company and co-owner of the Kansas City Royals baseball team (net worth: $1.3 billion)
- Trammell Crow, who leads the largest real estate firm in the country (net worth: $600 million)
- Donald Hall, chairman of Hallmark Cards (net worth: $450 million)
- Fred Smith, who started Federal Express (net worth: $295 million)
- John Weinberg, chairman of Goldman Sachs (net worth: $225 million)

Whether these men would like to be known as "nice guys," their employees consider them terrific employers. As a group, they refute the widely held belief that the only way to get rich is to exploit your employees. They have taken a lot of people with them while going to the top. Their employees have not only benefited financially from their work, but many of them report that their lives have been enriched from the working environment they have enjoyed. Without exception, these men ascribe their success largely to their people-oriented philosophies.

Resolving a Contradiction

We have then a contradiction. On the one hand, there's a wide-spread belief that the only way to get rich is to take advantage of other people. On other hand, there are many examples of people who worked their way into the ranks of the superrich while being generous employers.

How can we explain this discrepancy? A partial answer comes from looking more closely at how good employers behave in other aspects of their businesses. Some of the best employers are also ferocious competitors, tenaciously seeking gain from every business transaction. Retail clerks may find Wal-Mart a terrific company to work for, but executives at K mart or Sears probably consider Sam Walton anything but nice. They would see him as a tough-minded competitor who's bent on becoming the largest retailer in America within the next decade.

In the marketplace, a firm (or an individual) is expected to bargain and compete aggressively because it's the nature of market exchanges for each party to try to get the most while giving up the least. This can be done without being unfair or violating the rules of the marketplace game. It's a far different matter, however, when aggressive behavior is carried out within the company—that is, between employer and employees. As explained earlier, a great workplace requires relationships built on trust rather than pure self-interest. By nature, trust interactions are nonaggressive and sharing, requiring a different mode of behavior from marketplace exchanges.

On the other hand, ethical considerations have their place in marketplace transactions. Few policies destroy employee morale more quickly than a cavalier attitude toward business ethics. Several good employers I have visited place tremendous stress on the importance of honesty and integrity and fairness in competing with other firms.

It's not only in the marketplace that good employers can be tough. They can also be very demanding on their own employees. Hallmark Cards, which has long had a no-layoff policy, fires nonperformers. It considers workers who don't pull their own weight as endangering the ability of the company to guarantee job security in economically depressed times. Good employers communicate clearly to their employees that the company is not a sugar daddy. A good employer is attuned to those who abuse trust. Any trust interaction involves expectations. And good employers often have very high expectations of employees.

At the same time, good employers understand that any relationship goes both ways. IBM, for instance, prides itself on being hard on supervisors who mistreat employees. As one IBM executive told me: "The easiest way to get fired around here is for a supervisor to be capricious or unfair in dealing with subordinates."

Some companies take this concern about reciprocity one step further. They make sure *all* managers, including those at the very top, are held accountable for their actions. Bad management ranks among the most demoralizing aspects of many workplaces. This can be seen as the betrayal of the trust of technical competence. Employees have faith that the company's management will do its job properly, just as the management has faith that employees will do their jobs right.

The dispiriting effects of bad business decisions get further compounded when the offending managers are totally insulated from criticism, let alone the kinds of sanctions employees face when they make errors. To make matters even worse, these same managers have free rein to punish employees for even minor mistakes. Good employers are aware of this problem. Pitney Bowes, for instance, holds annual jobholders' meetings at which employees have a chance to question and challenge those in high management positions about their decisions. As one Pitney Bowes executive explains: "You've got to learn to stand up there and take it. Most managers at other companies wouldn't believe that we make ourselves that vulnerable."

From time to time, *Fortune* publishes a list of the "Ten Toughest Bosses." They are often cited because they routinely abuse employees or they make what are considered "tough" decisions, like closing down plants or lopping dozens or hundreds of employees off the company payroll. In the *Fortune* survey, toughness is equated with acting the role of a bully. Although not the conventional meaning of *tough*, it may require more toughness to preside over a jobholders' meeting at Pitney Bowes because, as the executive pointed out, the managers have permitted themselves to be "vulnerable." That's the kind of toughness that many good employers have in abundance.

Studies, Studies, Studies

So far we have explored some of the reasons why people are skeptical about the financial viability of good workplaces. But we have skirted around the question raised at the very beginning of this chapter: What about the bottom line? How do good workplaces stack up?

That question puzzled Patrick McVeigh, a stock analyst at Franklin Research & Development, a Boston-based private money manager. Shortly after the publication of *The 100 Best Companies to Work for in America* in 1984, he made some comparisons between a broad sampling of other companies (the Standard & Poor 500) and the *100 Best* companies (the seventy firms with publicly traded stock). McVeigh measured the two groups of companies using two conventional financial yardsticks—growth in profits over time (in terms of earnings per share) and increase in the price of stock (stock appreciation).

The results were spectacular. Over the previous decade, the *100 Best* companies outperformed the S & P 500 by a wide margin. The *100 Best* companies were more than twice as profitable as the average for the S & P 500. During the same time period (1975–84), the stock price of the *100 Best* grew at nearly three times the rate of the others.

A year and a half later, stockbrokers Theodore A. Brown and Thomas Van Dyck conducted a similar study for Dean Witter Reynolds. In a booklet aimed at potential investors entitled "Socially Responsible Investing: The Financial and Socio/Economic Issues," Brown and Van Dyck analyzed the financial performance of the *100 Best* companies using a technical criterion familiar to serious investors—average compounded total return on investment. Over the five-year period from 1981 to 1985, the publicly traded of the *100 Best* companies earned investors a substantial 17.69 percent more money than investors in the S & P 500 companies. Brown and Van Dyck asserted:

The evidence is strong that companies that treat their workers well benefit on the bottom line. The prudent investor can no longer ignore the quality of the workplace as an investment issue.

These two surveys are not unique. Far from it. The extensive literature on this subject overwhelmingly supports the notion that a great workplace is typically a more productive one. By using the *100 Best* list of good workplaces, the Franklin Research and Dean Witter analysts used a broad characterization of good workplaces. Other researchers have defined their criteria more narrowly. They've tried to determine the effect of such practices as employee stock ownership, participatory management, and profit sharing on productivity or profitability. The following three studies illustrate recent research along these lines:

• A 1985 study of 101 industrial firms found that those employing participative-management techniques outscored other firms on 13 of the 14 *Value Line Investors Survey* measurements, including financial strength, earnings per share, average annual earnings yield, net profit, etc. (The only measure on which these firms did not beat the *Value Line* average was "earnings predictability.") This survey, reported in *Personnel* magazine, also indicated that the companies with participative-management techniques showed lower employee turnover, absenteeism, and grievances than other firms. What's more, S. Andrew Carson, the financial researcher and business-school professor who conducted the survey, concluded: "Overall, the study clearly showed that the more participatory the firm, the higher its level of financial and behavioral success."

• In 1986, the National Center for Employee Ownership (NCEO) released its study of forty-five companies with ESOPs (employee stock ownership plans) to determine what effect employee ownership had on performance. Compared with firms in their industries without ESOP plans, the ESOP companies grew on average 7.1 percent faster in terms of sales and 6.5 percent faster per year in number of employees. The same study also revealed that the ESOP firms experienced significantly higher rates of growth after the introduction of employee

S & P 500 VS. 100 BEST COMPANIES

EPS INDEX COMPARISON

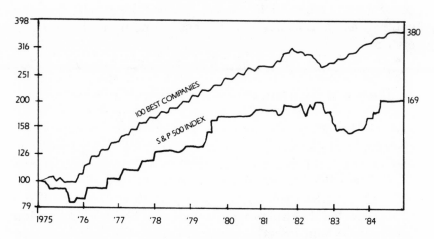

S & P 500 VS. 100 BEST COMPANIES

STOCK PRICE INDEX

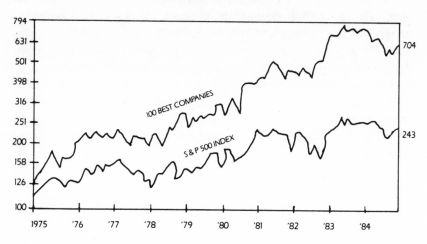

ownership than before. According to NCEO's projections, over a ten-year period "the ESOP companies would generate 46 percent more jobs and 40 percent higher sales growth than the companies would have experienced without employee ownership."

• In 1982, the New York Stock Exchange surveyed a representative sample of companies with more than a hundred employees to determine the effect of a variety of human-resource programs ranging from formal training, profit sharing, and quality circles to employee attitude surveys, suggestion systems, and flexible work hours. New York Stock Exchange economists William C. Freund and Eugene Epstein asked firms to evaluate the impact of these programs. Based on the responses of 1,158 companies, more than three quarters of the firms reported that the programs were successful in improving productivity and lowering costs. (None of the firms reported that the programs were unsuccessful; most of the remainder suggested that it was "too early to evaluate" the results of such programs.) Freund and Epstein found these conclusions significant because three quarters of the firms stated they had "specific means for measuring productivity."

Other studies could be cited, such as the Work in America Institute analysis of more than two hundred studies on worker-productivity experiments conducted between 1971 and 1981 or a recent book entitled *The Schuster Report: The Proven Connection Between People and Profits* (John Wiley & Sons) based on a survey of 592 large industrial and service companies. The evidence consistently shows that companies with progressive employment practices *tend* to do better than competitors without similar policies. The research does *not* prove that good employers *always* perform better. Nor does it indicate that companies that exploit their workers never profit. But the research demonstrates that in general, the better employers enjoy more financial success than their competitors. I could find *no* study that could be used to argue the opposite viewpoint—that bad or mediocre employers perform better financially than good employers.

Chicken or the Egg?

Before we accept as a definitive conclusion that there is a positive link between good workplace practices and financial success, we should address the obvious chicken-or-the-egg question: Which came first, good employment practices or financial success? Perhaps the studies merely show that successful companies can afford to be generous to their employees. Stated more positively, one might argue that good workplace practices are a byproduct of profitability. Therefore, employers should keep their eyes fixed on the bottom line. If the company succeeds well enough, it can afford the luxury of treating its people better. It's a version of the trickle-down theory in economics.

This argument has serious problems. For one thing, it ignores that two of the studies cited above, by the NCEO and the New York Stock Exchange, explicitly tried to pinpoint the effect of the introduction of certain techniques. They clearly showed that the more progressive practices preceded the improved financial performance.

It's also been my observation of the 100 Best companies that good employment practices were explicit goals of the company from the outset. (Preston Trucking was one of the few exceptions to that rule.) Being founded with high ideals about creating a good working environment does not, of course, distinguish good workplaces. Many other companies may be founded with similar ideals but give up when the going gets rough. What makes good employers good is that they avoid compromising their people during difficult times.

Similarly, I can think of no examples of firms that became good employers after achieving financial success. As a company prospers, it may have more to share with employees. But if sharing the spoils of success has not been a pattern before prosperity strikes, it is highly unlikely to become the policy afterward. Besides, if being generous appears to be an afterthought, it certainly will appear to the employees to be a paternalistic act of gift giving. It's not the absolute amount of money or benefits given to employees that makes the difference. It's the fairness with which the rewards of the enterprise are divided that matters.

At the same time, it's undeniable that being successful by

itself is a terrific morale booster. Being successful feeds on itself. Everybody likes being number one. There's nothing wrong with trying to be the best or the biggest or the most profitable unless you use questionable means to achieve those goals. On the contrary, having high competitive goals—that everybody feels a stake in achieving—can be a major factor in eradicating the traditional gulf between management and employees. But everybody does have to have a genuine stake in the outcome. Otherwise, attempts to boost team spirit and morale will backfire because they will be correctly perceived as yet another manipulative technique.

Perhaps we can explain the apparent success of good workplaces in a straightforward way. Good workplaces are defined by having a high degree of trust in the workplace relationships. In general, we could assume that where the level of trust is higher, people cooperate better than where it is lower. So good workplaces would have an edge since cooperation is the name of the game in complex businesses. With hundreds or thousands of people doing many different but interrelated tasks, it matters a great deal how well the people are able to coordinate their activities.

Doug Strain, founder of Electro Scientific Instruments, a 100 Best company, gives this example of how trust improves cooperation in a business:

> We were very fortunate in our beginnings because the four of us founders had known each other for years and had gone through school together. We just trusted one another. That releases a lot of energy to apply to tasks rather than wondering, for instance, whether if you go off on a long trip that you'll come back and find out somebody has stabbed you in the back or killed the project or done something without letting you know about it. Not having to watch that sort of thing really releases a lot of energy for the work.
>
> It takes awhile to evolve that sort of thing. That is, trust isn't built up overnight. You really have to watch yourself all the time to be sure that you've explained your motivation for doing things and make sure you put yourself in the other person's shoes. But once trust happens, it just seems to me that there's just so much more energy released for the important things. I think trust is the real grease that makes an organization run.

Obviously trust is not a cure-all for every organizational ill. Even a well-coordinated company can't survive selling obsolete products as, for instance, the horse carriage makers learned after the turn of the century. But trust does, as Strain suggests, provide an awfully good grease.

This explanation differs from the prescription of many management theorists that the key to higher productivity is a more highly motivated workforce. What is needed, they say, is to get employees to work harder, or, looked at the other way, keep them from withholding so much. But this approach has within it a subtle us-versus-them bias that hinders building trust. Worse, they've tried to get employees to put out more *without* yielding significant power or economic rewards. In other words, they have sought to solve the mystery of motivation without changing the effective power of the managerial class. As discussed earlier, there have been a variety of answers to the motivation problem, ranging from higher wages (Taylor) to more humane supervisory techniques (Mayo) to more explicitly articulated objectives (Drucker) to emotional rallying of the troops (Peters). The emphasis has been on practical techniques, each of which is initially proclaimed as the panacea to the motivational ills that plague the American labor force.

Great workplaces may offer a slightly different approach to productivity. They implicitly say that people tend to work more cooperatively when they are treated with respect, are given a say in what they do, and are given what they consider a fair share of the rewards for their efforts. To do all that may require disturbing the traditional role given to managers. But it is an answer—a nonmanipulative answer—to the mystery of motivation. And it may also work.

A final caveat must be inserted, however. Just because good workplaces tend to be more productive and profitable does not mean that good employers are primarily motivated to treat their people well in order to improve profitability. In other words, we could view everything in this chapter more cynically and conclude that a great workplace is ultimately only a more sophisticated manipulative technique to achieve higher profits.

Ewing Kauffman, founder of Marion Labs, offers an interesting perspective on this point. He told a gathering of company employees:

> Don't be ashamed to say that we are profitable. Hold your head high and your chest out and say, "We're the best in the industry, with more sales and more profits per associate than any other company." Be proud of it. Glory in it!

He then went on to say that the more important question was: "Does your company have a heart?" His answer, of course, was a resounding yes: Marion's products help humanity, it shares its success with its employees, it has a sense of corporate responsibility.

As far as this one good employer is concerned, there is no conflict between being profitable and being a good employer. He's saying that profitability isn't the only, or even the most important, criterion by which the firm should be judged. Profits have their place. Without profits, a private enterprise will die. But a firm's bottom line isn't how we should ultimately judge the enterprise. We need to eat in order to live. It's a far different matter to say that we should live in order to eat.

What's important about a great workplace is that profits are not something to be achieved at the expense of the people responsible for creating them. A great workplace suggests that it's possible to achieve that success while enriching the lives of the people who work there. The growth they achieve through more trusting relationships also helps the firm grow and prosper. What's more, because fairness is a fundamental characteristic of a great workplace, a highly profitable good workplace literally enriches its employees, too. This is not merely a utopian vision, either. It's already a working reality at good workplaces throughout the land.

18
TOWARD A
NEW WORKPLACE
ETHIC

Work is so central to our lives that it is how we typically identify ourselves ("I'm an engineer"; "I'm a cashier"). Work defines our role in society. It determines our level of income and hence our standard of living. All this is obvious, but more than our social identity is determined by our work. *How* we work, the quality of the workplace, also affects our personal lives.

The state of our personal health, for example, can be affected by our work. Looking at the issue negatively, there are up to 100,000 deaths and 340,000 disabilities each year resulting from work-related diseases. One government agency estimated that 2.3 million workers in such industries as mining, foundry work, ceramics, and plastic manufacturing risk contracting a lung disease called silicosis.

Similarly, work affects our mental health as well. Here is an excerpt from a recent report by the National Institute for Occupational Safety and Health:

There is increasing evidence that an unsatisfactory work environment may contribute to psychological disorders. Studies have shown that factors contributing to an unsatisfactory work environment may include work overload, lack of control over one's work, nonsupportive supervisors or co-workers, limited job opportunities, role ambiguity or conflict, rotating shift-work, and machine-paced work.

As we've seen repeatedly throughout this book, good work-places address most of these pathological problems of what this government report is calling "unsatisfactory work envi-ronments." The issue of increasing employees' control over their own work, for instance, is of crucial concern in a good workplace. It is a key issue in creating a better employee re-lationship with his or her job.

It's worth noting that the question of executive stress has been a popular subject among psychologists and others for years. The image projected in numerous books and articles has been of the hard-driving executive whose health gets destroyed by the terrible pressures of his or her job. This is a real problem that has affected many individuals. But what has been almost universally ignored in the focus on executive stress has been the terrible toll workplace stress has placed on the people who work underneath the hard-driving executives. Four studies conducted among more than five thousand Swedish and Amer-ican men disclosed that the lower tenth of workers, measured in terms of their ability to control their own jobs, were five times more likely to develop heart disease than the top tenth of the workplace hierarchy, who had the greatest control over their own jobs. According to one of the researchers, Dr. Robert Karasek of Columbia University, the health risk of low job control is "roughly the same order of magnitude as smoking or an elevated serum cholesterol level." Karasek pointed his finger directly at the influence of Frederick Taylor and sci-entific management in creating a class of middle managers who oversee those who are merely supposed to engage in the phys-ical or routine work of the organization. According to Karasek, "Once power is vested in a class or group, it sticks. It's fun to control things."

These physical and mental-health problems arising from bad-workplace practices aren't just personal problems of in-dividuals. They have a great impact on the entire society as well. The problem is more than the literally billions of dollars that are lost as a result of these illnesses. For just as our per-sonal lives are affected by *how* we do our work, so is society's physical and mental well-being affected by *how* its people do their work. The question of how work is accomplished is at root a question of society's ideals and priorities. The workplace simply reflects the real-life implications of those ideals.

Workplace-related illnesses, therefore, should be viewed as symptoms of the effect of bad workplaces on the people who work in them and on society. Throughout this book, we've seen that the bad workplaces subscribe to the notion, held by society at large, that serving employees cannot be a principal purpose of an enterprise. At best people are seen as a means to an end, the end being higher productivity or higher profitability. By contrast, the underlying message of good workplaces is that a company does not have to sacrifice its people for the good of the enterprise. In a profound sense, good workplaces declare that the people working for a company *are* the enterprise, and their needs should not always be subordinated to other goals of the organization.

Robert Greenleaf, a former management educator for AT&T, made an eloquent plea for a new workplace ethic in a little-noticed volume, *Servant Leadership*, published a decade ago. He wrote that "work, all work, exists as much for the enrichment of the life of the worker as it does for the service of the one who pays for it." If this assumption was genuinely accepted by business at large, Greenleaf says:

> When a business manager who is fully committed to this ethic is asked, "What are you in business for?" the answer may be: "*I am in the business of growing people*—people who are stronger, healthier, more autonomous, more self-reliant, more competent. Incidentally, we also make and sell for a profit things that people want to buy so we can pay for all this. We play that game hard and well and we are successful by the usual standards, but that is really incidental. . . ."

Does this sound farfetched? Impractical? Absolutely not. Several years ago, Milton Moskowitz, Michael Katz, and I co-authored a book entitled *The Computer Entrepreneurs*, composed of profiles of sixty-five men and women who founded companies that were part of the then-infant personal-computer industry. Because most of them had recently founded their companies, it was easy to explore with them their motivations for becoming entrepreneurs. What we heard is no surprise to anyone who has talked to entrepeneurs. They started their companies because they were frustrated in their previous jobs. Either they had ideas that they couldn't get their previous employers to go along with, or they simply couldn't tolerate the working atmosphere at their previous employers. Almost unanimously they wanted to create a new company where they would be able to grow and do work that was meaningful to them. Many of them sincerely wanted the same for their employees as well. Sure, they hoped they would get rich. They subscribed to the American dream enough to believe that was a possibility. But that wasn't their underlying reason for creating the company. They wanted a place to work that was fulfilling and meaningful.

The tragedy of the workplace in America is that the founder's vision of the company as a place for personal growth and fulfillment gets lost over time. That goal typically becomes subordinated to the quest for the almighty dollar. What's especially disturbing is that "more meaningful work" itself becomes a technique imposed to bolster productivity instead of an end in and of itself. Good workplaces demonstrate that it is not necessary to lose that original vision, that clarity about the essential goals of an enterprise.

Our society is in many ways at an economic crossroads. The recent stock market crash, the mergers and takeover binge, the mind-boggling trade deficits with Japan, West Germany, and other countries—these events point to a new era for the United States. The post-World War II era of America as the biggest and most important economic power on earth is coming to a close. There will be those who will refuse to face this reality and say that if only we can improve productivity, can we regain our competitive edge. Unfortunately, calls for higher productivity have usually been translated into prescriptions that mangle people in the workplace. Such calls solidify the notion that the only thing that matters is more, faster, bigger.

Instead of falling back on old reflexes because of this crisis, we should use this opportunity to engage in a major rethinking not just about where we're going but about how we expect to get there. One of the strongest messages of good workplaces is that being biggest is not as important as being best. Instead of being the world's biggest producer, our face to the world could be that of being the best producer. Being the best means

not just producing the best quality. We could be the best producer in the ways in which we produce things. We could
become known as the place where all people at all levels are
treated decently because work is seen as an end in and of itself.
The workplace, in this vision, becomes a place for people, not
for people who feel like robots.

BIBLIOGRAPHY

PART I. PIECES OF THE PUZZLE

Arendt, Hannah. *The Human Condition*. Chicago: University of Chicago Press, 1958.

Argyris, Chris. *Integrating the Individual and the Organization*. New York: John Wiley & Sons, 1964.

Auletta, Ken. *Greed and Glory on Wall Street: The Fall of the House of Lehman*. New York: Random House, 1986.

Kanter, Rosabeth Moss. *Men and Women of the Corporation*. New York: Basic Books, 1977.

————, and Stein, Barry A., eds. *Life in Organizations: Workplaces as People Experience Them*. New York: Basic Books, 1979.

Levering, Robert, Moskowitz, Milton, and Katz, Michael. *The 100 Best Companies to Work for in America*. New York: New American Library, 1985.

O'Toole, James, ed. *Work and the Quality of Life: Resource Papers for Work in America*. Cambridge: MIT Press, 1974.

————. *Work in America: Report of a Special Task Force to the Secretary of Health, Education, and Welfare*. Cambridge: MIT Press, 1973.

Schrank, Robert. *Ten Thousand Working Days*. Cambridge: MIT Press, 1978.

Shorris, Earl. *Scenes from Corporate Life: The Politics of Middle Management*. New York: Penguin Books, 1981.

Terkel, Studs. *Working: People Talk About What They Do All Day and How They Feel About What They Do*. New York: Avon Books, 1972.

PART II. DELIVERING ON WHAT THEY PROMISE

Cahn, William. *The Story of Pitney Bowes*. New York: Harper & Brothers, 1961.

Cole, Margaret. *Robert Owen of New Lanark*. New York: Oxford University Press, 1953.

Congress of the United States, Office of Technology Assessment. *The Electronic Supervisor: New Technology, New Tensions*. Washington: Government Printing Office (052-003-01082-8), 1987.

Dahl, Robert A. *A Preface to Economic Democracy*. Berkeley: University of California Press, 1985.

Gurda, John. *The Quiet Company: A Modern History of Northwestern Mutual Life*. Milwaukee: Northwestern Mutual Life Insurance Company, 1983.

Harrison, J.F.C. *Quest for the New Moral World: Robert Owen and the Owenites in Britain and America*. New York: Charles Scribner's Sons, 1969.

Herzberg, Frederick. *Work and the Nature of Man*. New York: New American Library, 1966.

———, Mausner, Bernard, Peterson, Richard O., and Capwell, Dora F. *Job Attitudes: Review of Research and Opinion*. Pittsburgh: Psychological Service of Pittsburgh, 1957.

———, and Snyderman, Barbara Bloch. *The Motivation to Work*. New York: John Wiley & Sons, 1959.

Howe, Louise Kapp. *Pink Collar Workers: Inside the World of Women's Work*. New York: Avon, 1977.

Lee, Marshall M. *Winning with People: The First 40 Years of Tektronix*. Portland: Tektronix, 1986.

Maslow, Abraham H. *Motivation and Personality*. New York: Harper & Brothers, 1954.

Morton, A.L. *The Life and Ideas of Robert Owen*. New York: International Publishers, 1962.

Owen, Robert. *A New View of Society and Report to the County of Lanark*. Gatrell, V.A.C., ed. Harmondsworth, England: Penguin Books, 1969.

———. *Life of Robert Owen*. New York: Augustus M. Kelley, 1967, reprint of 1857 edition.

Pollard, Sidney, and Salt, John, eds. *Robert Owen: Prophet of the Poor: Essays in Honor of the Two Hundredth Anniversary of His Birth*. Lewisburg, Pa.: Bucknell University Press, 1971.

Watters, Pat. *Fifty Years of Pleasure: The Illustrated History of Publix*

Super Markets, Inc. Lakeland, Fla.: Publix Super Markets, 1980.

Westin, Alan F. *The Guaranteed Fair Treatment Procedure at Federal Express Corporation: An In-Depth Profile.* New York: The Educational Fund for Individual Rights, 1985.

PART III. HOW MANAGEMENT GETS IN THE WAY

Aitken, Hugh G.J. *Taylorism at Watertown Arsenal: Scientific Management in Action 1908–1915.* Cambridge: Harvard University Press, 1960.

Bell, Daniel. *Work and Its Discontents: The Cult of Efficiency in America.* Boston: Beacon Press, 1956.

Bendix, Reinhard. *Work and Authority in Industry: Ideologies of Management in the Course of Industrialization, 1956.* Berkeley: University of California Press, 1974.

Bonaparte, Tony H., and Flaherty, John E., eds. *Peter Drucker: Contribution to Business Enterprise.* New York: New York University Press, 1970.

Braverman, Harry. *Labor and Monopoly Capital: The Degradation of Work in the Twentieth Century.* New York: Monthly Review Press, 1974.

Carnegie, Dale. *How to Win Friends and Influence People.* New York: Pocket Books, 1936.

Chandler, Alfred D., Jr. *The Visible Hand: The Managerial Revolution in American Business.* Cambridge: Harvard University Press, 1977.

Cole, Robert E. *Work, Mobility & Participation: A Comparative Study of American and Japanese Industry.* Berkeley: University of California Press, 1979.

Copley, Frank Barkley. *Frederick W. Taylor: Father of Scientific Management.* New York: Augustus M. Kelley, 1969.

Deci, Edward L., and Ryan, Richard M. *Intrinsic Motivation and Self-Determination in Human Behavior.* New York: Plenum Press, 1985.

Drucker, Peter F. *The End of Economic Man.* New York: John Day, 1939.

———. *The Future of Industrial Man: A Conservative Approach.* Westport, Conn.: Greenwood Press, 1942.

———. *Concept of the Corporation.* 1946. Second revised edition. New York: New American Library, 1983.

———. *The New Society: The Anatomy of the Industrial Order.* New York: Harper & Brothers, 1949.

———. *The Practice of Management.* New York: Harper & Row, 1954.

———. *Management: Tasks, Responsibilities, Practices.* New York: Harper & Row, 1973.

———. *Adventures of a Bystander.* New York: Harper & Row, 1978.

Durkhein, Emile. *The Division of Labor in Society.* New York: The Free Press, 1964.

Ezorsky, Gertrude, ed. *Moral Rights in the Workplace.* Albany: State University of New York Press, 1987.

Ford, Henry. *My Life and Work.* Garden City, N.Y.: Garden City Publishers, 1922.

Fromm, Erich. *Marx's Concept of Man.* New York: Roderick Ungar Publishing, 1961.

George, Claude S., Jr. *The History of Management Thought.* Englewood Cliffs, N.J.: Prentice-Hall, 1968.

Hobsbawm, E. J. *Industry and Empire.* New York: Penguin Books, 1968.

Lacey, Robert. *Ford: The Men and the Machine.* Boston: Little, Brown, 1986.

Landsberger, Henry A. *Hawthorne Revisited: Management and the Worker, Its Critics, and Developments in Human Relations in Industry.* Ithaca: Cornell University, 1958.

Lee, James A. *The Gold and the Garbage in Management Theories and Prescriptions.* Athens: Ohio University Press, 1980.

McClelland, David C., and Steele, Robert S., eds. *Human Motivation: A Book of Readings.* Morristown, N.J.: General Learning Press, 1973.

McGregor, Douglas. *The Human Side of Enterprise.* New York: McGraw-Hill, 25th anniversary printing, 1985.

Mayo, Elton. *The Human Problems of an Industrial Civilization.* New York: Macmillan, 1933.

———. *The Social Problems of an Industrial Civilization.* Cambridge: Harvard University Press, 1945.

Nadworny, Milton J. *Scientific Management and the Unions 1900–1932.* Cambridge: Harvard University Press, 1955.

Noble, David F. *America by Design: Science, Technology, and the Rise of Corporate Capitalism.* New York: Oxford University Press, 1977.

———. *Forces of Production: A Social History of Industrial Automation.* New York: Alfred A. Knopf, 1984.

Ouchi, William G. *Theory Z: How American Business Can Meet the Japanese Challenge.* New York: Avon, 1981.

Patton, John A. *Patton's Complete Guide to Productivity Improvement.* New York: American Management Association, 1982.

Peters, Tom. *Thriving on Chaos: Handbook for a Management Revolution.* New York: Alfred A. Knopf, 1987.

————, and Waterman, Robert H., Jr. *In Search of Excellence: Lessons from America's Best-Run Companies.* New York: Harper & Row, 1982.

————, and Austin, Nancy. *A Passion for Excellence: The Leadership Difference.* New York: Random House, 1985.

Reich, Robert B. *The Next American Frontier: A Provocative Program for Economic Renewal.* New York: Penguin Books, 1983.

Roethlisberger, F.J., and Dickson, William J. *Management and the Worker: An Account of a Research Program Conducted by the Western Electric Company, Hawthorne Works, Chicago.* Cambridge: Harvard University Press, 1943.

Tarrant, John J. *Drucker: The Man Who Invented the Corporate Society.* New York: Warner Books, 1976.

Taylor, Frederick Winslow. *The Principles of Scientific Management.* New York: W. W. Norton, 1967 reprint of 1911 edition.

————. *Taylor's Testimony Before the Special House Committee.* New York: Harper & Brothers, 1912.

Trahair, Richard C.S. *The Humanist Temper: The Life and Work of Elton Mayo.* New Brunswick, N.J.: Transaction, 1984.

Vroom, Victor H. *Work and Motivation.* New York: John Wiley & Sons, 1964.

————, and Deci, Edward L., eds. *Management and Motivation: Selected Readings.* Baltimore: Penguin Books, 1970.

Waterman, Robert H., Jr. *The Renewal Factor: How the Best Get and Keep the Competitive Edge.* New York: Bantam Books, 1987.

Watson, Thomas J., Jr. *A Business and Its Beliefs: The Ideas That Helped Build IBM.* New York: McGraw-Hill, 1963.

Whitehead, T.N. *The Industrial Worker: A Statistical Study of Human Relations in a Group of Manual Workers.* Cambridge: Harvard University Press, 1938.

Wren, Daniel A. *The Evolution of Management Thought.* New York: John Wiley & Sons, 1979.

PART IV. TWO CASE STUDIES

Buder, Stanley. *Pullman: An Experiment in Industrial Order and Community Planning 1880–1930.* New York: Oxford University Press, 1967.

Heskett, James L. *Managing in the Service Economy.* Boston: Harvard Business School Press, 1986.

Lindsey, Almont. *The Pullman Strike: The Story of a Unique Experiment and of a Great Labor Upheaval.* Chicago: University of Chicago Press, 1942.

McGregor, Douglas. *The Human Side of Enterprise*. New York: McGraw-Hill, 25th anniversary printing, 1985.

Naisbitt, John, and Aburdene, Patricia. *Re-inventing the Corporation: Transforming Your Job and Your Company for the New Information Age*. New York: Warner Books, 1985.

Peters, Tom, and Austin, Nancy. *A Passion for Excellence: The Leadership Difference*. New York: Random House, 1985.

Ramsey, Douglas K. *The Corporate Warriors: Six Classic Cases in American Business*. Boston: Houghton Mifflin, 1987.

PART V. PUTTING IT ALL TOGETHER

Arendt, Hannah. *The Human Condition*. Chicago: University of Chicago Press, 1958.

Barber, Bernard. *The Logic and Limits of Trust*. New Brunswick, N.J.: Rutgers University Press, 1983.

Beniger, James R. *The Control Revolution: Technological and Economic Origins of the Information Society*. Cambridge: Harvard University Press, 1986.

Berger, Peter L., ed. *The Human Shape of Work: Studies in the Sociology of Occupations*. New York: Macmillan, 1964.

Bernstein, Paul. *Workplace Democratization: Its Internal Dynamics*. New Brunswick, N.J.: Transaction, 1980.

Bok, Sissela. *Secrets: On the Ethics of Concealment and Revelation*. New York: Vintage Books, 1983.

Burritt, Arthur W., Kendall, H.P., Dennison, H.S., et al., *Profit Sharing: Its Principles and Practice*. New York: Harper & Brothers, 1918.

De Grazia, Sebastian. *Of Time, Work, and Leisure*. Garden City, N.Y.: Doubleday, 1962.

De Man, Henri. *Joy in Work*. Eden and Cedar Paul, trs., from the German. London: George Allen & Unwin, 1939.

Edwards, Richard. *Contested Terrain: The Transformation of the Workplace in the Twentieth Century*. New York: Basic Books, 1979.

Engels, Friedrich. *The Condition of the Working Class in England: From Personal Observations and Authentic Sources*. London: Granada, 1969.

Ewing, David W. *Freedom Inside the Organization: Bringing Civil Liberties to the Workplace*. New York: E. P. Dutton, 1977.

————. *"Do It My Way Or You're Fired!": Employee Rights and the Changing Role of Management Prerogatives*. New York: John Wiley & Sons, 1983.

Filley, Alan C., House, Robert J., and Kerr, Steven. *Managerial Pro-

cess and Organizational Behavior. Second Edition. Glenview, Ill.: Scott, Foresman, 1976.

Frankel, S. Herbert. *Money: Two Philosophies.* Oxford: Basil Blackwell, 1977.

Garson, Barbara. *All the Livelong Day: The Meaning and Demeaning of Routine Work.* Garden City, N.Y.: Doubleday, 1972.

Gouldner, Alvin W. *Wildcat Strike: A Study in Worker-Management Relationships.* New York: Harper & Row, 1954.

Gutchess, Jocelyn F. *Employment Security in Action: Strategies That Work.* New York: Pergamon Press/Work in America Institute, 1985.

Halle, David. *America's Working Man: Work, Home, and Politics Among Blue-Collar Property Owners.* Chicago: University of Chicago Press, 1984.

Hill, Melvyn A. *Hannah Arendt: The Recovery of the Public World.* New York: St. Martin's Press, 1979.

Hirschhorn, Larry. *Beyond Mechanization: Work and Technology in a Postindustrial Age.* Cambridge: MIT Press, 1984.

Hobson, J.A. *Work and Wealth: A Human Valuation.* London: George Allen & Unwin, 1914.

Howard, Robert. *Brave New Workplace.* New York: Penguin Books, 1985.

Howe, Louise Kapp. *Pink Collar Workers: Inside the World of Women's Work.* New York: Avon, 1977.

Hoyt, Elizabeth Ellis. *Primitive Trade: Its Psychology and Economics.* London: Kegan Paul, Trench, Trubner & Co., 1926.

Hyde, Lewis. *The Gift: Imagination and the Erotic Life of Property.* New York: Vintage Books, 1983.

Jenkins, David. *Job Power: Blue and White Collar Democracy.* New York: Penguin Books, 1974.

Kelley, Robert E. *The Gold-Collar Worker: Harnessing the Brainpower of the New Work Force.* Menlo Park, Calif.: Addison-Wesley, 1985.

Kuczynski, Jurgen. *The Rise of the Working Class.* New York: McGraw-Hill, 1967.

Luhmann, Niklas. *Trust and Power.* New York: John Wiley & Sons, 1979.

Mandel, Ernest. *An Introduction to Marxist Economic Theory.* New York: Pathfinder Press, 1970.

Marx, Karl. *Capital: A Critique of Political Economy: Vol. I, The Process of Capitalist Production.* Friedrich Engels, ed., Ernest Untermann, tr. New York: Modern Library, 1906.

Mauss, Marcel. *The Gift: Forms and Functions of Exchange in Archaic Societies.* Ian Cunnison, tr. New York: W. W. Norton, 1967.

Myers, Milton L. *The Soul of Modern Economic Man: Ideas of Self-*

Interest, Thomas Hobbes to Adam Smith. Chicago: University of Chicago Press, 1983.

Nadworny, Milton J. *Scientific Management and the Unions 1900–1932.* Cambridge: Harvard University Press, 1955.

Nightingale, Donald V. *Workplace Democracy: An Inquiry into Employee Participation in Canadian Work Organizations.* Toronto: University of Toronto Press, 1982.

Outten, Wayne N., with Kinigstein, Noah A. *The Rights of Employees: The Basic American Civil Liberties Union Guide to an Employee's Rights.* New York: Bantam Books, 1983.

Parker, Mike. *Inside the Circle: A Union Guide to QWL.* Boston: South End Press, 1985.

Pelling, Henry. *American Labor.* Chicago: University of Chicago Press, 1960.

Pfeffer, Richard M. *Working for Capitalism.* New York: Columbia University Press, 1979.

Reich, Robert B. *Tales of a New America.* New York: Times Books, 1987.

Rifkin, Jeremy. *Own Your Own Job: Economic Democracy for Working Americans.* New York: Bantam Books, 1977.

Rosow, Jerome M., ed. *Teamwork: Joint Labor-Management Programs in America.* New York: Pergamon Press, 1986.

———, and Zager, Robert, eds. *Employment Security in a Free Economy.* New York: Pergamon Press, 1984.

Schumacher, E.F. *Small Is Beautiful: Economics as if People Mattered.* San Francisco: Harper & Row, 1973.

Scitovsky, Tibor. *The Joyless Economy: An Inquiry into Human Satisfaction and Consumer Dissatisfaction.* New York: Oxford University Press, 1976.

Sennett, Richard. *Authority.* New York: Vintage, 1981.

Shaiken, Harley. *Work Transformed: Automation and Labor in the Computer Age.* New York: Holt, Rinehart and Winston, 1984.

Sheppard, Harold L., and Herrick, Neal Q. *Where Have All the Robots Gone? Worker Dissatisfaction in the '70s.* New York: Free Press/Macmillan, 1972.

Shostrom, Everett L. *Man, the Manipulator: The Inner Journey from Manipulation to Actualization.* New York: Bantam Books, 1968.

Simmons, John, and Mares, William. *Working Together.* New York: Alfred A. Knopf, 1983.

Sinclair, Upton. *The Jungle.* New York: New American Library, 1980.

Smith, Robert Ellis. *Workrights.* New York: E. P. Dutton, 1983.

Taylor, Sedley. *Profit-Sharing Between Capital and Labour.* London: Kegan, Paul, Trench & Co., 1884.

Terkel, Studs. *Working: People Talk About What They Do All Day and How They Feel About What They Do.* New York: Avon Books, 1972.

Torbert, William R., with Rogers, Malcolm P. *Being for the Most Part Puppets: Interactions Among Men's Labor, Leisure, and Politics.* Cambridge: Schenkman Publishers, 1973.

Vanek, Jaroslav. *The Participatory Economy: An Evolutionary Hypothesis and a Strategy for Development.* Ithaca: Cornell University Press, 1971.

Veninga, Robert L., and Spradley, James P. *The Work Stress Connection: How to Cope with Job Burnout.* New York: Ballantine Books, 1981.

Walker, Charles R., and Guest, Robert H. *The Man on the Assembly Line.* Cambridge: Harvard University Press, 1952.

Warr, Peter, and Wall, Toby. *Work and Well-Being.* Middlesex, England: Penguin, 1975.

Westin, Alan F., and Salisbury, Stephan, eds. *Individual Rights in the Corporation: A Reader on Employee Rights.* New York: Random House, 1980.

Zand, Dale E. *Information, Organization, and Power: Effective Management in the Knowledge Society.* New York: McGraw-Hill, 1981.

Zwerdling, Daniel. *Workplace Democracy: A Guide to Workplace Ownership, Participation & Self-Management Experiments in the United States and Europe.* New York: Harper & Row, 1980.

PART VI. WORKPLACE AND SOCIETY

Bateson, Gregory. *Steps to an Ecology of Mind.* New York: Ballantine, 1972.

Berle, Adolf A., Jr., and Means, Gardiner C. *The Modern Corporation & Private Property.* New York: Macmillan, 1934.

Blasi, Joseph Raphael. *Employee Ownership: Revolution or Ripoff?* Cambridge: Ballinger, 1988.

Bowles, Samuel, and Gintis, Herbert. *Democracy and Capitalism: Property, Community, and the Contradictions of Modern Social Thought.* New York: Basic Books, 1986.

Brooks, John. *The Takeover Game.* New York: E. P. Dutton, 1987.

Burnham, James. *The Managerial Revolution.* Bloomington, Ind.: Indiana University Press, 1941.

Drucker, Peter F. *The Future of Industrial Man: A Conservative Approach.* Westport, Conn.: Greenwood Press, 1942.

————. *The Unseen Revolution: How Pension Fund Socialism Came to America.* New York: Harper & Row, 1976.

Freeman, Richard B., and Medoff, James L. *What Do Unions Do?* New York: Basic Books, 1984.

Freund, William D., and Epstein, Eugene. *People and Productivity: The New York Stock Exchange Guide to Financial Incentives and the Quality of Work Life.* Homewood, Ill.: Dow Jones-Irwin, 1984.

Galbraith, John Kenneth. *The New Industrial State.* Revised edition. Boston: Houghton Mifflin, 1971.

Geneen, Harold, with Moscow, Alvin. *Managing.* New York: Avon, 1984.

Greenleaf, Robert K. *Servant Leadership: A Journey into the Nature of Legitimate Power and Greatness.* New York: Paulist Press, 1977.

Guzzo, Richard A., and Bondy, Jeffrey S. *A Guide to Worker Productivity Experiments in the United States 1976–81.* New York: Pergamon Press, 1983.

Herman, Edward S. *Corporate Control, Corporate Power.* New York: Cambridge University Press, 1981.

Jones, Derek C., and Svejnar, Jan, eds. *Participatory and Self-Managed Firms: Evaluating Economic Performance.* Lexington, Mass.: Lexington Books, 1982.

Kelso, Louis O., and Hetter, Patricia. *How to Turn Eighty Million Workers into Capitalists on Borrowed Money.* New York: Random House, 1967.

———, and Kelso, Patricia Hetter. *Democracy and Economic Power: Extending the ESOP Revolution.* Cambridge: Ballinger, 1986.

Levering, Robert, Katz, Michael, and Moskowitz, Milton. *The Computer Entrepreneurs: Who's Making It Big and How in America's Upstart Industry.* New York: New American Library, 1984.

Levinson, Harry. *Executive Stress.* New York: Harper & Row, 1970.

New York Stock Exchange. *Direct Ownership Employee Stock Purchase Plans.* New York: New York Stock Exchange, 1984.

Quarrey, Michael, Blasi, Joseph, and Rosen, Correy. *Taking Stock: Employee Ownership at Work.* Cambridge: Ballinger, 1986.

Reich, Robert B., and Donahue, John D. *New Deals: The Chrysler Revival and the American System.* New York: Times Books, 1985.

Rifkin, Jeremy, with Howard, Ted. *Entropy: A New World View.* New York: Bantam Books, 1981.

Rosen, Corey, Klein, Katherine J., and Young, Karen M. *Employee Ownership in America: The Equity Solution.* Lexington, Mass.: Lexington Books, 1986.

Rosow, Jerome M., and Zager, Robert, eds. *Productivity Through Work Innovations: A Work in America Institute Policy Study.* New York: Pergamon Press/Work in America Institute, 1982.

Schuster, Frederick E. *The Schuster Report: The Proven Connection Between People and Profits.* New York: John Wiley & Sons, 1986.

Weber, Max. *Max Weber: Selections from His Work.* New York: Thomas Y. Crowell, 1963.

Whyte, William H., Jr. *The Organization Man* Doubleday, 1956.

Wiener, Norbert. *The Human Use of Human Be Society.* New York: Doubleday, 1950.

Yankelovich, Daniel. *New Rules: Searching for World Turned Upside Down.* New York: Ban

———, and Immerwahr, John. *Putting the W* Public Agenda Report on Restoring America ity. New York: Public Agenda Foundation, 1

NOTES

(Unless noted below, all quotations from employees and top executives in the text are from interviews conducted by the author between 1983 and 1987.)

Introduction

Page

xx 27 percent turned on by jobs: *Industry Week*, August 6, 1979, p. 61.

xx Over half: Yankelovich, Daniel, and Immerwahr, John, *Putting the Work Ethic to Work: A Public Agenda Report on Restoring America's Competitive Vitality*, Public Agenda Foundation, 1983, pp. 19, 21, 25. The 52 percent of the Americans who answered affirmatively to the work ethic question was exactly double the 26 percent of the Germans who responded to the same question.

Chapter 1. Inside Great Workplaces: What Employees Say

5 "I found": Schrank, p. 79.

7 "An interest": Kanter, *Men and Women of the Corporation*, pp. 164–65.

8 "Within the layers": Shorris, *The Politics of Middle Management*, p. 216.

8 "minimum of infighting": *Forbes*, October 23, 1983.

11 "Without work": quoted in O'Toole, *Work in America*, p. 186.

11 labor and work: Arendt, pp. 79–81.

Chapter 2. In Search of a Definition: What Is a Great Place to Work?

20 Crow's wealth: *Forbes*, October 26, 1987, p. 152.

21 "discovered that no ownership plan": *New York Times*, May 3, 1987, p. 3–1.

Chapter 3. Showing Good Faith: New Lanark, Publix Super Markets, Marion Labs

Page

29 "The workpeople": Owen, pp. 62–64.

30 "Owen was in no hurry": Cole, pp. 53–54.

31 "This proceeding": Owen, pp. 62–64.

31 "contributed more than a little": Pollard, pp. 149, 153.

31 "I never knew": Cole, p. 58.

31 "ability to win": Pollard, p. 148.

32 "[Owen] has as little": ibid., p. 209.

32 "We view it": ibid., p. 189.

37 previous president sending cards: Watters, p. 163.

44 company newspaper quotes: The Associate, March/April 1983, p. 8.

Chapter 4. Redesigning Jobs: Northwestern Mutual Life

48 1910 milestone: New York Times, August 15, 1986, p. 26.

48 1970 census data: Howe, p. 135.

48 overwhelmingly female statistics: Congress, p. 7.

48 more than half women clerical: Howe, p. 135.

49 keystroke-counting attachments: Congress, p. 18.

53 "I think it is great": The 100 Best Companies to Work for in America, p. 252.

54 "the assorted we're-all": Howe, p. 139.

55 personnel officer quotes: ibid., pp. 153–56.

56 "Everybody's afraid": ibid., p. 139.

57 "No, those": ibid., p. 155.

58 "but since they're": ibid., p. 160.

Chapter 5. Promoting Fairness: Federal Express, Pitney Bowes, Tektronix

62 Intimidation story from Federal Express company newspaper, UpDate, December 1984, p. 6.

64 "employee participation": Westin, p. 102.

65 most rate system fair: ibid., pp. 72, 89.

65 "Given the inevitable": ibid., pp. 96–97.

67 "the glue": ibid., p. 5.

71 recent report: Pitney Bowes Jobholders' Report, 1985, p. 29.

71 "Most employees": Cahn, The Story of Pitney Bowes, p. 169.

72 "When things": Tekweek, May 15, 1987, p. 3.

73 Tek influenced by General Radio: Lee, p. 139.

73 Murdock impressed by McCormick: ibid., p. 143.

76 "If democracy": Dahl, p. 111.

Chapter 6. Scientific Manager: Frederick Winslow Taylor

Page

79 "Most companies": from National Public Radio interview in 1985.

79 Taylor's impact on Detroit: Lacey, pp. 107, 110.

79 DuPont and General Electric: Chandler, pp. 430, 438, 445.

80 United Parcel Service: *Wall Street Journal*, April 22, 1986, p. 1.

80 Drucker quote: *Practice of Management*, p. 280.

80 "The possibility": Braverman, p. 12.

80 tennis championship: Copley, Volume I, p. 117.

80 photo: ibid., facing page 90.

81 "Fred was always": ibid., pp. 56–57.

81 "the greatest evil": Taylor, *Principles* pp. 13, 14.

81 "the natural instinct": ibid., p. 19.

81 "systematic soldiering": ibid., p. 21.

82 "harmonious cooperation": ibid., pp. 52–53.

82 "Every single act": ibid., p. 64.

82 "a first-class": ibid., p. 65.

82 "conducted thousands": ibid., p. 67.

83 "substituting exact": ibid., pp. 124–25.

83 seven different bosses: *Taylor's Testimony*, p. 31.

84 "traditional knowledge": Taylor, *Principles*, p. 32.

84 "It is only through": ibid., p. 83.

85 "Work today": Karen Young, unpublished thesis, p. 2.

86 "It will make": Aitken, pp. 214–15.

86 "They can give us": ibid., pp. 214–15.

87 "They felt": Aitken, pp. 120–21.

87 "management, upper": "The Revolt against 'Working Smarter' " by Bill Saporito, *Fortune*, July 21, 1986, pp. 58–65.

89 "In the past": Taylor, *Principles*, p. 7.

Chapter 7. Psychological Manager: Elton Mayo

91 "The 'factory' ": Hobsbawm, p. 68.

92 lighting experiment: Roethlisberger, pp. 14–19.

93 relay-assembly experiment: ibid., pp. 19–188.

94 "Everyone, with the exception": Trahair, pp. 10–11.

94 "When he entered": ibid., p. 349.

94 "Dr. Mayo": ibid., p. 356.

95 "Hawthorne effect": This so-called effect has been subject to considerable debate among social scientists for decades. For a survey of recent literature on the subject, see "The Haw-

thorne Defect: Persistence of a Flawed Theory" by Berkeley
Rice in *Psychology Today*, February 1982, pp. 70–74.

Page

95 "a new industrial milieu": Mayo, *Human Problems*, p. 73.

95 interviewing program: Roethlisberger, pp. 189–376.

96 bank-wiring room study: ibid., p. 379–548.

97 "The discoveries of Mayo": Noble, p. 319.

97 "It is amusing": *Social Problems*, p. 83.

98 "Mayo was not a systematic thinker": from Roethlisberger's
introduction to a reprint of Mayo's *The Human Problems of
an Industrial Civilization*, New York: Compass/Viking, 1960,
p. IX.

99 "a healer of disease": Trahair, p. 355.

99 "One woman worker": *Social Problems*, p. 78.

100 "It was evident": Roethlisberger, pp. 307–15.

100 "a Company definitely committed": *Human Problems*, p. 100.

101 "The ends of the enterprise": Bell, p. 28.

103 "It was typically assumed": Vroom, *Work and Motivation*, p.
226.

104 "There had been a remarkable change": *Human Problems*,
pp. 71–72.

105 "Mayo preferred the American approach": Trahair, p. 208.

105 "The administrator of the future": *Social Problems*, p. 122.

105 "We do not lack": *Human Problems*, p. 177.

Chapter 8. Professional Manager: Peter F. Drucker

108 "I first presented": *New Management*, Winter 1985, p. 7.

108 "probably had more impact": ibid., p. 29.

108 "I am credited": Drucker, *Concept of the Corporation*, second
revised edition, p. 245.

108 "the management equivalent": *Financial Times*, September
1, 1986, p. 12.

108 "Each manager": Drucker, *Practice of Management*, p. 126.

109 "In practice": Tarrant, pp. 78–79.

110 "It is not the business": *Practice of Management*, p. 279.

110 "must definitely be subordinated": Drucker, *The New Society*,
p. 99.

110 "They use terms": Drucker, *Management*, pp. 243–44.

111 Drucker–Mayo encounter: Trahair, pp. 337–38.

112 for Drucker on IBM's policies, see *Practice of Management*,
pp. 255–61.

112 "transportation to and from work": *The New Society*, p. 283.

112 "I have always considered": *Concept of the Corporation*, p.
247.

Page

112 "The rank-and-file": *The New Society*, p. 290.

113 "Management, its competence": *Practice of Management*, pp. 4–5.

114 "America's professional managers": Reich, p. 140ff.

Chapter 9. Evangelical Manager: Tom Peters

116 twenty management crazes, *Business Week*, January 20, 1986.

117 mention of Organizational Dynamics article: *Financial Times*, August 18, 1986.

118 "There's absolutely nothing new": *Advertising Age*, November 7, 1985, pp. 4–5.

118 "American industry": *San Francisco Examiner*, December 14, 1986.

118 "There is good news": Peters, *In Search of Excellence*, p. xxv.

119 financial measurements: ibid., p. 22.

119 "the management practices": p. 118.

119 "a direct descendant": ibid., p. 42.

119 "What our framework": ibid., p. 11.

120 "It has become clear": *New Management*, Winter 1985, p. 16. Though Peters had not read Drucker's *The Practice of Management* before writing *In Search of Excellence*, he discovered upon reading it later that much to "my amazement (perhaps dismay is a better word), I found everything we had written—in some corner or other" in that 1954 classic.

120 "as His Eminence": *Wall Street Journal*, July 28, 1987, p. 1.

120 "a book for juveniles": *Business Week*, November 5, 1984, p. 77.

121 "people are not very rational": *In Search of Excellence*, p. 55.

121 "We all think we're tops": ibid., pp. 57–58.

122 "the excellent companies": ibid., p. 80.

122 "Psychologists study": ibid., p. 80.

123 "the emotional": ibid., p. 60.

124 "To manipulate": Ezorsky, p. 106.

125 "What we're suggesting": Peters, *A Passion for Excellence*, p. 258.

125 "You can't fake": ibid., p. 261.

125 "Motivation management": Ezorsky, p. 109.

127 "authors, who leave no doubt": Daniel Carroll in *Harvard Business Review*, November-December 1983, p. 88.

128 "You know, one of the things": *In Search of Excellence*, p. xx.

128 "McDonald's is a place": *The 100 Best Companies to Work for in America*, p. 390.

Page

129 "A well-run restaurant": *In Search of Excellence*, p. 255.

129 "Treat people as adults": ibid., p. 238.

130 "As businessmen": Watson, p. 18.

130 "end of the era": Peters, *Thriving on Chaos*, p. 3.

133 "When you have": *A Passion for Excellence*, p. 419.

133 "he is concerned with the tricks": *In Search of Excellence*, pp. 82–83.

133 "We are frequently asked": *A Passion for Excellence*, p. 419.

Chapter 10. Can a Bad Workplace Become Good?: Preston Trucking

141 "Letting Labor": *Business Week*, February 13, 1984.

141 "no detractors": *Washington Post*, April 30, 1984, p. 30.

153 "a special case of delegation": McGregor, p. 130.

153 "safety needs are thwarted": ibid., p. 41.

154 *Fortune*, July 21, 1986, pp. 58–59.

Chapter 11. The Role Model That Crashed: People Express

162 "elevated and refined": Buder, pp. 44, 45, 184.

163 "The single predominant reason": Harvard business school case study, 1983, number 483–103, p. 4.

163 "the most comprehensive": *Business Week*, November 25, 1986, p. 81.

163 "Anyone who isn't studying": *New York Times Magazine*, December 23, 1984, p. 18.

164 "As hokey": *Inc.*, January 1984, p. 48.

164 "Burr never misses": *New York Times Magazine*, December 23, 1984, p. 29.

165 "Don Burr is a motivational": *New York Times*, September 23, 1986, p. 1.

165 paid $28,200: ibid.

165 ibid.

165 *Wall Street Journal*, January 7, 1985.

167 "And start-up team members": Harvard case study 483–103, p. 17.

168 "Now there are a lot of people": ibid., p. 18.

168 "Leadership is not pandering": *Business Week*, November 25, 1985, pp. 91, 94.

170 "create an environment": *Inc.*, January 1984, p. 44.

171 "Every worker": *Wall Street Journal*, January 7, 1985.

174 "I came to People": *Bergen Record*, p. B-1.

Chapter 12. Beyond a Workplace of "Robots": A "People" Company

177 "It's kind of a family": *The 100 Best Companies to Work for in America*, p. 114.

Page
178 "The blue-collar blues": Terkel, p. xiv.
179 "They seem to think": Howe, p. 160.
180 feeling of being in control related to participation discussed in Deci and Ryan.
180 "With the growth": Veninga, p. 202.
181 $150 billion stress-related losses: National Institute for Occupational Safety and Health of the Centers for Disease Control, weekly report for October 3, 1986, pp. 613–21.
181 "The first thing that happens": Terkel, p. 5.
182 "Wait a minute!": Garson, p. xi.
182 "For most people": ibid., p. xii.
184 "The machine dictates": Terkel, pp. 57–60.
184 "Nobody really likes large-scale": Schumacher, p. 242.

Chapter 13. Trust at Work: The Difference Between Commodity and Gift Interactions
191 "This systemic erosion": Reich, p. 143.
192 "That art that matters": Hyde, p. xii.
192 A classic survey of anthropological studies of the gift economies is also called *The Gift* by Marcel Mauss.
193 "It is the cardinal": Hyde, p. 56.
195 "trust of technical competence": Barker, *The Logic and Limits of Trust*, pp. 7–25.
198 "an object or article": Hoyt, p. 105.
198 In *The Human Condition*, Chapter 3, Hannah Arendt makes the same critique of Marx. That is, by failing to distinguish between work and labor, Marx reduces everything to "labor power." We could add that this makes Marx oblivious to the reality of gift exchange and its implications for improving the workplace conditions he rightfully deplores.

Chapter 14. What Makes Some Workplaces So Good
206 "every worker aims": de Man, p. 11.
211 "The United States must resolve": Smith, p. 27.
219 "are no longer mere journeymen": Taylor, pp. 9–10.

Chapter 15. Spotting Bad Workplaces: From Exploitation to Paternalism
224 "Saxon serf": Engels, p. 211.
224 "detected speaking": ibid., pp. 205–7.
224 "Here was Durham's": Sinclair, p. 63.
226 "The only word I know": Gouldner, p. 73.
227 "These people": Sinclair, p. 102.
227 25 percent of OSHA cases willful violations: *Business Week*, June 8, 1987, p. 128J.

Page

228 "The assembly line": Walker, pp. 51, 54, 60.

228 "robots": ibid., pp. 137, 138, 161.

229 "Bureaucratic control": Edwards, p. 131.

230 industrial engineers cooperated with unions: see Nadworny.

231 "the corporation is conceived": Howard, p. 7.

233 "Spoil them": Sennett, p. 82. He does not mention Luce by name.

234 "the essential quality": ibid.

Chapter 16. The Rise and Corruption of the Managerial Class:
A Case for Employee Ownership

239 Crown executives' farewell party: *San Francisco Chronicle*, April 30, 1986, p. 30.

240 half million thrown out of work: *Business Week*, November 14, 1986, p. 76.

240 "Many of my friends": *San Francisco Chronicle*, November 23, 1986.

241 General Electric and U.S. Steel's stockholders, Berle, p. 109.

242 "passive property owners": ibid., p. 354.

242 "In ever widening sectors": Burnham, p. 78.

243 "Whenever enterprises": Bendix, p. 1.

244 "Polite lip service": Geneen, pp. 260–61.

244 "There are few": ibid., p. 262.

244 "for the sole benefit": Berle, pp. 354–57.

244 "essential if the corporate system": ibid.

245 "There has never been a more efficient": Drucker, *The Future of Industrial Man*, p. 99.

245 "technostructure": Galbraith, pp. 70–71.

245 "management does not go out ruthlessly": ibid., pp. 115–17.

246 comparison between American and Japanese executive pay: *Wall Street Journal*, January 3, 1987.

246 CEO pay: "Executive Pay," *Business Week*, May 4, 1987, pp. 50–94.

247 "Mr. Iacocca, don't you": "Executive Pay," *Business Week*, May 5, 1986, p. 48.

248 Thomas Wyman's $11 million parachute: "Executive Pay": *Business Week*, May 4, 1987, p. 51.

249 "cult of the CEO": *New Republic*, May 13, 1985.

249 Donald Kelly's $200 million: *Forbes*, October 26, 1987.

250 "trust of fiduciary responsibility": Barber, *The Logic and Limits of Trust*, p. 000.

Chapter 17. Do Nice Companies Finish Last?

Page

255 "Keep killing": *Wall Street Journal*, April 14, 1987, pp. 1, 28.

255 "Greedy, Greedy, Greedy": *People*, May 2, 1988.

256 estimates of wealth of Walton, et al.: *Forbes*, October 26, 1987.

258 "trust of technical competence": Barker, *The Logic and Limits of Trust*, pp. 7–25.

259 Brown-Van Dyck study: "Socially Responsible Investing: The Financial and Socio/Economic Issues," by Theodore A. Brown and Thomas Van Dyck, May 1986, p. 11.

260 *Personnel* study: "Participatory Management Beefs Up the Bottom Line" by S. Andrew Carson, *Personnel*, July 1985, pp. 45–48.

260 NCEO study: "Employee Ownership and Corporate Performance" by Michael Quarrey, National Center for Employee Ownership, 1986, pp. 28–29.

261 NYSE study: *People and Productivity: The New York Stock Exchange Guide to Financial Incentives and the Quality of Work Life* by William C. Freund and Eugene Epstein, pp. 134–35. On page 121, the authors noted: "One of our startling findings is how few companies have any formal human resources programs to improve productivity. We estimate that only 14 percent of corporations with 100 or more employees have such programs. . . . Furthermore, even in companies with programs, 4 of every 10 employees do not participate. . . . From our survey we estimated that only about 13 million of workers in companies in the United States are presently included in human resource programs."

262 survey of 200 productivity experiments: *A Guide to Worker Productivity Experiments in the United States 1976–81* by Richard A. Guzzo and Jeffery S. Bondy, New York: Pergamon Press/Work in America Institute Series, 1983.

262 Schuster study: *The Schuster Report: The Proven Connection Between People and Profits*, by Frederick E. Schuster, New York: John Wiley & Sons, 1986.

264 "We were very fortunate": On a more theoretical level, German sociologist Niklas Luhmann argues in his essay "Trust" that the principal function of trust in human affairs is to "reduce social complexity."

Chapter 18. Toward a New Workplace Ethic

Page
267 silicosis ailments: *Business Week*, June 8, 1987, p. 128F.
267 "There is increasing": NIOSH, weekly report, October 3, 1986, p. 613.
268 "roughly the same order of magnitude": *New York Times*, April 3, 1983.
268 "work, all work": Greenleaf, p. 156.
268 "When a business manager": ibid., p. 146.

INDEX

ROBERT LEVERING has been a labor and business journalist for more than fifteen years. His insight into the corporate workplace comes from personal visits to more than a hundred companies. He has coauthored several books including: *Everybody's Business: An Almanac*, *The Computer Entrepreneurs*, and *The 100 Best Companies to Work for in America*. A graduate of Swarthmore College, Mr. Levering lives in San Francisco, California.